Nino *Rota*

Music,
Film
and
Feeling

Richard DYER

A BFI book published by Palgrave Macmillan

First published in 2010 by
PALGRAVE MACMILLAN

on behalf of the

BRITISH FILM INSTITUTE
21 Stephen Street, London W1T 1LN
www.bfi.org.uk

There's more to discover about film and television through the BFI.
Our world-renowned archive, cinemas, festivals, films, publications and learning resources are
here to inspire you.

Palgrave Macmillan in the UK is an imprint of Macmillan Publishers Limited, registered in
England, company number 785998, of Houndmills, Basingstoke, Hampshire RG21 6XS. Palgrave
Macmillan in the US is a division of St Martin's Press LLC, 175 Fifth Avenue, New York, NY
10010. Palgrave Macmillan is the global academic imprint of the above companies and has
companies and representatives throughout the world. Palgrave® and Macmillan® are registered
trademarks in the United States, the United Kingdom, Europe and other countries.

Cover design: couch
Cover image: *Le notti di Cabiria* (Federico Fellini, 1957), © Dino De Laurentiis Cinematografica
Text design: couch

Set by Cambrian Typesetters, Camberley, Surrey
Printed in China

This book is printed on paper suitable for recycling and made from fully managed and sustained
forest sources. Logging, pulping and manufacturing processes are expected to conform to the
environmental regulations of the country of origin.

British Library Cataloguing-in-Publication Data
A catalogue record for this book is available from the British Library
A catalog record for this book is available from the Library of Congress
10 9 8 7 6 5 4 3 2 1
19 18 17 16 15 14 131 2 11 10

ISBN 978–1–84457–210–6 (pbk)
ISBN 978–1–84457–209–0 (hbk)

Contents

Introduction

Nino Rota's music is touching, funny, direct and affecting and yet it is also held back, uncommitted, every emotion always limned with another. It produces a very particular, albeit extremely flexible, way of feeling. This is the subject of this book.

He was one of the most successful of all film composers: prolific, esteemed, honoured, beloved. Yet his work does not exactly conform to prevalent models of music in film. In particular, the music, in itself and how it is deployed, is not entirely bound up with a film's characters and situations. It does not deal in identification and illusionism, the supposedly dominant qualities of film prevalent in film (music) analysis. This book is then also an exploration of the ways his music does and does not do what music in film is generally held to do. Given his success, and mainly in mainstream popular cinema, Rota's different approach suggests that the standard accounts of how music typically functions in films may need modification or extension.

His music is familiar and recognisable, yet at the same time he extensively re-used his own material, was chameleonic in adapting himself to different directors, genres and *mises en scène* and wrote music full of reference and pastiche. This has sometimes been held against him, not least because originality continues to be such a fundamental term in aesthetic understanding. However, the very high regard in which he is held as well as his popularity also suggest that not being original may have aesthetic benefits, and this too is what this book explores.

The first two chapters situate his films in relation to some of the circumstances of their production. Through a consideration of three interrelated films, the first chapter explores the way Rota was in practice caught up in the intertwining of commercial considerations, artistic assumptions and his propensity for re-use and pastiche. The second chapter provides basic information on his career and a characterisation of his music within and without film. The rest of the book considers first his general practice in relation to film music, organised around a notion of ironic attachment, that sense of music that is close, very close to, but not quite wholly engaged or subsumed by, what is going on on screen. The last two chapters look at two particular bodies of work. On the one hand, comedy, Rota's most common mode, elicits scores in some ways more involved in the workings of the film than elsewhere in his work, but this is because comedy, and especially as Rota inflects it, is itself a mode that stands in an unusual relation to what it depicts. The final chapter, on the other hand, looks at the body of work where there is the most productive realisation of Rota's musically within-and-without stance, namely the long collaboration with Federico Fellini.

* * *

I have taught Rota in relation to music and film at Warwick, Stockholm, Copenhagen and Bergamo universities and King's College London; I want to thank all those who took these classes for the myriad ways they opened up, supplemented and challenged my take on his work. I have also presented aspects of the work published here in many places, and should like to thank accordingly those who invited me and came and discussed: in the UK, the universities of Birmingham, Coventry, Kent, Lancaster, Leeds (Music and Film Conference), London (Birkbeck, University College (Centre for Italian Studies), Queen Mary and Westfield, King's College (Popular Italian Cinema Conference)), Sheffield Hallam, Southampton (Royal Society of Music Conference) and Surrey, as well as the Italian Cultural Institute, National Film Theatre and Warwick Arts Centre; in mainland Europe and Ireland: the universities of Bergamo, Bergen (Cultural Disorder Seminar), Bologna, Dublin (University College), Gothenburg, Łódź, Lund, Turku and Zürich; in North America, the universities of Minneapolis (Music and Film Conference), Columbia, Pittsburgh and Syracuse; and the Australian Film, Television and Radio School, Sydney. I am also grateful for support and leave from Warwick University and King's College and owe a special debit of gratitude to the Internationales Kolleg für Kulturtechnikforschung und Medienphilosophie (the IKKM) at the Bauhaus University of Weimar for a fellowship that afforded me both the time and the intellectual context in which to complete this book. I originally thought of writing on Rota when approached by Frank Burke re an anthology on Fellini; although I was not able to deliver this, I am grateful for his encouragement and suggestions at that point. I have published aspects or versions of this material elsewhere and should like to thank the following: Jostein Gripsrud (for Dyer, 2001), Nick James (Dyer, 2004), Mattias Brütsch (Dyer, 2005), Miguel Mera and David Burnand (Dyer, 2006), Daniel Goldmark, Lawrence Kramer and Richard Leppert (Dyer, 2007a), Serena Guarracino and Marina Vitale (Dyer, 2009).

Many others have helped in the preparation of this book, in practical and intellectual ways, including Andrew Lockett (who commissioned it), Rebecca Barden (who took over as the most supportive of editors), Sophie Contento (who saw it insightfully through production) and Louis Bayman (for the index) as well as Charles Barr, Louis Bayman, Thies Brunner, Carlo Cenciarelli, Lauro Crisman, Luisella Farinotti, Diane Gabrysiak, Barbara Grespi, Giacomo Manzoni, Giorgio Marini, Mandy Merck, Aldo Miceli,

Bruno Moretti, Geoffrey Nowell-Smith, Alastair Phillips, Elisabetta Piccolomini, Victor Perkins, Irmbert Schenck, Rinaldo Sordelli and Sabine Süße. I want especially to thank Giorgio. In many circles in Italy, to be enthusiastic about Rota is not considered a sign of great aesthetic acumen: I am grateful to him for his forbearance, patience and good humour.

1
Tales of Plagiarism And Pastiche

THE GODFATHER, IL GATTOPARDO and THE GLASS MOUNTAIN
In 1972 the American Academy of Motion Picture Arts and Sciences refused the nomination of *The Godfather* for an Oscar in the category of Best Original Dramatic Score. They argued that for the love theme its composer, Nino Rota, had re-used music from an earlier film, *Fortunella* (1957), and thus that the *Godfather* score could not be deemed original.[1] They seem not to have realised that the main theme is based on a motif already used by Rota in *Fellini-Satyricon* (1969) and Michael's theme on one used for the funeral at the end of *I clowns* (1970).[2]

Many, then and subsequently, would consider the music for *The Godfather* among the finest of all film scores, certainly more distinguished than the others nominated (*Images, Napoleon and Samantha, The Poseidon Adventure, Sleuth*[3] (all 1972)); bizarrely, the score that won was for *Limelight*, a film made twenty years earlier, whose nomination was accepted on a technicality.[4] Besides, Rota had after all re-used his own music, and when he did so again, in *Godfather II* (1974), he was awarded the Oscar. Yet *Godfather II* contains very much more of his music for *The Godfather* than the latter does of *Fortunella*. Nonetheless, on this occasion the Academy saw no problems of unoriginality in his nomination and award. They probably did not know that several of the new elements in *Godfather II* were also recycled: the song the child Vito sings while waiting in quarantine on Ellis Island is taken from Rota's music for Visconti's 1957 stage production of Goldoni's *L'impresario delle Smirne*; the theme for Kay is taken from his music for the television series *Il giornalino di Gian Burrasca* (1965), hugely successful and fondly remembered in Italy but unknown outside It; and the important new motif, known as 'The Immigrant', reworked the fourth (andante sostenuto ed espressivo) of his fifteen *Preludes* for piano (1964).

In its own terms, the Academy's decision on the first *Godfather* was correct. The primary burden of 'original' in the category's designation is that the music be expressly written for the film in question. Rota's use of music from *Fortunella* for *The Godfather* was not in this sense original; it was, in the most exacting sense of the term, plagiarism. He knew he was using music he'd used before and does not appear to have made that clear to Coppola or Paramount. They thought they were getting new ('original') music from him; he knew they weren't, and he presumably presumed that no one would realise because *Fortunella* was a pretty obscure film. Presenting something already heard as never heard before in circumstances where you assume you can get away with it are hallmarks of plagiarism. However, the *Godfather–Fortunella* link is only a point of entry to a trail of connections, which in turn open onto readily confused meanings of (un)originality, to wit, plagiarism and pastiche.

It seems to have been a product of a kind of laziness. Rota was, as always, extremely busy when Coppola made a late request for a theme for the Sicily sequence. Deeming it 'inutile che mi spremessi le miningi' ('a waste of time racking my brains') to come up with a new tune, Rota pulled out a number of old ones and, 'secondo il mio solito' ('as is my way'), ran them past a few friends to see which they thought best (Comuzio and Vecchi, 1986: 10). In any case, said Rota later, all composers re-use material, sometimes an idea jotted down waiting for the right moment, but other times 'an idea already made use of but transformed, re-elaborated'.[5] It is only one theme out of the whole score, about twenty minutes in a nearly three-hour film, and played very differently from its previous use. In *Fortunella* it appears first as a fast march, played with the kind of reckless enthusiasm that Rota often used to suggest the circus or amateur town band; Rota (Comuzio and Vecchi, 1986: 10) refers to it as 'una marcetta sfottente' ('a nice little send-up of a march'). It then goes through a number of variations, including ones much closer in tempo to its reappearance in *The Godfather* (although in context even the more sentimental variant is either comic or sad, neither of which it is in *The Godfather*). At no point is it used, as in *The Godfather*, in an arrangement for mandolins and strings, nor played fortissimo over the images or in relation to the romantic evocation of landscape and love. Aside from the tune itself, the actual sequence of the melodic line, it is really quite far musically and affectively from its appearance in *The Godfather*. This is unlike the re-use of the song from *L' impresario delle Smirne* in *Godfather II*, where the feeling evoked in both cases is very similar: in its earlier incarnation, it is an intensely melancholic serenade sung by a small, lonely boy in prison, just like Vito on Ellis Island.

All of the markers and mitigations of plagiarism in the *Fortunella–Godfather* case contrast with another instance of Rota's re-use of a (different) melody in *Fortunella*. In a contemporary review, 'm.m.' (Morando Morandini) observed that in *Fortunella*, Rota 'arriva al punto di plagiare se stesso' ('goes so far as to plagiarise himself').[6] However, unless plagiarism means here (as it often does) stale but not literal repetition of previous work, only one element of the *Fortunella* score actually comes from an earlier film and thus might on the face of it be thought auto-plagiarism. This is a fanfare-like motif composed for *Il bidone*. However, as the latter was made only two years earlier (1955) and was directed by one of *Fortunella*'s scriptwriters, Federico Fellini, it is unlikely that no one knew what Rota was up to. The theme is very little altered between the two films, punctuating events on and off; the bitter, and in the end tragic, feeling of the earlier film,

The Godfather: Johnny
Fontane (Al Martino)
croons for Connie Corleone
(Talia Shire) on her wedding
day

carried in this theme, makes available an undertow to the more whimsical tone of the later one. Not only did those making *Fortunella* know the theme was being re-used, but in fact the film works better if the audience pick up on it too. Declared and purposeful re-use is not plagiarism.

Compared to this, Rota's re-use of a *Fortunella* theme in *The Godfather* is indisputably, technically, plagiarism yet all the same it seems pretty innocent at the level of intention and affect. As already noted, it is musically very different, really only involving a melody, and constituting only a small part of the score. It only became plagiarism that mattered when it started to make money. Much to Rota's surprise, Paramount chose the last minute, *Fortunella*-derived theme for the short Sicily sequence as 'The Theme from *The Godfather*'. It was widely used in the promotion of the film, including in the form of the hit ballad 'Speak Softly Love' (words by Larry Kusik), recorded by, among many others, Johnny Mathis, Andy Williams and Al Martino, who plays the crooner Johnny Fontane in the film.[7] It thus became seen as the principal musical element of the film, sidelining the film's other much more pervasive and expressly written motifs and perhaps giving the Sicily sequence an undue significance. Paramount had reduced the score to a single marketable element, a tune that could be made into a song. It was this though that caused a problem for the Academy.

It is in fact rather surprising that the latter had even heard of *Fortunella*. In Italy it had been a flop, albeit a high-profile one, involving as it did a notable line-up: Eduardo De Filippo, the most famous name in Italian theatre, as director and co-star; Giulietta Masina and Alberto Sordi, very well-established stars by this time; an American star, Paul Douglas; Fellini as one of the scriptwriters;[8] and Rota's music. Masina, Fellini and Rota were riding high from the success of *La strada* (1956), which had won the Oscar for Best Foreign Film, and the character of Nanda (nicknamed 'Fortunella') is clearly built on Gelsomina, the winsome character played by Masina in *La strada*. Rota was also now internationally known for his music for *War and Peace* (1957). None of this though could secure *Fortunella* art-house success abroad any more than it could box-office success in Italy. The tune that Paramount had promoted to main-theme status and that was under fire from the Academy was from a film most people had never even heard of. The Academy only learnt of the prior existence of the theme from a telegram, signed by 'I compositori italiani di colonne sonore' ('The Italian film music composers'). It seems probable that Dino De Laurentiis, the producer of *Fortunella*, was behind this, as he hoped to make money from the huge success of 'Speak Softly Love' by claiming his rights in it, even though he had never paid Rota for the music for *Fortunella*, nor even got him to sign a contract (Lombardi, 2000: 152). In short, plagiarism was an issue because Paramount promoted a tune to main theme status and put words to it to make it at once a money-spinner and a form of advertising, but only really became one when Di Laurentiis thought he could profit from it too. The underlying economic imperative for both Paramount and Di Laurentiis was in turn wittily highlighted when in 1972 the record company Cora reissued the *Fortunella* soundtrack on LP with the by-line (in much bigger letters than the title itself) 'La madrina del padrino' ('The Godmother of the Godfather'), thus brazenly milking the scandal, and money-making potential, of the accusation of plagiarism.

The *Fortunella* score repackaged by Cora Records as 'The Godmother of the Godfather'

Rota had never particularly wanted to write the music for *The Godfather*. By 1971, with a string of successes behind him, to say nothing of a very active life as a composer and teacher, he was not interested in taking on yet more work, especially with a then-unknown American director, Francis Ford Coppola.[9] The latter, against the wishes of the studio, who wanted Henry Mancini (Cowie, 1997: 63–4), went specially to visit Rota in Rome to beg him to take it on; when Rota, to shake him off, imposed extravagant conditions (such as that he would only compose the music when the film was finished, would never himself come to the USA and would send someone else to conduct it and adjust the score in synchronising it for the image), Coppola went ahead and accepted. It is interesting that he so much wanted Rota (and that, with more promise than track record behind him, he was able to get his way with Paramount). Rota had only once, with *War and Peace*, worked on a Hollywood film, and then not actually in Hollywood as it was shot in Rome, and though he had worked in many genres, including one or two psychological thrillers, he had never done a Mafia or gangster film. Coppola, however, did not want him to write action thriller music. Rather, as Rota recounted (in De Santi, 1992: 104–5), he wanted music that would evoke, rather broadly, even vaguely, Sicily, such as to suggest how far away it was from America.

In short, what Coppola wanted from Rota was pastiche, music that, precisely by not actually being Sicilian, suggested Sicily as an idea, that at once communicated directly the feeling of Sicilianness while indicating the fact that this is a notion carried in the fading memories and passed-on values of the characters. Pastiche is able to convey the emotional pull of this notion even while signalling it as a notion, and it is precisely the affective power of everything suggested by this Sicilianness (notably family, loyalty, honour, male bonding) that draws the characters (and especially Michael) inexorably into crime and violence. Rota provided this sense of culturally and historically constructed feeling, above all in the film's real main theme, a slow waltz, first heard on a solo trumpet recorded with considerable echo, to give a blowsy sound suggesting faraway, nostalgia, longing, loneliness, melancholy.

The theme that caused all the trouble for the Academy (now usually referred to as the love theme) ratchets pastiche up a further notch. The main theme insinuates itself into the texture of the soundtrack, often reticently. The love theme, withheld for just under an hour and three-quarters, appears only in the Sicily sequence; the orchestra plunges straight into the melody, first with gloopy massed strings, then augmented by mandolins insistently to the fore, thus combining, almost to excess, the folkloristic/touristic aural image of Sicily and the conventions of Hollywoodian romanticism. It seems to underline the fantasy of Sicily that the character of Michael experiences, even when, indeed only when, he is actually in Sicily – a fantasy coloured by the American culture that he is in reality so much a part of. You don't have to take it this way: it is possible to take the Sicily episode straight, as a largely idyllic escape from the tension and carnage of New York. But neither Coppola or Rota are straight in that way, and the ambiguity of pastiche, poised exactly on the cusp of straight and ironic, is at the heart of both artists' work.

Rota's love theme for *The Godfather* was not original in the Academy's sense. Melodically, it was plagiarism (albeit auto-plagiarist and guileless), though in all other musical aspects (harmony, tempo, orchestration) it was not, to say nothing of the fact that it was such a small fraction of the whole score that was, nominally, nominated. The theme was also, in all its musical dimensions, pastiche. This is almost by definition not original, except in a technical sense (that is, it is not plagiarism). Yet Coppola seems to have recognised in Rota's pastiching both a consummate skill and an unusual complexity of relationship between the pastiche, that which it is pastiching and the context (the film) in which it is being deployed. It is a vindication of pastiche.

* * *

There is virtually no original music, in the Academy's sense, in *Il gattopardo* (1963). It comes from one of Rota's symphonies and two of his earlier films, together with a Verdi waltz.[10] There is, but in a markedly different sense from above, pastiche.

The non-diegetic score has two main elements. A rising stately romantic theme in a predominantly string arrangement accompanies the credits (a tracking shot taking us into the grounds of the di Salina palazzo near Palermo) and such sequences as Tancredi leaving the palazzo to join Garibaldi and the Risorgimento, Tancredi and Angelina exploring the palazzo in Donnafugata during their courtship and Don Fabrizio contemplating his mortality in the final moments of the film. Second, there is a poundingly dramatic theme, carried principally on violins with brass and timpani, mostly used for the Risorgimento battle sequences. The themes are drawn respectively from the third (andante sostenuto)[11] and fourth (allegro impetuoso) movements of Rota's *Sinfonia sopra una canzone d'amore* (Symphony on a Love Song), written in 1947. Although the director, Luchino Visconti, did use expressly written scores in some of his films (including by Rota in *Le notti bianche*, 1957, and *Rocco e i suoi fratelli*, 1960), he more commonly used already existing music for the resonances they carried with them (e.g., Donizetti in *Bellissima*, 1951; Bruckner in *Senso*, 1954; Mahler in *Morte in Venezia*, 1972). According to Rota, Visconti had considered Massenet, Wagner and Gounod's *Faust* for *Il gattopardo*, and Rota played some of these themes over as they discussed the matter, segueing distractedly into the andante from his symphony; Visconti at once recognised that 'this was the music of *Il gattopardo*' (De Santi, 1992: 90). On this occasion, Visconti could not be using the music for its associations, since it had never been published or performed,[12] yet it is almost uncannily appropriate for the film. A symphony of the period, which would have been new in the period, would sound familiar and be encrusted with association. The Rota symphony can have a sense of newness (unfamiliarity) while at the same time being recognisable as old (the style of the period) and this fits with the general aesthetic strategies of the film.

Il gattopardo is based on the novel by Giuseppe Tomasi di Lampedusa, written between 1954 and 1957 and published in 1958. It is set principally between 1860 and 1862 (with later episodes omitted from the film) and tells of the moment of the Risorgimento, the mid-nineteenth-century movement for the unification of Italy, through its impact on an aristocratic Sicilian, Prince Fabrizio, and his family. It is written in a faintly ironic realist style, untouched by twentieth-century literary modernism. Rota's *Sinfonia sopra una canzone d'amore* was written ten years earlier, yet it too could have been written a hundred years before: Suso Cecchi D'Amico, in the critical study that came out with the film, simply refers to it as a 'nineteenth century style symphony' (1963: 172). It uses large orchestral forces, but with none of the exotic instrumentation, lush chromaticism or folk and jazz inflections that were to come in symphonic composition (and not least in classic film music: Steiner, Rózsa, Korngold, Herrman). If the credits did not indicate to the contrary, you might think it was a mid-nineteenth-century symphony you happen never to have heard, by Tchaikovsky perhaps. The film *Il gattopardo* is shot largely on locations carefully restored to how they would have looked in the period (Bertetto, 2000: 203–6), with costumes meticulously recreated by Piero Tosi; its style approximates nineteenth-century art, both painting (composition within the 'landscape' (that is, scope) frame that is reminiscent of, and sometimes specifically refers to, nineteenth-century Italian painting, a quality brought out by an overall 'tempo rallentato' (slowed-down pace) (Severi, 2001)) and also the novel (naturalistic accumulation of physical detail; 'omniscient narration with a plurality of unsubjective points of view' (Bertetto, 2000: 218), achieved by long takes and, mainly, pans, techniques that hold back from a scene rather than entering it and fostering identifica-tion). In short, the novel, symphony and film, produced within fifteen years of each other, all evoke an older world in something approaching the style of that world.

One might say that this is what a film – and score – of *Il gattopardo* would have been like if there had been cinema in the 1860s. It is more nine-teenth century than mainstream cinema, strongly marked though that is by both the novel and melodrama. It was, moreover, made by a high-profile director in a period when cinema's nineteenth-century inheritance was under attack, the period, to mention only Italian examples, of *Accattone* (1961, Pasolini), *La commare secca* (1962, Bertolucci), *L'eclisse* (1962, Antonioni) and *8½* (1963, Fellini). The score is likewise out of step with prevailing styles of film music, the Cinecittà/Hollywood mainstream as well as the spare atonality of Giovanni Fusco (*L'eclisse*), Bach cantatas over sordid imagery (*Accattone*) or the exuberant collage of evident pastiche, quotation and parody of the Rota of *8½*. If it could never be possible to make a nineteenth-century film, it was even more remarkable to be trying to do so in this period.

Some aspects of the film may even seem to underline this. The *mise en scène* is excessive in its detail, always in danger of drawing attention to its pictorial sources and the pains that have been taken; the casting of stars, notably Burt Lancaster, Alain Delon and Claudia Cardinale, puts familiar, twentieth-century faces amid all this strenuous recreation; and as the film's central source of understanding, Don Fabrizio's perspective 'at times seems too advanced and twentieth century to fit realistically and coherently with the film's diegetic world' (Bertetto, 2000: 219). Even without these elements, the film would have to be considered anachronistic, albeit anachronism of a peculiar kind, for it seems to want to recreate a form that never in fact existed, the nineteenth-century film. It is, if not pastiche proper, at any rate in that neck of the woods, an imitation that, in context (a film and score out of synch with its time) and perhaps textually (*mise en scène*, stars, central character), is evidently an imitation, but in a medium that the thing imitated neither did nor could have deployed. Much of the melancholy of the film resides not only in Don Fabrizio's sense of the ironies of history and his own mortality, but in the fact that the film itself, including its score, cannot be what it wants to be, cannot achieve the imagined fullness and presence of nineteenth-century cinema.

Rota also composed the dances for the ballroom sequence that makes up the last third of the film. These are diegetic music: you wouldn't necessarily know that they were written by Rota at all, and indeed one of them, a valzer brillant (a gay waltz), is in fact by Giuseppe Verdi.[13] It was discovered by a friend of Visconti's on a bookstall in autographed manuscript form, scored for piano and dedicated to Countess Maffei, whose Milanese salon played a significant role in the Risorgimento; Verdi himself has also been considered 'Il vate del Risorgimento' (the Bard of the Risorgimento).[14] Rota arranged it for orchestra along with six other dances, including another waltz. The Verdi waltz carries particular narrative weight in the film: it is the first dance we hear and see and is also the music for the dance between Don Fabrizio and Angelica, a dance startlingly erotically charged and pregnant with class significance, the aristocracy dancing with the rising bourgeoisie. However, I find it hard to believe that one could pick out the Verdi dance from the Rota

The Verdi waltz in
Il gattopardo

ones – the orchestration ensures that they seem all of a piece. So does the playing. A local orchestra was used during the shooting, and their playing is less polished, with smaller orchestral forces, than originally planned. Visconti and Rota, however, liked this less-than-perfect sound, perhaps on grounds of realism, but in any case folding Verdi and Rota on a par into the film's processes of recreation.

All of the dances sound nineteenth century. As with the score, their unfamiliarity to the film audience is well judged: they sound of their period, they carry no baggage and, for the characters, they are present-day. They are a memory of something that the film's audience in fact has never known. One at least though may be more. This is another waltz that Rota had used in an earlier film, *Appassionatamente* (1954), with just the same orchestration. Here too there is a long ball sequence, where questions of shifts of class structure (in this case, an aristocratic woman marrying into the rising new professional class) are played out in the gyrations and couplings of the dance floor. *Appassionatamente* is unashamedly a period melodrama, but clearly Rota saw no incongruity in transposing the music from one film representing social relations through interpersonal ones to another doing the same thing within the more highbrow accurate period gloss of *Il gattopardo*. Visconti seems not to have known of the borrowing.

There is also a galop in *Appassionatamente* that is re-used in *Il gattopardo* (as well as a polka that, entirely in keeping with the style of the other dances, is nonetheless not re-used). The only other dance in *Appassionatamente* (*Il gattopardo* has four others) is a then well-known old waltz tune that gives the film its title, composed by Dino Rulli in 1928 (and acknowledged in the credits). Thus there is here no question of plagiarism: though also used non-diegetically, the film's title and the credit to Rulli draw attention to the tune as a reference. This is also part of the way *Appassionatamente* works differently to *Il gattopardo* as a historical film. The former assumes that the audience will recognise its eponymous theme, suggesting an attitude of awareness of the past as past, and perhaps of nostalgia, in its visual and aural *mise en scène* (even while being modern in its contemporary melodramatic identity, not least by virtue of stars specialised in the genre, Myriam Bru and Amadeo Nazzari). *Il gattopardo*, in contrast, works on the assumption that, though obviously old fashioned, everything about the film is nonetheless contemporary with the characters.

In 1947 Romeo Carreri observed, in the course of an enthusiastic article on Rota's film music, 'Who could forget the delicate waltz in *Un americano in vacanza?*' (Carreri, 2000: 40). Yet clearly many could (forget), since this is the waltz in *Appassionatamente* and *Il gattopardo*. *Un americano in vacanza* (1945) tells of an encounter between Dick, an American GI on a few days' leave in Rome, and a young Italian teacher, Maria. She resists his advances, thinking he just wants a fling, like other GIs and indeed many Italian girls, a situation illustrated in the 'Melody Club' (sic) and its hot swing music (which, as is common in films of this period, is associated with loose morals[15]). Later Dick takes her to an American reception held in an old

Italian villa; Maria is not dressed for the occasion, but the villa's owner, the Countess Arcieri, lends her an elegant ballroom gown; as she dances with Dick, she finally comes to believe in the honourableness of his intentions. The music they dance to is the 'unforgettable' waltz. The villa, the ball gown, the waltz all affirm the values of an older age, still alive despite fascism, the war and the American invasion of jazz and loose morals (emphasised by a brutal cut from the waltz to blaring swing later at the party). It is not actually an old waltz – it is the idea or echo of one.

In the ball in *Il gattopardo*, where it is called the 'valzer del commiato' (parting waltz), it occurs twice. The first time it accompanies Tancredi introducing Don Calogero (Angelica's father, representative of the petit bourgeois class who have profited from the Risorgimento) to the hostess, a princess of ancient noble family; it continues behind Don Fabrizio looking on at the new vulgarity of the young aristocrats at the ball and with the first intimation of his own death. It appears at the end, as the ball is breaking up, coming in on the soundtrack as Don Fabrizio looks at himself in the mirror, next to a room full of unemptied piss pots, and sheds a tear.

In *Un americano in vacanza*, the waltz represents the survival of old values in a world imperilled by modernity; eleven years later, in *Appassionatamente*, it suggests the tension between values; in *Il gattopardo*, another nine years on, set nearly a hundred years earlier, it is an elegy for the eclipse of those values. Both the score and the dances in *Il gattopardo* are

Il gattopardo: Don Fabrizio, the gattopardo (Burt Lancaster), contemplates his demise

pastiche, in that they are imitations that know themselves to be such (rather than simply imitating prevalent styles, the basis of nearly all cultural production) but they are not textually marked as pastiche (unlike the *Godfather* score). They contribute to the creative anachronism of the film and to its melancholy, for a world that is passed, for a film form that never was.

*   *   *

Il gattopardo is not the only film with music in common with the *Sinfonia sopra una canzone d'amore*. The latter's first movement (allegro) uses music written for an earlier film, *La donna della montagna* (1943), which Rota then re-used, after writing the symphony, in what was in its time one of his greatest hits, *The Glass Mountain* (1948). Both films are about the lure – the beauty and danger – of mountains; in each, a dead woman is associated with that lure. The *Sinfonia*'s allegro theme is associated with the lure in both cases, though the films' overall tones are very different: *La donna della montagna*, made and not really completed in the last year of the war in Italy (Trasati, 1984: 33–6), is bleak and perverse, whereas *The Glass Mountain*, a British film, with Italy figuring as a place of wartime heroism and peacetime exoticism, tempers melodrama with sweetness and light. Ostensibly, both end happily, but the reconciliation of the couple in *La donna* is perfunctory and formulaic and we have never seen love between them anywhere else in the film, whereas we have idyllic scenes of love and marriage between the couple in *The Glass Mountain*, and they come together at the end as a result of an arduous journey towards each other. The use of the *Sinfonia* theme in the two films underlines the difference. In *La donna* it is used throughout the film, broken down into phrases and not given a full, orchestrally affirmative statement at the end. In *The Glass Mountain*, there is an alternative theme for the central (married English) couple, Anne and Richard Wilder, and it is this that accompanies their reconciliation. After this, *The Glass Mountain* does have a full statement of the *Sinfonia* theme, but over a panorama of the mountains as the couple and rescue party ski safely away from them. The most important statement of the theme occurs in the opera, 'The Glass Mountain', composed by Richard (and in fact of course by Rota), which is about a fateful love story, wherein a woman scorned kills herself in the mountains and then in turn, perhaps only in his imagination, lures her fickle lover to his death with her plaintive song. Here, within the opera, there prevails something of the sense of emotional doom that pervades *La donna della montagna*, albeit more grandiose, less bleak, and the return to the theme at the very end of the film itself, as the English couple leaves the mountains, perhaps suggests the abiding presence, and lure, of such terrain.

Rota's re-use of the *La donna/Sinfonia* theme in *The Glass Mountain* is a different case from his use of the *Fortunella* theme in *The Godfather*. In the latter instance, there is a radical reorchestration and change of tempo in the theme in the context of huge differences in setting, period, story and tone, whereas the orchestration alters only slightly between the two mountain films. Although one would be hard put to it to claim that there is something intrinsically 'mountainy' about the music (it does not, for instance, draw on the music of the German Bergfilm of the 1930s), it is reasonable to assume that Rota heard doomed love in it (whether in the cadences of the theme itself or in its association with the events in *La donna della montagna*), not least because it is the *canzone d'amore* on which the symphony is built, and in undoubtedly dark, turbulent colours. While it is probably the case that Rota assumed that few if any would see both films and make the musical connection between them, it would also not matter aesthetically if they did, since their emotional material is so close.

As a piece of film music the allegro (and other music) in *La donna della montagna* and *The Glass Mountain* conforms to what had become standard practice by the mid-twentieth century: formally modified nineteenth-century symphonic in style, subordinate to the story-telling, offering the audience emotional response cues. Perhaps because, unlike the symphony's andante sostenuto and allegro impetuoso movements, the allegro was originally conceived as a piece of film music, and perhaps also because, unlike *Il gattopardo*, the setting of both films is contemporary, there is nothing remarkable about the allegro here. If it is, in relation to developments in both highbrow (atonality, serialism) and popular (hit songs, jazz) music, anachronistic, then this is because film music in general was. Anachronism is put to particular ends in *Il gattopardo*, but in *The Glass Mountain* it is just business as usual.

As already noted, the allegro theme also occurs in the opera-within-the-film, 'The Glass Mountain'. Works-within-works have a propensity to seem to be being held up for stylistic inspection, but this does not have to be the case and is not so here, and this despite the fact that 'The Glass Mountain' is an amalgam of musical styles. There is the allegro theme, here sung by both lovers, whereas it only functions as purely orchestral, non-diegetic music for the surrounding story. It also draws on the modes of operatic verismo associated especially with the Mascagni of *Cavalleria rusticana*; four years later, Rota arranged and supplemented the music for the Mascagni biopic, *Melodie immortali* (1952). As in 'The Glass Mountain', Mascagnian verismo promotes a chimera of noble poverty and peasant vitality. The opera also quotes a song, 'La montanara' ('The Song of the Mountains'), sung by the mountaineers in the surrounding story. This combination of references in a work which is moreover, as far as the film is concerned, written by an Englishman, might suggest multiple foregrounding of the constructedness of musical affect.

Yet this is not how the opera works in the film. This is partly because the musical elements are themselves related: opera, and especially verismo, had a direct influence on film scoring, especially in Italy, and, notionally at any rate, verismo gestured towards folk sources (a point made in many biopics, including *Melodie immortali*). Even were this not so, the scoring of the opera folds all the elements into a stylistically unified whole. Most suggestive of all is the presence of the Italian male lead in the film, Tito Gobbi, the most famous baritone (and perhaps male opera star) of the period, not least by

virtue of his many film appearances. As with the films of other opera stars
(e.g., Beniamino Gigli, Gino Bechi) and the biopic *Enrico Caruso: leggenda
di una voce* (1951), Gobbi's films present him as a man of the people, even
often of poor origins, able to move musically and naturally between opera,
folk and music hall, an embodiment of an ideal of unified Italian identity
achieved through music (e.g., *Musica proibita* (1943), *O sole mio* (1946),
Avanti a lui tremava tutta Roma (1946)). The different musical styles are not
seen as inimical but quite the contrary, wholly compatible, as both Gobbi's
practice and star persona, and the opera in the film, demonstrate. Further
authentication is provided by the fact that Gobbi plays a character in the surrounding story who sings in the opera, suggesting the continuity between
the two realms.

The Glass Mountain is in part about the recovery of past, perhaps lost
emotion. For Richard, the opera itself seeks to recapture his feelings for
Alida, the woman he fell in love with when his plane crashed in the Alps
during the war; and he remembers her through a legend she told him, about
a man whose dead fiancée forces him to remember her forever. Like *Il gattopardo*, the opera recalls a past moment in the musical language of that
moment – except that the musical language of the opera, both its verismo
and its folklore, were already past by the time the film was made and in
which is set. The anomaly of its style is highlighted by the fact that it is supposedly premiered at La Fenice in Venice, which in the immediately following years premiered two unmistakably mid-twentieth century operas, *The
Rake's Progress* (1951, Igor Stravinsky) and *The Turn of the Screw* (1954,
Benjamin Britten). Moreover, Britten had had remarkable success with *Peter
Grimes* (1945), premiered just after the war (that is, before *The Glass*

The Glass Mountain: Richard Wilder (Michael Denison) composing

Mountain and 'The Glass Mountain'), establishing a contemporary British approach to opera very different to Richard Wilder's unselfconsciously anachronistic style.

The Glass Mountain, in its use of 'La montanara', also takes us back to the question of plagiarism. The song had been found / composed by Antonio Ortelli and Luigi Pigarelli, specifically for the Coro della Società Alpinisti Tridentini (cf. Borgna, 1992: 102),[16] and presented probably by the composers and certainly by the film as an authentic emanation of the alpine spirit. The credits of the film clearly attribute 'La montanara' to Ortelli and Pigarelli, and Rota seems to have tried to sort out his right to use it before leaving for London to complete the score;[17] in the programme of music for the film, Rota claims that every single second of use of 'La montanara', as song or as cited in the non-diegetic score, was spelled out.[18]

In the film, the people of the village of San Felice (including Tito Gobbi) are seen singing it, so that when it appears in the non-diegetic score it can readily be understood as having been picked up and reworked from this source. Most viewers are perhaps unlikely to take in the small print (literally) of the credits and might well take 'La montanara' to be Rota's invention or, even more probably, a genuine folk song. This last was how it was referred to in coverage in 1948 in the British magazine *The Cinema*,[19] apparently on the basis of interviewing Rota, and the song was well known in Italy, certainly in the Dolomites, at least since the late 1920s. Besides, as so often with folk song, to what extent one should consider it composed rather than collected by Ortelli and Pigarelli is unclear, as is what (artistic as well as legal) right of ownership collection would give them. Folk music is characterised by just such fudges of composition and discovery, authenticity and invention.

In all these ways, there may have been aesthetic conundrums about originality, but no clear-cut issues of ownership. However, Rota was persuaded to produce a version of the much-admired score in the form of a piece for piano and orchestra, aiming at the same market that had made hits out of other British 'concertos' such as the *Warsaw Concerto* (Richard Addinsell, from *Dangerous Moonlight*, 1941), the *Cornish Rhapsody* (Hubert Bath, *Love Story*, 1945) and *The Dream of Olwen* (Charles Williams, *While I Live*, 1947), to say nothing of the popular success of Rachmaninov's Second Piano Concerto following its use in *Brief Encounter* (1945, much admired by Rota[20]). This 'concerto' (short enough – just over four minutes – to fit on one side of a 78 rpm record), entitled *The Legend of the Glass Mountain*, had a phenomenal success in Britain, on radio, in record and sheet music sales (De Santi, 1983: 48), appearing in the top ten of the hit parade for over a year. *The Legend* incorporated phrases from 'La montanara' and, as 'Song of the Mountains', it appeared in non-vocal form on the B-side the disc; with English words, it became a popular song, sung by the most beloved star of her generation, Gracie Fields, at the Royal Variety Show in 1950. Royalties poured in. As with 'Speak Softly Love', who owned the song came to be of considerable significance. What, within the discourse of folk music, ought to have been considered traditional, autochthonous, and thus beyond issues of individual authorship and ownership, of originality and copyright, came to matter financially a great deal in those terms. Rota commented later (De Santi, 1992: 61):

> With 'La montanara' I did the same sort of thing that Tchaikovsky did with our folk music in *Capriccio italiano*. But there was nothing for it: along with the success came the first accusation against me of plagiarism. And I did feel aggrieved about it, even though the tribunal came down on my side.[21]

The score of *The Glass Mountain* also a couple of times incorporates a snatch of the tune 'Lilliburlero',[22] to underline moments of cheerfulness between Richard and Anne. This is a standard item of British light music, and thus a familiar musical point of reference in the middle-class culture to which the couple belong, a tune seen as so traditional as to be beyond questions of origin or authorship and thus beyond those of plagiarism. It is an overt citation, perhaps also constituting some kind of homage by an Italian composer working in a British context.

* * *

Nino Rota was a composer responsive to what was asked of him, enormously at ease with generic and historical musical styles, delighting in the possibilities of irony and pastiche and, not least, always very busy. At the same time he was caught up in the legal, financial, practical and aesthetic realities of the situation in which he worked. *The Godfather*, *Il gattopardo* and *The Glass Mountain* illustrate the interaction of this compositional sensibility with these production circumstances. They also throw into relief the matter of imitation.

Imitation is the foundation of all expression and performance but it also constitutes a faultline in modern Western culture. On the one hand, it is viewed with disdain from the perspectives of individualism, expressive and autographic notions of authorship, and copyright. On the other hand, the centrality of genre and branding to capitalist cultural production and the rise of identity politics and multiculturalism emphasise the value of similarity, which, whether fully perceived or not, entails imitation. Within academic discourse, imitation's other, originality, has been resoundingly routed by critiques of romanticism and the rise of post- and post-postmodernism, yet in public intellectual life, in highbrow journalism, in examination guidelines, the criterion of originality continues unaffected.

Plagiarism and pastiche are two registers of this. They are two forms of imitation that share the characteristic of being formally very close to that which they imitate, so close as to be on occasion mistakenly taken to be that which they imitate (pastiche) or deliberately intended to be taken as it (plagiarism): this is the first way in which they straddle the discursive faultline of imitation. At the same time they are near-opposites: plagiarism only works as plagiarism if it is not recognised as such, whereas pastiche has to be recognised as pastiche to work as pastiche. Yet despite this glaring difference, in practice, because of their closeness to their referent, they are also often taken for one another: that is, in given circumstances, the accusation of plagiarism is often levelled at a work pastiching another work, while pastiche is often condemned as nothing better than plagiarism. This confounding of the two is a second way in which they throw into relief the faultline of imitation.

Plagiarism and pastiche both violate the culturally privileged principle of originality, but this doesn't need to matter. Plagiarism flouts the principle of originality by directly ripping off a previous work and even claiming itself as original. Though the examples here do not go that far, the initial proposal that *The Godfather* score be nominated did so inadvertently. However, plagiarism's deceit only matters when something – money or acclaim, or it might be status or competitive examination – is at stake. Pastiche signals the issue of unoriginality because it acknowledges that all expression and performance involve imitation. However, pastiche may nonetheless take that which it imitates at face value, as if acknowledging its own activity of imitation without perceiving that that which it imitates is also involved in imitation. *The Glass Mountain* knows that it is producing a new version of verismo and reproducing an established version of folk, but shows no recognition of the problem of authenticity in both of these traditions. *Il gattopardo* and *The Godfather*, in contrast, recognise that they are in the realm of the already said and use it, not to spuriously authenticate nor yet, as in much modernist and postmodernist consideration of such recognition, to distance or critique, but to get close, formally (*Il gattopardo*) and/or affectively (*The Godfather*), to acknowledge the sources of imagination and emotion without in the process extinguishing them.

2
Nino Rota: Life, Works and Times

When I am at the piano, when I'm working on a piece of music, I am on the whole happy; but as a man, how can one be happy in the midst of the unhappiness of other people? The feeling that underlines my music is aimed at giving those who hear it at least a moment of serenity.

Nino Rota[1]

Nino Rota wrote the music for 158 films (five for television),[2] most famously the *Godfather* trilogy, the Zeffirelli Shakespeare adaptations, three Visconti films and all of Fellini up to *Prova d'orchestra* (1978), but also comedies, melodramas and other genre films, both period and contemporary settings, working in Italy, the USA, Britain, France and Russia. He also wrote thirty-three concert and fifty-one chamber works, five ballet scores, ten operas and incidental music for ten plays. Born in Milan in 1911, he died, unmarried, in Rome in 1979.

In this chapter, I both give an overview of this prodigious output[3] and seek to characterise it. The first section below gives an account of his musical formation, while the next attempts to describe some of the typical musical qualities of his work, in particular the centrality of melody and the paradoxical combination of immediacy and reticence, of irony and straightforwardness. This is followed by a survey of his film work, particularly in terms of genre and directors. Finally, I look briefly at his life, a life that seems to have consisted of almost nothing but music making, but which may provide a further clue in his sexuality to the source of his music's ironically attached stance.

* * *

Nino is an angelic friend made of music, with always an angel of music by his side, with its huge wings about him.

Federico Fellini[4]

Nino Rota was born in 1911 into a well-to-do and highly musical Milanese family.[5] His maternal grandfather, Giovanni Rinaldi, was a composer,[6] his mother an accomplished pianist and his cousin, Maria Rota, a concert singer; the family had subscriptions to opera and concert series and held musical evenings, and visitors included Puccini, Leoncavallo, Ravel, Stravinsky, Toscanini and leading contemporary Italian composers such as Ildebrando Pizzetti (1880–1968) and Alfredo Casella (1883–1947). Nino, 'the pet of the Milanese salons',[7] was playing the piano at the age of four and composing at eight. In 1923, aged twelve, he had his first work publicly performed, an oratorio *L'infanzia di San Giovanni Battista* (The Childhood of St John the Baptist); he himself conducted its second performance, at Tourcoing in France, with his cousin Maria as soloist. He was seen as an infant prodigy, even referred to as the new Mozart by *Il mattino* and the Mozart of the twentieth century by the *New York Times*.

He was exceptionally gifted musically and brought up in the most fertile musical environment imaginable. Together, they gave him outstanding musical facility. Stories of it abound. He was improvising at the piano with perfect harmony at the age of eight and at eleven he came home from a performance of Pizzetti's new opera *Debora e Jaele* and wrote out its opening bars. He could compose one tune while listening to another, composing while listening to the radio (Lombardi, 2000: xiv). He wrote the music-hall songs for *Zazà* (1943) on the set at the last minute[8] and composed all the scores for *The Valley of the Eagles* (1951) and *Star of India* (1953) on the train journeys from Bari to London.[9] Fedele D'Amico, a musicologist, champion of Rota's work and husband of Rota's close friend Suso Cecchi D'Amico, recounts:[10]

> I remember once Luigi Zampa rang me at home to ask Nino if he had done the music for his film. Nino had completely forgotten about it. What's more, he was right that moment writing the music for another soundtrack. But he didn't have the nerve to tell Zampa that he hadn't done it and Zampa asked him to come to Cinecittà at half-past one to play him the music. It was midday. Nino had lunch and left for Cinecittà. He sat at the piano and, having checked on the length of each piece of music needed for each sequence, he played Zampa all the music for the film. ... I remember an evening when Visconti got Nino to play 'E lucean le stelle'[[11]] in the style of the great composers, from Bach to Debussy.

Franco Mannino (1994: 32) tells a similar story of he and the ethnomusicologist Diego Carpitella taking the oldest example the latter could find of a 'rota', a form of medieval canon,[12] playing Rota only part of it and asking him 'to improvise the composition for six voices, just as in the original. Unperturbed, he sat down at the piano and calmly played all six voices!'[13]

Such facility, having all that musical culture at his fingertips, meant that he could produce almost any style of music. Many of the operas seem to evoke predecessors: *Ariodante* (Donizetti),[14] *Torquemada* (Verdi), *Il cappelo di paglia di Firenze* (Rossini). For theatre and film, he could readily summon up and make instantly recognisable, say, a Renaissance court (*Romeo and Juliet*[15]), eighteenth-century Venice (*L'impresario delle Smirne*[16]), a nineteenth-century battlefield (*Waterloo*, 1970) or contemporary Italian night life (*La dolce vita*, 1960), or else Naples (*Napoli milionaria*[17]), Southern Italy

(*Rocco e i suoi fratelli*) or Sicily (*The Godfather*), Indochina (*This Angry Age*, 1956) or Samoa (*Hurricane*, 1979).

There is another sense in which Rota's gift and early immersion in music produces facility. This is music that communicates immediately but is also often not retained. As Rota himself observed:[18] 'My music seems easy and quite a few people say that they have the impression of "knowing it already"; but then, in the end, no one remembers a thing because the notes vanish before them.' With exceptions, a Rota tune is one you can grasp instantly, readily recognise when it is re-used and forget immediately after. This is very effective for film music, where easy recognisability and unobtrusiveness are equally prized. The fact that the music came easily to him seems also to be expressed by the music itself. It seems natural, unaffected, unlaboured. In the concert works, melodies often come straight in, with no preparatory passages, something even more striking in first movements: the Violin Sonata (1936) starts with a slightly atonal chord that at once segues into the allegretto cantabile theme; the piano in the E major Piano Concerto (1978) comes in straightaway, a dreamy, slowly descending tune over a bed of strings. In *Un americano in vacanza*, when Dick finally catches sight of Maria again outside St Peter's, a romantic tune comes in the moment he sees her, no hanging about, straight in on a downward phrase. Of course, the effect of an unforced outpouring of melody is not necessarily achieved by writing down the first thing that comes into your head, but in Rota's case the evidence suggests it was like this and certainly it feels as if it is.

The easiness and readiness of melody for Rota accounts not only for its centrality to his work but also perhaps for his lack of preciousness about his tunes, and indeed other people's. He frequently re-used his own material[19] and seems never quite to have understood why there should be fuss about drawing upon others':

> I'm absolutely convinced that there's no such thing as plagiarism in music. There is musical material at one's disposal: if one takes it and makes it one's own, there's still the gratitude that a new author owes to the old one, but what could be more beautiful between we musicians?[20]

And if his melodies were not so precious that they couldn't be recycled, nor were they so precious that they couldn't be used once and then discarded. There is an astonishing sense of squandering tunes in Rota. In *Vivere in pace* (1947), for instance, there is early on an exquisite tarantella theme accompanying the children looking for a runaway pig, but it's never heard again nor, as far as I can tell, did Rota ever use it again in other works; other examples include the lovely sad melody on high strings as the two GIs walk among war ruins towards the beginning of *Un americano in vacanza* and the ruefully melancholic music in *Molti sogni per le strade* (1948) as Linda looks round the flat as she is about to leave it and her husband. Often too scores are played so quietly you can barely hear them and they can seem indifferent to what is going on on-screen, a key quality to his work.

The emphasis on melody in his work meant that he was out of critical fashion: to be melodic was, according to the canons of modernism, old-fashioned, out of touch; but Rota seems not to have been bothered: he never felt, he says, the need to be 'à la page'.[21] Yet he was not oblivious. He knew what was going on around him, was very much part of musical life and friendly with, for instance, Stravinsky, Petrassi (even dedicating his first symphony to him) and Dallapiccola. His *Mysterium* (1962) suggests lessons learnt now from Stravinsky's *Symphony of Psalms* (1930),[22] now William Walton's *Belshazzar's Feast* (1931), now Carl Orff's *Carmina Burana* (1937), now Miklós Rózsa's *Ben Hur* score (1956). As we have seen, he had a vast musical knowledge, which shows up in the prolific use of citation and pastiche in the film music. If his music sang out unaffectedly, it was not because he didn't know what he was doing.

The 'new Mozart' studied with Pizzetti (from 1924 to 1926) and Casella (1926–30), and at the Accademia di Santa Cecilia, the national conservatory of music in Rome. Casella was the focus for a generation of Italian composers that, as his pupil, Rota came to know well: Ferrucio Busoni (1866–1924), Ottorino Respighi (1879–1936), Gianfranco Malipiero (1882–1973), Mario Castelnuovo-Tedesco (1895–1968). Touched by the nationalist impulse current across Western music in the period, this generation rebelled against the overwhelming dominance of opera in Italian musical life, a form which seemed provincial, backward and musically impure, swamped by narrative and theatricality. They looked back to pre-nineteenth-century traditions of music, today canonical but then, especially in Italy, eclipsed by romanticism: to Bach, Haydn, Mozart, and especially Italian music from when Italy had been one of the defining musical cultures internationally: Corelli, Gabrieli, Monteverdi, Pergolesi, Scarlatti, Vivaldi. Sometimes the work produced referred directly to these forebears. At the same time, the so-called (indeed misnamed) 'Generazione dell'ottanta' (eighties generation) also looked to contemporary musical developments in Europe, especially France (Fauré, Ravel, Debussy), but also Stravinsky, Richard Strauss, de Falla, Schoenberg. The project was, in Casella's phrase, 'la creazione di uno stile moderno nostro' ('to create our own modern style'),[23] at once definitely Italian but new and up to the minute. The result was a form of music that favoured spare over thick or lush instrumentation, astringent over ripe or melting harmonics, musical over dramatic form, the emotionally sharp, contradictory or withdrawn over the soaring and passionate.

Generations are never chronologically sealed off. Opera continued to be composed, often itself influenced by some of these ideas: Giacomo Puccini (1858–1924), Ermanno Wolf-Ferrari (1876–1948). Younger composers emerged (Luigi Dallapiccola (1904–75), Goffredo Petrassi (1904–2003), Luigi Nono (1924–90), Luciano Berio (1925–2003)) who embraced both the turn to folk music that had characterised earlier generations elsewhere (e.g., Austria, Bohemia, Britain, Hungary, Norway, the USA) and hard-line modernism. Some of the 'Generazione dell'ottanta', including Casella, went part way down these paths.

Nino Rota belongs with this generation. Some of his works are either explicitly dedicated or else clearly written in homage to them: Pizzetti with his early songs (1923–5), Malipiero with the Canzona for Chamber Orchestra 1935, Casella with the *Petite offrande musicale* (1943)[24] and the *Cantico in memoria di Alfredo Casella* (1947); De Santi writes of the latter that Rota renders homage 'with the clarity of construction and transparency of polyphonic texture that were the hallmarks of the founder of Italian musical neo-classicism' (1992: 156).[25] Much of his music has the instrumental and harmonic colouring of Casella and company, especially in the 1920s and 30s. Characteristic is the score for *Il Casanova di Federico Fellini*, especially the mini-opera 'L'intermezzo della mantide religiosa' (The Religious Mantis's Intermezzo), at once obviously eighteenth century in reference and yet nothing like eighteenth-century music in its sour tones and manic tempi. However, in other ways Rota is also very much not of the 'Generazione dell'ottanta'.

He was not so literally: he was born when they were well into their late twenties and thirties. Perhaps for this reason (as well as, by all accounts, temperament), there seems not be the animus in him against romanticism. His music hardly ever has the bombast or ardour, the straining emotional rhetoric, of nineteenth-century Italian opera, but it readily embraces the softer, dreamier, more sentimental or open-hearted strains of musical romanticism. Second, he too had an interest in music of the past – indeed, it is the prerequisite for his consummate chameleonic skills – and in 1937 he wrote a PhD thesis on the Italian Renaissance music theorist Gioseffo Zarlino. However, in his own practice, when he was neo-classical he was often more strictly so than the Casella generation, the structures and melodic form of the classical precedent showing clearly through the modern gloss, in much the same way as in the exemplary neo-classical work *Pulcinella* (Stravinsky's 1920 ballet drawing directly on the work of Pergolesi): Variations and Fugue on a Theme of Bach (1950), Fantasia on twelve notes from *Don Giovanni* by W. A. Mozart (1960), the Nonet (1959/74/77), the late Cello concertos (1972 and 1973) and the music for *The Taming of the Shrew* (1967) and *Romeo and Juliet* (1968) and the ballet *Le Molière imaginaire* (1976).

Having gained a degree in composition from Santa Cecilia in 1930, the next year Rota went on a two-year scholarship to the Curtis Institute in Philadelphia. Here his historical musical education was widened still further and, through his close friendship with Aaron Copland, he also came into contact with American popular and film music. Not only was he able to draw on this in, especially, his film work but also it seems to have freed him to embrace commercially popular Italian music traditions (operetta, Neapolitan song, Italian swing and pop) and incorporate them into his work, starting with the songs and score for his first film *Treno popolare* in 1933. In Philadelphia he became friendly with Samuel Barber (1910–1981) and Gian Carlo Menotti (1911–2006), both forging a romantic style of music for the twentieth century, comparable to Korngold and Rózsa and to the Rota of, notably, the piano concertos and much of the chamber and film music.

On his return to Italy, Rota made more or less a living as a composer and wrote his PhD (at Milan University) on Zarlino. In 1937 he went to teach at the music college of Taranto in Puglia, transferring to the Bari Conservatory in 1939, first as a lecturer in harmony and counterpoint, then becoming Director ten years later and staying there until his death.

He was extraordinarily musically productive throughout his life. In addition to the film scores he wrote: four works for solo piano (three of them substantial sets of variations), two for organ, one each for solo harp and flute; two pieces for bells; two song cycles and sixteen songs (usually with piano but twice with other instrumental accompaniment); sonatas for violin (3), flute (3), flute and harp (2), viola (1), clarinet (2), oboe (1), bassoon (1), trombone (1), harpsichord (1) and two pianos (1); two trios (flute, violin and piano; clarinet, cello and piano); two works for string quartet; one quintet (for flute, oboe, viola, cello and harp); two other chamber works; concertos (or equivalent works for solo instrument and orchestra) for piano (4), cello (3), bassoon (2), harp (1), French horn (1) and double bass (1), together with one concerto for strings and one for orchestra; four symphonies; nine other orchestral works (two with chorus); incidental music for ten plays (including one cabaret); five ballet scores;[26] ten operas; one cantata; five oratorios; one short Mass.

This large output is consistently professional, never in the least careless, with no cutting of musical corners. Compared with the film music, there is also surprisingly little re-use of material within the concert music, but much transfer of ideas to the film scores (and occasionally vice versa), and both concert and film work show up in the theatrical works. This is part of the point in two cases of the latter: both the ballet *La strada*[27] and the opera *Napoli milionaria* (1973–7) draw on music from the two eponymous films but also Rota's other work with Fellini and Eduardo De Filippo respectively.

Rota was a successful, as well as prolific, composer. The first Viola Sonata (1934–5) was a favourite for several years throughout Europe, notably in the repertoire of the most important violist of the period, Ruben Grimlow, while the Violin Sonata (1936–7) was a staple of the recitals given by Sandro Materassi and Luigi Dallapicola (the latter to become one of the key modernist Italian composers). *Il cappello di paglia di Firenze*, first produced in Palermo in 1955, was subsequently produced at La Scala by Giorgio Strehler, the leading theatre director of the period, for two seasons in a row (1957–8, 1958–9) and has been produced many times since, in Italy and abroad. The critic Guido Agosti praised the Variations and Fugue on Bach (1950) for solo piano in the highest terms:[28]

> Here the composer demonstrates to the full a technique and knowledge of the instrument and the keyboard (he himself played the piano with extreme facility), comparable in its extraordinary intuitive grasp of different resonances and musical equilibrium to Chopin and Ravel.

Rota won prizes, much of the work was published (by no means to be taken for granted with concert music scores) and recorded; recently there has been a minor resurgence of his music on CD, both reissues and new recordings; he has been championed by conductor Riccardo Muti, violinist Gideon Kremer and pianist Caetano Veloso. Yet despite all this Rota has never become part of the basic twentieth-century concert repertoire, nor has he had great and widespread critical acclaim, and particularly not in Italy.

* * *

> In truth this composer is always 'double', caught between light-heartedness and sadness, irony and pathos, great music and minor jobs; he is available and refractory, modest and self-aware, realistic and full of beautiful illusions. He is falsely simple.
>
> Ermanno Comuzio[29]

Melody is primary in Rota's music. His tunes are seldom long and have clean lines, with no slurring or huge jumps. There are two main types: slower and gently romantic, perky and bustling. Very often the melodic line of the former has an overall downward trajectory, often coming in on descending notes, and even when rising, very seldom straining and usually sinking back by the end. Yet this can often also go along with a slightly emphasised underlying rhythm, pretty little phrases or embellishments that prevent the melody ever being really tragic, bleak or despairing.[30]

The perky melodies provide a contrast of cheerfulness, running merrily along, never excessively busy or manic, occasionally brought to a sudden, comic pause, and often using instruments with known comic potential (flute, trombone, bassoon). This is not pounding or driven music, but it does have a breezy, propellant energy. Sergio Miceli (1982: 250) writes of a typical rhythmic organisation in Rota's work, a thickening of polyphonic texture leading to growing conflict between a hyperactive contrapuntalism and the original rhythm, which then, however, returns to imperturbability. This kind of music has affinities with the circus music that Rota wrote for Fellini and is often thought of as quintessential Rota. I remember once being on the underground in London and a trio of musicians coming into the carriage and starting to play in just this manner and the person with me saying, 'There's some Nino Rota for you' (though they were not literally playing Rota). But really this is Rota–Fellini, by no means characterising all or even most of his output.

Rota's melodies are generally cantabile, that is, within the normal singing range, his music 'canta ed il suo canto possiede la suggestione popolare di una lirica semplicità' ('sings and his song has the suggestion of simple, popular lyricism').[31] His 'facile vena melodica' ('ready melodic gift'), as one dictionary of music has it (Vignal, 1995: 171), along with his pleasing harmonies and charming rhythms, gives his music a quality that a collection of essays in his honour calls *candore* (Morelli, 2001a). It's a notion that the English word 'candour' doesn't quite catch, suggesting rather simplicity, straightforwardness, transparency, lack of affectation. The music seems unpremeditated; as already noted, it gives the impression of spontaneity, tunes pouring out of him. It aims to communicate directly; as Rota himself put it, he did not 'fear to be melodic and catchy', the important thing for him was 'that music be at once perceptible, that is, that it follows the canons of immediacy'.[32]

And yet. For all the recognition of the music's unaffected affectivity, most attempts to characterise it also find a need to offset it: it is sad but never really tragic, bleak or despairing, romantic but not ardent, sentimental but not tearjerking, cheerfully energetic but never, or never for long, excessively busy or manic. Somehow it is never quite emotionally straightforward. Two characterisations are typical and evocative, one from one of the only sustained scholarly analyses of Rota's music, the other from a classical music website.

[His music is] witty, ironic, always ready to temper its own self-consciousness with the most disarming and forceful melodic vein. (Miceli, 1982: 255)[33]

Rota's film music style is characterised by a certain good-humoured energy verging on satire. … He didn't completely ignore the emotional side of the films he scored, but avoided the overly sentimental by seemingly coming at the subject obliquely with a slight sense of the absurd. … While on the surface this description might sound like a lack of caring, it has often resulted in artistically

pleasing and often very poignant, true-to-life stories when compared to the
inevitable over-simplified Hollywood remakes.[34]

Mario Soldati puts the point differently again, speaking of the sense of death
in Rota, and yet a death without weight, producing a mysteriously happy
melancholy.[35]

Rota's music is paradoxical, combining directness and pastiche, naivety
and knowledge. The Morelli *candore* collection comes up with various for-
mulations to address what Massimo Bontempelli termed oxymoronically
'consapevole candore' (conscious candour) (Finotti, 2001: 10). Comparison
is made with baroque music and its 'dissumulazione onesta' (honest or open
faking) (Steffan, 2001: 57), its 'imprestiti senza camouflage' (undisguised
borrowings) (Morelli, 2001b: 389).

It suggests a particular relation to the past. Fabio Finotti (2001) situates
Rota in relation to the ideas of the poet and critic Massimo Bontempelli. As
has happened recurrently in modernity, Bontempelli voiced a desire for a
return to simplicity and connection, reacting against the bustle, scale and
fragmentation of contemporary life; yet he also recognised that one could
not produce simplicity as if there were not bustle. Discussing this in terms
of the primitive (nowadays a dodgy term), Bontempelli acknowledges that
there cannot be a straightforward primitivism, a return to precivilised values
as if there had not been civilisation. Instead, he calls for a 'primitivismo
cosciente' ('conscious primitivism'): 'Adam did not have a past, but we
cannot go back to being Adam, we must be primitives with a past.'[36] The
values of primitivism can be striven for – heartfelt expression, unpremeditated utterance, direct communication – in full awareness of the inescapable
inheritance of the forms and structures of expression. A straightforwardness
that can never be straightforward, affect that can never be unselfconscious
simplicity, and with that perhaps then always a sense of ruefulness, that one
can never quite inhabit the emotion any more. This is Rota.

* * *

After *Treno popolare* in 1933, Rota did not write another film score until *Il
birichino di papà* in 1942. This was at the invitation of Guido Gatti, at once a
leading figure in Italian musical life (critic, editor of the journal *Rassegna
musicale*, director of the Teatro di Torino) and the right-hand man of the
head of Lux film, Riccardo Gualino. Lux sought to produce commercial
films with artistic ambition, and, through Gatti's influence, employed a
number of the most highly regarded composers of the day: Giorgio
Federico Ghedini (for *Don Bosco*, 1934, Lux's first film), Pizzetti (*I promessi
sposi*, 1941), Fernando Previtali (*Una storia d'amore*, 1942), Giuseppe Rosati
(*Malombra*, 1942), Giovanni Fusco (*Ti ritroverò*, 1949), Petrassi (*Riso amaro*,
1949) (Calabretto, 2000). There was too an increasing official recognition of
film music, with courses established in the Santa Cecilia (Rome) and
Chigiana (Siena) conservatories. Often though Lux's use of established classical composers was not successful. As the composer and musicologist Mario

Labroca (1959: 14) put it some time later, established composers felt that the demands of film 'overturned systems and methods, depriving music of being itself narrative in its schema and traditional forms (the first movement of a sonata, adagio, scherzo, rondo and so on)':[37] for Pizzetti, for instance, the tempi of music and of film were not readily compatible (Calabretto, 2000: 93, 99) and many of the scores by name composers were felt not to work because such problems had not been resolved. Fedele D'Amico, however, in an article in Gatti's *Rassegno musicale*,[38] pointed to the example of Malipiero and Vincenzo Tommasini, whose acclaimed scores respectively for *Acciaio* (1933) and *Un colpo di pistola* (1942, a Lux production), could not be explained by reference to 'valori di pura musica' ('the values of pure music') but by their 'intelligente abilità' ('intelligent ability') to adapt themselves to the 'compito del momento' ('needs of the job').

Adaptation to the needs of film time, diegetic appropriateness, self-effacement with regard to action and dialogue, these were some of the notions and norms that provided a context for Rota's return to film composition. He became virtually the house composer for Lux, writing thirty films for them, but, starting with *Lo sbaglio di essere vivo* (1945), he worked also for other studios, and then abroad:[39] Britain (nine films), France (four), the USA (four[40]), USSR (one) and Japan (one). The work includes two cartoons for UNICEF (*Handicap* (1954), *Tutti i bambini* (1979)) and television work: documentaries (*Viaggio lungo la valle del Po* (1957), *Chi legge? Viaggio lungo le rive del Tirreno* (1960)) and serials (*Il giornalino di Gian Burrasca* (1965), *Alle origini della Mafia* (1976), *Il furto della Gioconda* (1978)). Among the projects he was wanted for were *Eugenie Grandet* (1946),[41] *Barabbas* (1961), *Darling* (1965, made after the success of *La dolce vita* and perhaps in emulation of it)[42] and *Barry Lyndon* (1975, but Rota found Kubrick too demanding to work with[43]), while his music was re-used without his involvement in *Roger-la-Honte* (1946) and, after his death, *I soliti ignoti vent' anni dopo* (1985), *The Godfather Part III* (1990), *Paranoid Park* (2007) and *Valentino – The Last Emperor* (2008). He also arranged the music for *Proibito* and *Senso* (in the same year, 1954) and a television play *Quei figuri di trent' anni fa* (1956).[44] Much of the music for *Melodie immortali*, a biopic about Pietro Mascagni, is taken from the latter's work, but much more rearranged than Brahms is in *Proibito* or Bruckner in *Senso*[45] and with original contributions. The score of *Amanti senza amore* (1947), adapted from Tolstoy's story 'The Kreutzer Sonata', in which the eponymous work kindles an elicit liaison, is based on that work,[46] and the score of *Il segreto di Don Giovanni* (1947, about a philandering opera singer) on themes from Donizetti's *La favorita* and Mozart's *Don Giovanni*; in both cases the themes are points of departure for musical variations (or, as the latter's credits have it, elaborations) throughout the film. From arrangement to variation and elaboration is one link in the succession that leads through analogy and citation to pastiche.

Rota worked in the mainstream of Italian commercial cinema. He wrote scores for films starring many of the major Italian stars of the period, including the key comedians (discussed in Chapter 4) and singing stars such as operatic tenor Gino Bechi, light soprano Chiaretta Gelli and pop singer Rita Pavone. He was involved many big box-office successes:[47] *Un americano in vacanza, Anna* (1951), *Boccaccio '70* (1962), *Come persi la guerra* (1947), *Come scopersi l'America* (1949), *La dolce vita, Donne e briganti* (1950), *L'eroe della strada* (1948), *Il gattopardo, La grande guerra* (1959), *Mambo* (1954), *Mio figlio professore* (1946), *Napoli milionaria, Le notti di Cabiria* (1957), *La regina di Saba* (1952), *Rocco e i suoi fratelli, Il segreto di Don Giovanni, Senza pietà* (1947), *La strada, Totò al giro d'Italia* (1948), *Vivere in pace, Zazà* and, internationally, *War and Peace, The Taming of the Shrew, Romeo and Juliet, The Godfather, Godfather II* and *Death on the Nile* (1978).

The bulk of his output was in genre cinema, notably melodrama and comedy, but also fantasy, musicals, war films, thrillers and epic/adventure films ranging from low-budget escapades (*I pirati di Capri* (1948), *Donne e briganti, Le meravigliose avventure di Guerrin Meschino* (1951), *Jolanda la figlia del Corsaro Nero* (1952), *La regina di Saba, I tre corsari* (1952), *L'amante de Paride* (1953), *La nave delle donne maledette* (1953), *Star of India*) through to international 'super-colossal' productions (*War and Peace, Il gattopardo, Waterloo, The Abdication* (1974), *Hurricane*). All this places him at the heart of Italian entertainment cinema. There is though a telling absence from his generic filmography, namely, that series of adventure/sensation cycles, centred on and presumed to be addressed to men: the peplum (c.1958–65, musclemen heroes in ancient times), the giallo (c.1962–82, a cross between detection and body horror) and spaghetti Westerns (c.1964–78). It is not so much the masculine subject matter of these genres that put them at odds with Rota's sensibility – his military and bellicose scores for war films, whether Napoleonic (*War and Peace, Waterloo*) or Second World War (e.g., *La grande speranza* (1953), *Divisione folgore* (1954), *Sotto dieci bandiere* (1960)) are highly effective. Rather the peplum, giallo and spaghetti Western all developed an aesthetic of visceral sensation, through, respectively, comic-book energy, stylised sadism or ritualised confrontation. This is the very antithesis of Rota's stance towards characters and worlds, not seeking to sweep the audience up in sensations stimulated by actions and events (and, for instance, jagged editing, vertiginous camerawork, strident music). The exemplary composer of gialli and spaghettis, Ennio Morricone, drew on both avant-garde composition and rock, neither of them close to Rota's musical repertoire, and his scores dominate the imagery, unlike Rota's unsubservient but discreet closeness.[48]

Whatever his limits, Rota was a prolific and versatile composer at the heart of the commercial film industry, from fly-by-night B-movies through respectable mainstream studio films to mega-budget international productions. At the same time, and mostly across all this, he was a regular collaborator with a large number of directors. He is most famous internationally for his work with Coppola, Fellini, Visconti and Zeffirelli, but he also worked together with several very well-established Italian directors, some journeymen (Giorgio Bianchi, Carlo Borghesio, Carlo Ludovico Bragaglia, Duilio

Coletti, Giacomo Gentilomo, Camillo Mastrocinque, Vittorio Metz and
Marcello Marchesi, Luigi Zampa), but some who deserve recognition out-
side Italy as auteurs, notably Renato Castellani (seven films), Alberto
Lattuada (4), Raffaele Matarazzo (4), Mario Monicelli (8)[49] and Mario
Soldati (11), as well as Mario Camerini, Luigi Comencini, Luciano Emmer,
Pietro Francisci, Mario Mattoli, Leopoldo Trieste and Lina Wertmüller
(one-offs) and the long collaboration, in theatre in addition to cinema, with
Eduardo De Filippo. In Italy Rota worked with distinguished expatriates
Christian-Jaque, René Clément, Robert Rossen, King Vidor and Bernard
Vorhaus, while internationally, in addition to Coppola, he worked with such
figures as Sergei Bondarchuk, Edward Dmytryk, John Guillermin,
Koreyyoshi Kurahara, Jan Troell and Henri Verneuil.

We should also note the Italian directors with whom he did not work. In
some cases, this may be chance: while the result would have been different
with Rota scores, there is enough warmth and ambivalence in Bernardo
Bertolucci and the Taviani brothers, for instance, to imagine him having
worked with them. But the unyielding modernisms of Michelangelo
Antonioni, Pier Paolo Pasolini, Roberto Rossellini, the very seriousness
with which their work takes itself, indicate the bounds of Rota's musical
sympathies.

There is of necessity in any composer's work for the cinema a negotia-
tion between what he/she brings to the music and what the films demand. In
Rota's case, the first includes his combination of melodic immediacy and
inclinations towards melancholy, perkiness, teasing, pastiche. This though
has to accommodate the needs of the film, whether generic or star-related or,
as I'll focus on here, directorial design. Rota often brings a perspective to the
film, of cultural memory, of ironic attachment, that is otherwise not in the
film, though this never goes so far as to undermine its emotional project.
More or less accommodation is needed. Castellani's films, for instance, often
focus on the eruption of sadness in carefree lives, something clearly in
accord with Rota's melodic inclinations, whereas Lattuada's are fiercer and
grimmer, granted a stronger, louder, more full-throttle vein of emotional
excess in Rota's scores. Rota's mimetic capacity provided for both Visconti
and Zeffirelli an element of cultural memory for their historical dramas, but
which then works out differently for each; perhaps because of their prestige,
and lack of irony, Rota rather abandons the latter in the music he produces
for them.

The complexity of emotional stance characterising Rota's work is most
in tune with Monicelli, Fellini and Coppola. All three, albeit differently, present characters and their world with insight and affection, but never quite
from their perspective. Both Monicelli and Coppola do use patterns of identification, but these are never the central building blocks of the narration. In
the case of Monicelli, gags and caricature, though never exaggerated,
nonetheless provide a patina of amusement that also stands back from the
characters, while the films are also often ready to slip into melancholy (*Vita
da cani* (1950), *Un eroe dei nostri tempi* (1955), *La grande guerra*), all very

'Rota'. For Coppola, as discussed in Chapter 1, the choice of Rota was cru-
cial to the approach of the *Godfather* films to their material: the music provides much of the emotional pull that goes along with the violence and
dehumanisation unfolded by the narrative, its pastiche indicates the sentimental cultural memory that draws the male characters into the action.
Fellini though is the most complicated and extensive case and for this reason
their collaboration has a chapter to itself.

* * *

La tua passione per la musica non è neanche una passione: è un vizio!

Luigi Rota[50]

Sono musicista e sono soltanto musicista.

Nino Rota[51]

Very little is known about Nino Rota's private life. You get the impression
that he virtually didn't have one. Perhaps he didn't have time: in addition to
his prodigious productivity, he was, when there, a conscientious and disci-
plined head of the Bari Conservatory, and he also occasionally conducted
and gave piano recitals. Virtually all accounts and footage of him show him
at the piano, doodling away even while talking and listening, as if he could
not be detached from music. Not only did he never marry but also his name
was never linked romantically to any woman. He did father a child when he
was in London, but although he sent money regularly he never had any contact with her. He was from childhood a very close friend of Suso Cecchi
D'Amico; in 1950 they co-wrote a short opera for radio, *I due timidi*, about
a man and a woman too shy to tell each other they loved one another. It was
Suso, already married to the music critic Fedele D'Amico, who kept in touch
with Nino's child.[52]

One can assemble a number of observations that could point to the conclusion that he was homosexual. I have been told that he was and also that he
wasn't (by the same person). Early photos (De Santi, 1992: 16, 22, 25) suggest that he was a rather feminine little boy and young man. His father died
when Nino was eleven and he was very close to his mother (although,
unusually for an Italian bachelor, he did not live with her). In the USA he
was an 'intimate friend' of (gay) Aaron Copland (De Santi, 1992: 10) and
taken under the wing of the gay couple Menotti and Barber. When I was
buying *La filmografia di Nino Rota* the bookseller told me that, when in his
youth he worked as a hotel valet, Rota, an utterly delightful person, had
asked him out of the blue if he would like to be his personal assistant. He
was notoriously and inexplicably late or absent when expected (gay readers
especially will recognise why that might be worth mentioning, although
cruising and casual sex seem wholly out of character). For most of his life
he lived with Vinicio (Vinci) Verginelli, described by Suso (1996: 171) as his
'amico fraterno' (fraternal friend) and by Pier Marco De Santi (1983: 109) as
'suo intimo amico' (his intimate friend); in the opera *Aladino*, for which

Verginelli wrote the libretto, the Magician says, in backwards language, 'I open my mouth in parable: Vinci Nino Rota'.[53] Equivocal gossip, stereotypical indicators, the opacity of close same-sex co-habitation and friendship – none are cast-iron and most have to be qualified.

This uncertainty though may provide a way into an understanding of any affective/erotic dimension to the work.[54] As with details about the life, it is possible to pick out more or less clearly homosexual elements in Rota's work, but they represent a tiny percentage of his output. The operina 'La mantide religiosa' in *Il Casanova di Federico Fellini*, composed prior to the film at Fellini's request, is the nearest thing to camp in Rota's output, with its falsetto duet introit, syncopated baroque metre and drag mantis singing not falsetto but tenor. However, although Rota said (before the film was shot) that this music 'might have something "likeable" about it even if the film as a whole certainly won't',[55] the sinister quality of the whole, notably its sharp, acidic harmonies, do not suggest an embrace of camp. The central male friendship in *Sotto il sole di Roma* (1947) is between handsome Ciro and odd-looking Geppa; when Ciro thinks that Geppa may have drowned and then realises he is alright, glowing lighting and an upswell of music combine to create a radiance of delight rarely so directly expressed in Rota's music; later, Ciro sleeps out with Geppa in the latter's cave, and the film's title song, set up as a (heterosexual) love song, is briefly heard, long before it is heard in connection with Ciro and his eventual girlfriend Iris. The reflective guitar

Il Casanova di Federico Fellini: The 'Praying Mantis' mini-opera, with Count Du Bois (Daniel Emilfork-Berenstein) as the female mantis and Gianbruno (Mariano Brancaccio) as the male

Satyricon: Encolpio (Martin Potter) and Gitone (Max Born)

in *Satyricon* accompanying the dissolves of Encolpio and Gitone starting to make love are about the only moment of tenderness in the film, all the more touching for also being the least strange of any of the music.

Amici per la pelle (1955) is a rather more complex case. This tells the story of a friendship between two schoolboys in early adolescence, Mario and Franco. The sense that this is more than just male bonding is suggested partly in the gender differentiation of the boys themselves: masculine Mario, with tumbling dark locks, full lips and athletic disposition, often lit with stronger areas of darkness on the face, and the more feminine Franco, with neat, slicked back, fair hair, neat clothes, no interest in games and often more glowingly lit.

The music suggests the tenderness of the relationship. Early on, Mario stands up to some boys who are bullying Franco on account of the latter's

Amici per la pelle: Mario (Geronimo Meynier) and Franco (Andrea Scirè), friends for life

fob watch and its pretty chime; in the process Mario is hurt and the two go into the locker-room for him to recover; here as Franco looks at Mario, a slow, violin version of the tune played by his watch chime seeps in and accompanies a shot/reverse shot series of radiantly lit, fond looks. The film's main sentimental theme comes in on a shot of them sharing Franco's umbrella, notably, after a pause, on the moment when Mario puts his arm in Franco's. Later, Mario develops a relationship with a girl, Margherita, and he asks Franco if he has a girl; Franco says yes. Later he shows Mario a picture of his girl: it is a portrait of his dead mother and at the point he shows him the portrait, the same sentimental music comes in. Quite apart from the common stereotype of gay boys being excessively fond of their mother, what is interesting here is the way the music evoked here in a quasi-heterosexual context (Franco has spoken of being in love with a woman) is the

Amici per la pelle: Franco shows Mario the portrait of his girl, his mother

same as that that accompanied moments of tenderness between the two boys. (Neither this theme nor any equivalent is used in the brief scene featuring Mario and Margherita.) When Franco tells Mario that he is leaving the town, to accompany his father to Brazil where his business takes him, a solo violin plays the most plaintive variation on the theme. The music, by virtue of drawing upon conventions of sentimentality, casts their relationship in terms of an intense tenderness seldom shown in stories of adolescent male friendship; it also associates this with heterosexual feeling, delicately suggesting an equivalence.

Sotto il sole di Roma, *Satyricon* and *Amici per la pelle* might just about suggest that Rota finds a strain of unbuttoned lyricism for such scenes that he does not deploy elsewhere. However, the only work where we can confidently attribute the subject as well as the treatment to Rota is the late opera *La visita meravigliosa* (1970), whose libretto is by Rota himself, based on an 1895 novel by H. G. Wells, *The Wonderful Visit*. It tells of a vicar, the Reverend Hilyer, in an English village who shoots down what he thinks is a huge bird flying overhead but discovers that he has shot and wounded a – handsome, male – angel. 'È un giovane, dal volto bellissimo, coi lunghi capelli, vestito di una tunica dorata, i ginocchi e i piedi nudi.'[56] He shelters and looks after him in the vicarage but his parishioners are scandalised. His housekeeper remarks: 'Ma Reverendo, che avete fatto? Un uomo mezzo nudo, vestito in modo sconcio, entrato in casa vostra.'[57] Perhaps in Wells's version the story is meant as a parable about the intolerance of difference. However, it is striking that the only other adaptation of this now rather obscure novel[58] is Marcel Carné's film *La Merveilleuse visite*, made four years later, where the homoerotic potential is rendered pretty well explicit (not least in the casting of a bare-chested pretty boy as the angel and dialogue speaking of the many forms of love).

At one point in Rota's opera, the angel picks up Hilyer's trumpet and starts to play a throbbing, ever-rising melody, that overwhelms the reverend: 'Vedo ... vedo ... un paese infinito, senza spazio senza tempo, è lui, è il suo paese. Altri mondi, altri cieli, tutto è luce.' The angel puts down the trumpet, but the reverend picks it up and gives it to him, saying 'Tenetola, è vostra' ('Keep it, it's yours').[59] The music reveals a hitherto unknown radiance to the reverend; it is life-

The angel (Gilles Kohler) in *La Merveilleuse visite*

changing. It is music that recalls two elements from Rota's film scores. In *Un ettaro di cielo* (1957), there is a strange scene in which the protagonist Severino goes to visit the Fat Lady (in fact a man) in a travelling sideshow and inside the tent there is a woman playing 'Casta Diva' from Bellini's *Norma* on solo trumpet. The woman who is in fact a man, a woman playing an instrument with strongly male associations,[60] an aria about worshipping the moon as a sexually chaste goddess, by a composer known to have had an intense, romantic relationship with another man, all suggest a strangeness that might also be not gender and sexuality normative. More strongly, and involving Rota's own music, the angel's trumpet song in *La visita meravi   gliosa* seems – and I am by no means the only person to have observed this – a reworking of the melody that the character of il Matto (the fool) teaches Gelsomina to play in *La strada*. Il Matto is first seen in the film doing his high-wire act, for which he wears, like an angel, wings. He is first heard playing the melody on a tiny, almost toy violin, a sound at once childlike and ethereal. The tune plays during a long talk between him and Gelsomina at night in which he instils in her a sense of self-worth; as he speaks, he curls his knees up under him and lies along the bench beside her, tucking his hands between his corduroy trousered legs, a decidedly unmasculine posi-   tion that is sensuous but not sexual. Later, when they part, he recognises that she would perhaps like to go away with him but laughs and says that is not possible. Later still, Zampanò kills him, perhaps for il Matto's constant teasing of his coarse masculinity, perhaps jealous of Gelsomina's feeling for him. It would be crass to claim that il Matto is really gay any more than he is really an angel, and yet there is something erotic about him that is clearly not heterosexually directed, just as he is touched by the angelic. The angel's

La strada: the fool, the angel (Richard Basehart)

trumpet song in *La visita meravigliosa*, so rousing, so radiant, has affinities with two androgynous, sexually ambivalent precedents in Rota's work.

It was Nino's cousin Titina who brought Wells's book to Nino's attention, telling him 'Questa è la storia della tua vita' ('this is story of your life').[61] Many people referred to Rota as angelic (including Fellini in the quote above), often relating it to his childlikeness,[62] his unworldliness and *candore*[63] and also to his ingenuous engagement with the esoteric. Perhaps what Titina may have perceived is just Nino's angelic quality and the way he was misunderstood and unappreciated. However, in an interview in 2000, Suso Cecchi D'Amico commented 'for me he was a bit …, how shall I put it?, a sort of asexual angel'.[64] The hesitation, the 'a bit', may be telling, as if on the brink of outing, although what she plumps for is asexuality and angelicness. Should we go where Suso did not?

Freudians, gay liberationists and queer theorists would all probably be inclined to see the angel trope as one of evasiveness, of suppression, closetry or equivocation. Perhaps this is the case with Rota. But there are two other possibilities. One is that he really was asexual, a way of being in the world that has some difficulty in gaining recognition in post-Freudian, post-sexological times. The other is that the angel expresses a desire for a sensuousness that is not tied to sex in the most directly genital sense of the word. Either understanding might catch better a sensuousness that is perhaps homoerotic (the boys of *Sotto il sole di Roma*, *Amici per la pelle* and even *Satyricon*, the Reverend Hilyer and the angel), but not drivingly homosexual.

It also illuminates a much wider, central feature of Rota's practice, what might be called a sense of absence. This relates to how he was in the world, the unworldliness already referred to. Fellini referred to Rota's *presenza-assenza*, recalling how he would 'try to leave by non-existent doors or through a window like a butterfly'.[65] In one of the few bits of footage of Rota where he is not at a piano, he is seen with a group of people visiting a possible beach location for *Satyricon*; while the others worry about suitability and practicality, he picks up a starfish and gazes at it in wonder, showing it to the others, their reactions ranging from fond acceptance to humouring.[66] It also relates to his working practice: he often wrote scores after a film was made without having seen it; he would sleep through projections. All of which means that he was not seeking to make music express himself emotionally nor to impress emotions on others, on narratives or on audiences. Hence the lack of emotional over-investment in his music, the strong melodic vein tempered by irony, the indifference at the heart of the lyricism; hence too the squandering of melodies and the copious re-use; hence his handling of the relation of the score to what's on-screen, going for, as he put it, 'the spirit of film, not following the succession of images'.[67]

* * *

Nino Rota belonged with the musical generation of the 1880s but was born twenty-odd years too late for them; his own generation went down the road of atonality, serialism and grim high seriousness that he was disinclined to follow. In a nation hypersensitive to regional difference, he was born in the North but spent most of his working life in the South. He was steeped in highbrow music culture yet worked at the heart of the commercial film industry. He lived as neither married nor an open homosexual, the commonest options of the period, and, despite possible glimpses of homoeroticism in his life and work, perhaps not as a homosexual at all. All of this begins to account for the sense of his not quite being in the music nor in the world of his films, of feelings not being quite unequivocally meant or fully inhabited. It needs though to be put together with the particularity of his temperament, unworldly, happiest when writing music and hoping to give 'those who hear it at least a moment of serenity', to get nearer to the sweetness and light of what is explored more in the next chapter, his characteristic stance of ironic attachment.

> Everyone was fascinated by his extreme availability and at the same time his total absence. In whatever setting or on whatever occasion you met him, whatever were or might be the reasons why he found himself there, he always gave the impression of landing there by chance, and yet at the same time made you feel that you could count on him, that he could keep you company for a bit.
>
> Federico Fellini[68]

3
Ironic Attachment

Rota's film scores sympathise with what is on-screen, but they do not cleave to the characters and events in ways that invite involvement or identification; they are in tune with what is on-screen but they do not respond to every movement, shift of emotion or minute plot development; they are close, very close, to the world of the film, but not at one with it, neither a part nor yet apart. They achieve this partly through his music's inherent qualities of immediacy and reticence, irony and straightforwardness, and also through a use of musical motifs that do not stick rigorously to characters, situations or ideas, the extensive deployment of forms of musical reference that register the fact of making reference, play on the difference between music emanating from the fictional world of the film and that coming from without it, and overall scoring that neither follows the film slavishly nor leads the way.

One can in fact find pretty much every standard procedure of film music in Rota's work: a strict use of motifs, familiar generic tropes, no meddling with where the music is coming from, within or without the film's world, detailed underscoring, impressive overscoring. Some of this has to do with his responsiveness to different directors, but when pretty much left to his own devices, it is the characteristics indicated in the previous paragraph that predominate. The method works supremely well with directors like Coppola, Fellini and Visconti, whose relation to their narrative worlds is also complexly close but not entirely identificatory, but the most effective achievements are not confined to them, in films as various (in terms of genre, brow and quality) as *Anni facili* (1953), *È primavera* (1949), *Un ettaro di cielo, Il maestro di Vigevano* (1963), *Molti sogni per le strada, Obsession* (1949), *Quel bandito sono io* (1949), *Vita da cani* and *Zazà*.

MOTIFS
Rota's deployment of motifs[1] is most often discreet and uninsistent. *La domenica della buona gente* (1953), for instance, a film of intertwined but mostly not directly connected stories, lends itself to, and gets, a series of musical motifs. The stories all take place on the day of a big football match in Rome between Rome and Naples. The themes include a boisterous tune for the football in general, a tarantella-ish one for the Naples supporters, a cheery one for the young lovers Sandra and Giulio, and two tragic in character, one

for Ines (come to Rome to find and, if he abandons her, shoot the rich, married man who has made her pregnant), the other for Bruno (ex-champion footballer, now unemployed and, as a result, becoming estranged from his wife and daughter). Yet the presence of these motifs is reserved, quiet, not mechanistic or underlined, guided more by the narrative tone of a particular sequence than any impulse to delineate character.

When a motif does become more noticeable, it is often for a comic effect. In *Le miserie del signor Travet* (1946), every time the character Camillo Barbarotti appears, there is a sudden, very brief, sparkling musical flourish, on what might be the high end of a xylophone; it sounds a bit tinny, very much suggesting the vivid phoniness and pushiness of the character, as well as pointing up the brilliance of Alberto Sordi's quick, deft and witty body language. The sound recalls the brief little shimmer of music that accompanies every appearance of the pearl necklace in *Roma città libera* (1946), little up-and-down runs on high woodwind and xylophone. This film was made pretty well contemporaneously with *signor Travet*, but, despite the immediate similarity (a brief, shimmering flourish), the motifs are different in character, the brilliance in *Roma città libera* alluringly pretty, appropriate to the role of the pearls in this story of petty theft and contributing to the odd tone of the film, part light comedy, part sub-neo-realist tale of ordinary, poor people.

However, despite the more usual discretion with which he deploys them, Rota's scores use motifs extensively. Credit sequences most often establish two elements, very often contrasting: boisterous and reflective, dramatic and romantic, perky and sentimental and so on. In *Death on the Nile*, it is one majestic but lively, with an echo of Lara's theme from *Dr Zhivago* (1965), and one mildly Orientalist harmonically and melodically (while eschewing

Death on the Nile: multi-star big-budget, exotic locations; middlebrow pedigree

Arab instruments or rhythms); the first aligns the film with contemporaneous middlebrow, multi-star, international megaproductions (although admirers of Boris Pasternak and David Lean may baulk at the alignment with Agatha Christie and John Guillermin), while the second, by staying musically well to the occidental side, suggests Orientalism and tourism rather than attempts at authentic local colour; in effect the motifs put the film in its cultural place. The music for the credits of *Fantasmi a Roma* (1961) is supplied first by a sprightly modern jazz combo, then by a barrel organ. This is appropriate for a film that is about the present and the past in two ways: ghosts occupying a palazzo in present-day Rome, and the destructive attempts of its new owners to modernise it, attempts thwarted by the ghosts. However, the ghosts' motifs are not always played on old instruments; while on their first appearance in the film, each one's motif is so introduced (organ for the friar Bartolomeo, clarinet for kittenish Flora, harpsichord for the rake Reginaldo), this often gives way to jazziness (jazz phrases mixed in with the organ for Bartolomeo, the clarinet played in a swingier way and then the motif played on flowing, distinctly mid-twentieth-century strings for Flora, the harpsichord replaced by a jazz combo for Reginaldo and later, when he visits a convent, the harpsichord itself, one of the least jazz-related of all instruments, played in a jazzy fashion). This play with motifs and instrumentations continues throughout the film and is appropriate: the ghosts are not anti-modern; they enjoy playing about in modern-day Rome while also wishing to preserve the inheritance of (their) past.

Not only may there be contrasting motifs, but very often a motif itself has two related elements. Cabiria's theme in *Le notti di Cabiria* consists of an upward sweeping melody and a somewhat hesitant section, while its prostitutes' theme, a mambo, has two parts, mainly quite close in character, but the first coming in on rather precipitate downward phrases and the second including a passage of a markedly different, stronger, staccato rhythm. 'The immigrant' theme in *Godfather II* has a first more tentative and introductory section, with sometimes a fast mounting passage, then a lyrical melody at once majestic and yearning. I discuss both these examples at further length elsewhere. The double-structured motif allows one or other element to be used separately, bringing out its particular flavour, while at the same time retaining the association with the other element. Together they offset each other musically and affectively; separately they allow for the echo of what is being offset.

A motif established in the credits may set up an expectation that can be played with. An obviously romantic theme appears with the names of the two stars, Anna Magnani and Massimo Girotti, in the credits of *Molti sogni per le strade*, but it is not heard again until nearly two-thirds of the way through the film, delaying the fulfilment of romance between the leads. Similarly, *Sotto il sole di Roma* establishes its titular song in the credits; we may expect it to be used in relation to the pair obviously destined to be the central couple, Ciro and Iris, but in fact we have to wait until well into the film, when they tentatively admit that they love one another, and even then the tune is only sketched in, only being fully heard again at the end of the film. It may be that the sketchiness is just reticence or expresses the uncertainty of their feelings, but it may also be because the song is too overtly and stereotypically a love song, suggesting an easy commercial culture of romance with which the film – because of its foot in neo-realism, because of its ambivalence about the central relationship, because of Rota's propensity to acknowledge the cultural sources of feeling – is uneasy.

The ambivalence of *Sotto il sole di Roma* has to do with its young male protagonist, at once charming and feckless, a common enough combination in the representation of the appeal of masculinity within heterosexuality, but one briefly borne with less assurance in the post-fascist, postwar years, where masculinity was doubly discredited for its involvement in the former and failure in the latter. The ambivalence runs through the very extensive use of the motif of the title song of *È primavera*,[2] associated with the central character, Beppe. An incorrigible flirt, barefaced stealer of his best friend's girlfriend and unabashed bigamist, he is also lively, charming and

È primavera: Beppe (Mario Angelotti) and one of his customers

ingenuous, seemingly utterly unaware of the impropriety of his behaviour. The opening phrase of the main motif suggests a fanfare, a musical trope of both the military and varietà. It accords with Beppe, a soldier, a show-off and, a stereotype connecting the two, a bit of lad. He is introduced doing his rounds as a bread delivery boy in Florence, cheerily flirting with his house-wife clients. There is a complex interplay between his motif and first wife Maria Antonia's at their parting in Catania, half way through the film, exu-berance alloyed with sadness, and this continues over shots of his journey to Milan; but once he gets there an oboe fanfare reintroduces 'È primavera' on its own. The fanfare not only reinserts him into barracks life but also gives that varietà sense of introducing the next act, Beppe on to his next escapade; having it on the oboe, though, gives an odd flavour, bright and yet perhaps tinged with melancholy or sourness. At the end of the film, the motif is played on a solo piano (almost as if for a silent movie), until giving way to full orchestra for the end cast list. The old-fashioned sound gives a faintly comic quality to the proceedings, perhaps softening what is a rather uneasy resolution (is everyone really going to be so happy?), perhaps in its rolling continuity suggesting that life goes on whatever, something stressed by ending with shots of another boy delivering bread to the strains of the same song.

It is not clear what *È primavera* feels about Beppe. The film was not a success, the director Renato Castellani observing that the public were not ready for its irony; Sergio Trasatti (1984: 52) concurs, seeing it as 'a cynical film, deliberately so, detached from the fate of its characters, at whose expense Castellani shows himself ready to be amused'.[3] However, a con-temporary review found it 'soft and light [so that] it melts in the mouth'.[4] Cynicism is not a characteristic part of Rota's affective repertoire and, though his music holds back from identification, it is seldom critical. Rota's score for *È primavera* does not undermine the cheeriness of the titular motif and supplies a range of touching variants and other motifs, and it is perhaps this that holds it somewhere awkward between deliberate cynicism and melt-ing in the mouth.

An unusual variant on setting up motifs in a credits sequence is the use in *La grande guerra* of Italian soldiers' songs from the First World War. Here each section of the film takes off from one of the songs, its title (or opening words) announced in an inter-title at the beginning of the section. They are nearly always first heard being sung by the soldiers before booom ing, with much modification and development, the basis of the score for the section. They suggest a signature tone for each section, although much of the tragic-comic effect of the film derives from the discrepancy between the maudlin or bawdy character of the songs and the cynicism of the central characters and the increasing wretchedness of the events.

Motifs do narrational work. They can, for instance, thicken a film's emo-tional texture. There is a scene between Agostina and the marshal in *Campane a martello* (1948) in which, just after Don Andrea's death, he signs a document permitting her to leave Ischia. The music intertwines three motifs. The main theme of the film is melancholic, associated from the beginning with war, farewell and disgrace; its continued presence is a reminder that Agostina is trapped by her past as a prostitute. At the moment the marshal, up to now mainly a comically pompous figure, signs the document, comic phrases are mixed in to the main theme, lightening the mood, although, because of the mixing, also bringing him more into the sympathetic side of the film. As Agostina thanks him, a third element is introduced, the music associated with her possible fiancé Marco. This, though played strongly in an earlier scene between them on the beach when they meet up again after she comes back to Ischia, is here played quietly and within the main theme, in keeping with his affective marginality in the film. The music keeps the different tones of the film in play – melancholy, comic, romantic – but also begins to blend them, as it does even more thoroughly in the last few minutes of the film.

Motifs, especially in Rota's hands, can also serve to reflect on the values they carry. 'Garibaldina' (*Cento anni d'amore*, 1953) has a love theme for its central couple, Maria, the ward of the parish priest, Don Pietro, and Rico, one of Garibaldi's men billeted on Don Pietro, much against the latter's will. The first time it occurs is conventional enough: Maria looks through a barred window in a door and sees Rico and the love theme (instantly recognisable generically as such) comes in and carries on over shot/reverse shots of them, until immediately fading when Don Pietro replaces Maria at the window (and in Rico's point of view). It next occurs when she holds up a cloth with Garibaldi embroidered on it in the window of her room as Rico

Francesco Hayez: *Il bacio*, the passion of the Risorgimento

passes and then again when she speaks Risorgimento slogans at the top of her voice in the room below his, continuing behind his pulling up a floorboard to look at and speak with her, the theme again only coming to an end when Rico's fellow militant tells him Don Pietro is coming back from church. These instances fuse young love and the patriotic fervour of the Risorgimento in a trope going back to one of the most famous of all Italian paintings, *Il bacio* ('The Kiss') 1859 by Francesco Hayez, very widely seen in its original form as well as in copies and above all reproductions.[5] Subsequently, although the Risorgimento connection is not made explicit, the use of the motif is informed by the association, charting various moments in the progress of their love. When the Papal forces regain control of the village, Maria and Rico escape together and Don Pietro, who has come round to blessing their love, persuades the commanding officer not to follow them, appealing to a sense of common humanity and Christian values. As Don Pietro makes this appeal, the love theme recurs: it references Maria and Rico's love, but also fuses this with the values of humanitarianism and Catholicism, values by the 1950s enshrined at the heart of the perception of the Risorgimento. Don Pietro's speech makes explicit this work of effecting a reconciliation of values, work already set in train by the musical motif.

'Garibaldina' affirms values through its motif; *Zazà* examines them. Here two themes are established diegetically as Zazà's, both songs that she sings in the café chantant of which she is the star; the first, 'Zazà', celebrates her own allure, the second, 'Canta con me', invites men to sing along with her (and, by implication, do much more). The songs celebrate her confidence and delight in her own glamorous sexiness; at the same time, shots of men in the audience and their enthusiastic joining in for the chorus of both songs (to the point that, in the case of 'Zazà', we only see and hear them in the final chorus) emphasise the accuracy of her affirmation of her sex appeal. The melodies of both songs are then used non-diegetically, though quite sparingly. 'Zazà' is heard in pretty, but very quiet variations as her lover Alberto lies at home on his bed by himself, and then again briefly a little later, when Zazà runs to answer the doorbell and finds him standing there. 'Canta con me' is used softly on cello when Alberto wakes Zazà at the hotel they are staying in in Paris and later, with unusually melodramatic force, when Zazà notes on the calendar his impending visit, at which she has self-sacrificingly decided to tell him the affair is over and sends him back to his wife. These are brief, if telling, moments in a film that has much other diegetic music (at the café chantant, on- and off-stage) and long stretches with no music of any kind.

The motifs are, however, elaborated in two musical set pieces, one at the end of each half of the film. The refrains of the two motifs are quite close, each based on a 'da-dà · da-dà' rhythm: 'Zazà! · Zazà!', 'Cantà · con me', and this makes the intertwining of them especially easy. At the end of the first half, Alberto returns to Paris, assuring Zazà that he will return; as she runs after the train carrying him away, 'Zazà' comes in in agitated form, achieved partly by the way it runs counter to an underlying train-like rhythm. Then, as Alberto falls asleep on the train and the film cuts between him asleep and the train wheels billowing with smoke, 'Zazà',

Zazà: café chantant brio

un film LUX
diretto da RENATO CASTELLANI

ZAZÀ

ISA MIRANDA
ANTONIO CENTA
ALDO SILVANI · ADA CONCINI · NICO PEPE

'Canta con me' and the rhythm of the train intertwine, 'Canta con me' slowed down and dramatic, becoming ever more tragic, decorated with urgent, staccato versions of the main 'Zazà' refrain. The sequence climaxes, getting faster, higher and louder, until Alberto wakes and throws away the key to Zazà's flat, thinking that he is breaking with her. Here the music mimics – or actually is – what is going round in his brain as he sleeps fitfully on the train: it is her music, the idea of her that she promotes in her song, that he can't get out of his mind. This is very different from the use of the motifs at the end of the film. As Zazà persuades Alberto to go back to his family, saying that she hopes he will have a good memory of her, 'Zazà' seeps in very quietly on high violins; as she bids him farewell, the melody goes through a series of variations for string orchestra, culminating in more tragic colours after he has gone and she staggers to the window to see him go; now the 'Canta con me' phrases also come in; on the last shots of her, first her eyes full of tears in extreme close-up, then led away by her old friend in the café chantant, the two refrains, 'Zazà' and 'Canta con me', become indistinguishable in a searing climax. This second elaboration of the motifs is clearly much more on Zazà's side, indicating or expressing her anguish, her tragedy.

What makes the use of the two motifs in *Zazà* powerful is the relation between their appearance as songs sung by her and their appearance in relation to Alberto and to Zazà herself. The songs affirm her pleasure in being an object of sexual desire, in having all the men adore her; the Alberto-on-the-train sequence suggests how this works on a male imagination, confirming her allure, but also seen as threatening, hysterical (so that when he wakes, he decides to break off with her); the final sequence expresses her tragedy through her own motifs, for it is precisely because she is a woman like that (a gorgeous sex object) that she cannot be a woman like that (a wife). Moreover, because the songs are pastiche,[6] the sense can be suggested that her sexy self-presentation is a cultural construction, which is nonetheless capable of inducing feverish dreams and, as an image of woman, sowing the seeds of tragedy for the real woman who embodies it.

As most of the examples above already indicate, motifs act as a kind of guide through a film. However, the guidance is not always straightforward: a motif may undergo many variations and it may not remain attached to one particular character or type of situation but may shift attitude and allegiance. I end this section by examining this, and Rota's use of motifs more generally, by looking at greater length at two of his most familiar scores, *Rocco e i suoi fratelli* and the *Godfather* films. In the case of the first, I trace the recurrence of the different motifs, and their shifting allegiances, across the film; for the second, I look at the way the motifs all come together in one short sequence in *Godfather II*.

Rocco e i suoi fratelli has one of Rota's most sustained use of motifs. Comparably perhaps to their use in Wagner's operas, they here serve the classic function of providing thematic clarity and continuity over the length of a sprawling, three-hour film. In particular they help to articulate not just the complex narrative of the Parondi family in Milan, but also its wider significance. The Parondis are part of the mass internal South–North migration in Italy in the late 1950s, the period of what was called the economic miracle; they are a microcosm not only of this broader socio-economic development, but also of the yet more vast historical movement from feudalism to capitalism.[7] What happens to each brother suggests ways that individuals cope, or do not, with the momentous historical forces that shape their lives. The motifs help to point up these resonances. They are musically distinct, suggesting associations and attachments to particular places and people, but they also undergo development and combination, sometimes shifting narrative allegiance and, if sometimes melodramatically inescapable, at others reticent to the point of unnoticeable.

Two motifs stick fairly rigorously to particular aspects of the narrative. One is the 'Milan' music that accompanies various sequences emphasising the city's modernity, an emphasis itself conveyed in the jazzy arrangement using electric organ (e.g., when the Parondis first arrive, gazing from the tram, 'See how beautiful it is!'; when Ginetta tells Vincenzo in no uncertain terms how he should treat her, not thinking he can use his old peasant ways).

Second, there is Nadia's theme. This is first briefly heard when Simone goes off with Nadia after his first successful boxing match (having previously agreed to celebrate with Duilio): it decorates the Milan music, thus explicitly linking Nadia with Milan and modernity. It is most extensively used in a scene between Nadia and Simone as their relationship develops, the theme supporting a monologue in which Nadia compares herself as a prostitute to Simone as a boxer, both selling their bodies for money. It is played on clarinet and then saxophone, with xylophone accompaniment, instruments, as well as the slow jazziness of the playing, reinforcing the link with modernity. At once lonely and sinuous, melancholy and sultry, it catches, and in some measure supplies, the sense of the sadness in Nadia as well as her sexiness. Later, less extended uses include a phrase from it on horns punctuating the suspense music as Simone goes in search of Rocco and Nadia to confront them[8] and some snatches of it triggered by Nadia telling Simone she hates him when he goes to find her where she is picking up clients on the outskirts of Milan. The earlier extended use of the theme established its association with Nadia and gave weight to her as a character; these later moments again give her some recognition as a character in her own right, although here the residual use of the motif may also reinforce the sense (often remarked upon) that Nadia is really no more than a function of the boys' destiny.

There is another, curious use of the theme in the scene where Duilio takes Simone back to his flat. Nadia has nothing to do with this scene, but perhaps the brief allusion to her theme links the scene back to her comparison of herself and Simone, for now Simone has become even more like her, a whore. The music links the corruption (for this is how the film presents it) via Nadia to modernity. Even in this case, then, the motif is not entirely fixed in terms of character allegiance and this is much less so with what may be considered the main motif of the film.

This is a mere five notes, yet it is the basis of the most sustained work and development in the film. Rota tells of working on the film, sitting with Visconti at the piano trying out various phrases; when Rota had got what Visconti was looking for,

> he stopped me and said 'That's what we want'. And then I elaborated on that thematic idea, because with Luchino it's not like little bits of music will do. You need fully developed themes. So, that first intuition was not enough – but that's what I started from.[9]

The sense of a brief phrase that feels just right but then needs to be worked up into longer themes characterises this main motif. There are two major variants. The first (A_1) follows two crashing, reverberating chords; behind the first half of the credits (themselves white on black copperplate lettering, solid, formal, unfussy), the phrase forms the basis of a dark, sombre melodic development, played on strings, with brass punctuations repeating the basic phrase. It is as if the melody wants to break free of this phrase but keeps being pulled back to it, until it finally sinks away beneath a final, harsh brass variant on it. A tone of high emotional seriousness is established. However, in the body of the film, when there is melodic development, it does not always take this brooding, gloomy character. For two of the great climaxes – Rocco renouncing Nadia on the roof of Milan Cathedral, Simone killing Nadia – the melody, in variant A_2, moves much further and higher away from the five-note phrase. It does also sink back at the end and the phrase is never long absent, but there is a brief, searing pulling away from it, usually on high strings, played loud and with a strong underlying pulse, a surge of aspiring energy. In either variant, this is classic romantic melodrama music, a long melodic line with a stepwise progression of notes and sudden large intervallic leaps, evocative of yearning, anguish and high passion (cf. Brownrigg, 2003: 154). Much of the play with the main motif is the co-presence of these variants and also the way they are held back, broken up and used as the basis for further variation.

After the credits, it is not heard at all in the first fifty minutes of the film. Then it occurs – just the five-note phrase, repeated twice, with a final warning brass punctuation – when Simone steals a shirt from the laundry where Rocco works, and then again – this time only once, with a different brass warning – when his hand runs down Luisa, the laundress, and he fingers her brooch. This is still only the basic phrase. Variant A_2 comes into the body of the film before A_1, first when Nadia gives Rocco the brooch that Simone had stolen to give her; at this point, the melody is not yet fully stated, even though it has started to move beyond the five-note phrase. It is heard next when Rocco speaks of the meeting to Simone, then when Nadia and Rocco meet by chance and have a coffee together (he on leave during military service, she just released from prison in the same town). Here the music, played first on an accordion, comes in when Rocco tells her that he feels such pity for her ('un bel complimento', she says ironically). The use of the accordion already softens the quality of the motif, perhaps giving it some affinity with the folk music played elsewhere in the film, although there is also briefly a use of electric guitar which gives it something of the feeling of the modernity of the Milan music and Nadia. At the point that Rocco tells her to have faith ('What in?', 'In everything', 'Including in you?', 'Yes, also in me'), the music shifts into the major key.[10] Its most romantic statement in the film is next, accompanying Rocco and Nadia in each others' arms on a tram in Milan. However, thereafter it returns to its more melancholic/tragic mode, supremely in a searingly melodramatic statement in the sequence on the roof of Milan Cathedral, where Rocco tells Nadia that she should go back to Simone, and in a broken up and desperate version, as Nadia confronts Simone for the last time, tells him she hates him and he kills her.

Variant A_1 comes into the film the first time (after the credits) in the sequence in which Ivo, one of Simone's hangers-on, tells him about Rocco and Nadia. First barely perceptible, very low and quiet behind the conversation and not yet quite the developed motif, then taking hold, still in very low strings with occasional horn punctuations, over a long close-up of Simone as he takes in what Ivo is telling him (that his girl is now Rocco's). It then develops, louder, always on low-register string and brass, over a dissolve to the bar where Simone, Ivo and others hang out, continuing on behind Ivo and Simone looking out of the window. Here the ominous quality of the sound and the repeated basic phrase contribute to a sense of danger and, after a brief sequence inside the bar (with diegetic juke-box music), it returns, faster, but still dark and low, creating a sense of mounting suspense as Simone and some of his mates run towards the waste land where they know Rocco and Nadia to be. As Simone goes in search of the lovers, the music becomes generic suspense music (a low treading rhythm and drawn-out quavering xylophone phrases) punctuated by brass variants on the five-note phrase, stopping when Simone crouches down to spy through bushes on Nadia and Rocco. There is no music for the confrontation, rape and fight, and when the motif returns, as Nadia staggers away and Rocco weeps, it is as A_2.

The main motif of *Rocco e i suoi fratelli* has been considered a theme of 'destiny'. According to Renzo D'Andrea (1986: 91), Visconti had planned to make use of the first movement of Tchaikovsky's Fourth Symphony, 'that brass fanfare and the "destiny theme" for strings', but dropped this idea and asked Rota to compose an 'harmonically similar Leitmotif', the phrase and its melodic variants now in the film. The link to the Tchaikovsky is suggested by having Nadia listen to the movement in question on her transistor radio in the scene where Ciro confronts her and Simone in the mother's flat. Given the element of fatalism in the film (cf. Canova, 2000: 178), this makes sense; it is also interesting to consider in relation to the film's putative Marxism. On the one hand, some notion of fate might be considered appropriate to a Marxist world-view, at any rate in the most deterministic version of this, where class and the economic order determine alike the lives of individuals and the direction of society; on the other hand, a Marxism based more on two mid-century rediscoveries, the early Marx and the writings of Antonio Gramsci, puts more emphasis on human agency, the interaction of individuals and situations, as in Marx's maxim 'People make their own history but not in circumstances of their own choosing'. This ambiguity in the film surrounding fate, determinism and Marxism may be clarified by considering the main motif in relation to character.

Henry Bacon (1998: 114) writes of the motif and its two variants, 'one dark, the other light, corresponding roughly to Simone and Rocco, respectively'. What I'm calling A_1 is associated with Simone's thefts and the lead-up to his rape of Nadia. A_2, on the other hand, first appears when Nadia speaks to Rocco about Simone and the brooch he has stolen; this is the moment when, as it were, the motif transfers from Simone to Rocco. Its development – especially in its optimistic mode (Nadia and Rocco having a coffee and later in the tram together) – remains with Rocco. However, its most agonised full statement, with Nadia and Rocco on the roof of Milan Cathedral, is also a scene that is about Simone and thereafter the theme comes in in other scenes where he is at issue even if not present (Ciro talking with Rocco about the latter's success in a boxing match, which Rocco connects to his hatred of Simone; Rocco saying he will do what he can to help Simone, after his theft from Duilio). The scene of Simone's killing of Nadia uses A_2, but chopped about, undercutting the urgent pulse and soaring melody of its use in the Milan Cathedral scene. All of this makes sense in that Simone's and Rocco's stories are so intertwined in the second half of the film, but it makes even more sense if one thinks of this as having to do with destiny. The main motif connects the two characters destroyed by the move to Milan, the two who cannot adjust to modernity, the one (Simone) corrupted by it, the other (Rocco) unable to live by its codes, unable to break free of feudal and patriarchal ideas of behaviour (the rights of elder brothers, the disposability of women). This is their destiny – but they are also the characters most prey to the very notion of destiny, of an inevitable fate. The other brothers adapt to the situation by taking on modern ideas, in work (Vincenzo as a construction worker; Ciro, who goes to night school to learn a trade, at Alfa Romeo) and in relationships (bourgeois, nuclear marriage). In short, if there is warrant to consider the main motif one of destiny, it may be that it allows us to see how the very notion of fate is itself what holds back and destroys the film's two major characters, Rocco and Simone. Variant A_1, more associated with Simone, keeps falling back musically, just as Simone is always dragged back and down; A_2 soars higher, suggesting melodramatic transcendence, even a glimpse of happiness, just as Rocco is elevated to the sanctity, or at any rate the beauty, of suffering.

In addition to the Fate, Nadia and Milan music, there are two folk-style motifs. One is provided by the song 'Paese mio', first heard sung behind the second half of the credits (displacing A_1). The words sing of how vast the world is and how the singer's heart is still in his beautiful 'paese', a word meaning both country and village and perhaps best understood as 'where I come from'. It is heard sung again at the very end of the film, as Luca skips home after talking with Ciro, but in between it is heard instrumentally, usually unobtrusively: on accordion, when Nadia, the first time she meets the family, asks them what they are doing in Milan and looks at an old photo of them together; very quietly, on muted trumpet, when Rocco gives his name, in reply to the boxing trainer Cerri, in the course of a conversation suggesting that Rocco train alongside Simone to keep an eye on him; behind Ciro and his mother talking about the situation of Nadia living with Simone in the flat, with the mother speaking of how she had always wanted to come North so that her sons could prosper and how it is now all falling apart; behind Rocco agreeing to sign to a long-term contract with Cerri, played here on horn over low strings, giving it some of the colouring of A_1 (with which the credits have already associated it, and made even more appropriate here because it follows on immediately from Rocco saying that signing on with Cerri, and condemning himself to a profession he hates, is 'the only way to save Simone from his fate'); behind Rocco speaking, at the celebration of his most recent victory in the ring, of how, back in their paese, when a master builder built a house he always threw away a stone at the shadow of the first passer-by, because 'there has to be a sacrifice to make the house strong'; intertwined with the main five-note figure as the camera tracks in on Rocco comforting Luca after Ciro has gone to the police to denounce Simone for the murder of Nadia, ending finally on Rocco's face in close-up.

The song, explicitly in its words but also in its form, is closely based on a traditional Southern Italian lullaby[11] and is often played on traditional instruments (accordion, or muted, ever so slightly blowsy trumpet; a folk balladeer accompanied by a guitar in the sung versions at the beginning and end of the film); it evokes the place the family have come from but always in the context of their not being there. Sometimes this goes with explicit reference to it: Nadia looking at the old photo, the mother lamenting having come north, Rocco (posed against the old photo of the family and one of him as a boxer, between the old and the modern) speaking of the builder casting the stone. At other times however it evokes that place even while not being referenced by characters or events. When Rocco agrees to train alongside Simone and later when he signs to a long-term contract, it signals these events as drawing him ever further and more definitively away from his paese, somewhere we know he longs to return to. The two sung versions are set markedly against images of modernity. The white lettering on a blank, dark background in the first part of the credits, with A_1 over, gives way to a rising crane shot, revealing the vast industrial ironwork of Milan railway station, just as the music gives way to the latter's antithesis, 'Paese mio'. At the end, Luca leaves Ciro, walks past hoardings advertising Rocco's boxing success and then skips away from the camera down a wide,

Rocco e i suoi fratelli: Rocco (Alain Delon) between family and boxing, past and future

empty, tarmac road towards high-rise developments (the kind that Vincenzo works on,
the kind springing up around the northern
towns of Italy in the period of the 'economic
miracle'). Some see the ending as optimistic,
either within the framework of the film's
Marxism (Luca has just been talking with
Ciro, the model worker at the Alfa Romeo
plant, and is moving towards ultra-modern
proletarian accommodation) or in relation to
the notion that, of all the brothers, perhaps

he is the one that will be able to return to the paese, or yet more generally, to
the notion of children as the hope for the future, a quite common trope of
postwar cinema (and not least neo-realism). To me the weight is more full

Luca (Rocco Vidolazzi)
skipping home at the end
of *Rocco e i suoi fratelli*

of sadness and loss, a soulless image set against the soulful evocation of the
paese that the child Luca can probably barely remember. There was originally to have been a scene at the beginning of the film in Lucania, showing
the family and the reasons for their move north.[12] Various factors, including
economic, meant that this was never shot. This diminishes the film tempo-
rally and geographically, depriving it of some epic sweep perhaps, but in
compensation it means that where the family came from, evoked only in
spoken words and above all in 'Paese mio', remains unseen, impalpable, a
trace, unrecoverable.

The other folk motif in *Rocco* is a waltz, reminiscent in some phrases of
The Godfather waltz. In its first two uses it accompanies quite long stretches
of film: the brothers getting up and dressed to go out to shovel snow, Rocco
on military service reading a letter from his mother about how everyone in
the family is getting on. Later versions are briefer: when Rocco, just back
from military service, speaks with his mother, and then again when he goes,
unlike her, to the christening of Vincenzo and Ginetta's first child; the conversation between Ciro and Luca near the very end of the film. The music,
with its lilting rhythm and cantabile melody played on accordion, like 'Paese
mio' suggests the past and the South, but cheerfully, with no sense of loss,
and accompanying family togetherness. However, that sense of all pulling
together functions more like a memory, above all in its final use in the conversation between Ciro and Luca, where togetherness is spoken about in a
context of fragmentation (Vincenzo in his own nuclear family and Ciro
about to be, Simone in prison, Rocco on tour).

The motifs in *Rocco e i suoi fratelli* clarify and articulate, but also shift
allegiance, suggesting, without insisting on, symbolic connections between
characters and situations. The same is true of the *Godfather* films, but here
I consider the way this works in just one section of the second part.
Godfather II moves back and forth, in long segments, between, on the one
hand, Vito Corleone's arrival as a child in the USA at the beginning of the
twentieth century, in flight from a vendetta against his family, and his establishing himself as a presence in Little Italy, and, on the other, his son

Michael's consolidation in the late 1950s of his hold over what has become a powerful Mafia business. Implicit in between is the period covered in *The Godfather*, the 1940s, Vito as head of one of the major New York Mafia families, an attempt on his life and his handing on the business to Michael. Towards the end of *II*, there is a sequence in which Don Vito takes his young family to visit his home town, Corleone in Sicily, to agree an olive oil importing scheme and also to the kill the man, Don Ciccio, who, as seen in the opening sequence of the film, murdered his father, mother and brother. The sequence brings together four of the motifs from the film in a manner that contributes to articulating the sequence, but they are also destabilised, by alterations of instrumentation and excessive or fleeting use, suggesting ways the characters are caught in a web of determinations and continuities, at once inexorable and elusive.

The sequence opens on a sudden cut from a scene, in the 1950s part of the film, in which Michael's wife Kay has told him that she has had an abortion (to put an end to 'this Sicilian thing') and he has forbidden her to go away, as she plans, with, in his words, 'my children'. The cut is sudden partly because it is one from a relatively dark interior to a relatively bright exterior, and from the tense silence following a quarrel to the cheerful sound of a brass band (playing to welcome the family at the station), and also partly because transitions between the two time frames in *Godfather II* are usually achieved by the softer means of a dissolve and often involve one or other of the characters involved (in either of the time frames) in a pose of contemplation. As always in the film the point of transition is suggestive, in the manner of classic montage juxtaposition. Here Kay has symbolically brought an end to the reproduction of the Mafia family line through a drastic act that has additional resonances in the context of the prohibition on abortion within Catholicism; the transition is to a sequence that shows the family in the warmest light, a charming group that seems the very antithesis of what Kay wants to end. Yet the seeds of what is to come (which, by virtue of the film's internal structure and its relation to *The Godfather*, we already know) are shown to be present in the sequence, not least by the use of musical motifs. Not only by virtue of these: most obviously, the killing of Don Ciccio shows the hold of the principle of revenge across time and space, and we may also note the combative disposition of the eldest son, Sonny (boxing with people around the table at the lunch in the family's honour), a disposition that will be his undoing.[13] However, the motifs suggest less obvious pre-echoes.

The local band playing a cheerful march with a certain reckless abandon (thumping percussion, slightly awry brass) at one level signifies Sicilianness, and true Sicilianness at that; it says, 'this is what [band] music was like in the old country'. However, the sudden cut to it and the manner of the playing also create a slightly comic quality, that might suggest the family's (and/or our) sophistication and distance from this peasant culture. The tune is played fully through, slightly petering out melodically to give way to the non-diegetic 'Love Theme' motif.

This motif, though so familiar, only appears in this sequence in *II* and in *The Godfather* only in the (one) Sicily sequence and the end credits. In *The Godfather*, it is first heard, the melody coming straight in on strings, quite loud, over a mid/close-up shot of Don Vito in bed, now back at home recuperating from an attempt on his life and watched over by middle son Fredo; the melody continues over an immediate dissolve to a long shot of a Sicilian hillside.

The Godfather: Don Vito (Marlon Brando) in New York; a Sicilian hillside

Perhaps the Don is thinking of his childhood or else of Michael in exile in Sicily (having shot the men responsible for the attempt on his father's life) or else there is just the juxtaposition of the Sicilian-in-America with actual Sicily. The transition is dreamy but also one of contrast, darkened interior to sun-drenched exterior, the quiet of Don Vito's room to music that is much fuller, much less reticent, than most of the music elsewhere in the film. The pastoral imagery – the sunlight, the sheep, the blue horizon – is picture-postcard pretty and the music is, with its sweet strings, in accord with this. As the sequence progresses, and Michael moves, literally and socially, deeper into Sicily, including seeing and meeting the woman he is to marry, Apollonia, the instrumentation becomes progressively more folkloric, first, on the road to Corleone, on harmonica, then in Corleone itself, on mandolins. The insistence of the melody, played over and over rather than broken down into phrases, suggests a romantic attachment, to Apollonia, to Sicily, but, as suggested in Chapter 1, also lightly signals this as romantic, acknowledging Sicily as, for Michael, for Vito, for Italian-Americans, a romantic construct rather than a fully known reality.

Some of this instrumentation recurs in the theme's use in the *Godfather II* sequence: mandolins over a welcoming lunch under an awning in a large garden, big strings at the beginning and end of shots of the family visiting an olive mill, mandolins and strings, mixed in with bells, outside the church after the murder of Don Ciccio. However, when it first comes in, it is on an almost piercing solo flute with very light string support and played just a bit slower than usual; if it would overstate it to say that this is more melancholy, it is certainly less whole-heartedly romantic. In *The Godfather*, the cut to the tune is a burst of sunshine and romance, whereas here its introduction sets up momentarily a much less enchanted relation to Sicily. This does give way to the more folkloric and rapturous versions just noted above, but these are fleeting statements (unlike the repetitions in *The Godfather*) and the last statement, outside the church, after the killing, is in fact over somewhat darker strings than before. In short, mandolins and high strings give us the romance again, but the opening flute and darker closing strings diminish its warmth.

In the olive mill, between statements of the love theme on strings, there is a shot of Vito holding a boy in his arms, feeding him an olive. The music used at this point has been associated since *The Godfather* with Michael and his gradual involvement, after an initial distance, in the family business. Marcia Citron (2005: 441), following Francis Ford Coppola, refers to this as a Fate motif. It consists of two main elements, usually heard together: a steady timpani beat and a darkly, mournfully descending melody. Here, in this brief shot in the olive mill, it functions first of all to identify the child as Michael (he is only named as such in the last moments of the whole sequence) and thence to associate this moment with what he is to become, the next Godfather. Yet the arrangement here is not fateful and brooding, but almost childlike, simple winds picking out the tune over what sounds like a music box. What is important is Vito cradling Michael, of the intimacy between father and son, something not shown with any of the other sons. It echoes the earlier shot of Vito cradling Michael at the end of the first part of *II*, just after Vito's assassination of the Black Hand boss Fanucci, the first step in establishing himself in the neighbourhood, the first step towards becoming a Mafia boss, an echo I will return to in a moment. The arrangement of the motif in the Sicily sequence links this softly lit moment of cradling in all its charm almost subliminally with Michael's descent into lonely monstrosity, suggesting, as the film does elsewhere, that it is precisely the intimacy, the almost atavistic memory of father–son love, that draws him inexorably into the business and his moral, emotional and spiritual desolation.

There is no music in the sequence of the murder of Don Ciccio except right at the end, as Vito and his accomplice Tommasino make their getaway, where we hear very briefly part of a theme introduced only in *Godfather II*. This is titled 'The Immigrant' on the CD of the soundtrack and named 'The Ethnic Longing Motive' by Citron. Its first, tentative part is first heard over a slow dissolve from the darkness of the streets in Corleone as the young Vito makes his getaway to a shot of the prow of a sailing ship in a pinkish dawn moving past the Statue of Liberty. Mounting phrases accompany a shot of people on board standing up, the camera following Vito as he walks along the ship. The big majestic and yearning melody (with decorating phrases from the first part) comes in with overhead shots of people looking up at the statue. The opening phrases together with the prow of the ship, Liberty and the dawn light suggest anticipation, promise, a new start,

Godfather II: the ship carrying young Vito arrives in New York

become more beatific when the main melody comes in. Later the melody is heard, played on mandolins, as Vito walks into the main street of Little Italy delivering groceries, the image, albeit in colour, made to look like an old photograph; the mandolins, the quasi-sepia quality of the image, the bustling scene, as well as the tune itself, convey warmth and nostalgia.

However, the motif does not remain exclusive to Vito. It is heard when Michael is

talking to his mother, after Cuba, with the
Kefauver hearings under way;[14] she tells him
one can never lose one's family, he says that
times are changing; as she speaks, the main
melodic element the motif comes in very
quietly indeed; then a developmental section
of the melody comes in fuller and on louder
strings with a dissolve to Vito, who is buying
fruit in the street. The dissolve, holding
Michael's and Vito's heads together, as well
as the music bridging the transition, link the
two of them. There is a further poignancy in the fact that Vito is buying
fruit, for it is when he is, as an older man, buying fruit in *The Godfather*, that
he is gunned down, an act leading to Michael's first involvement in the
family business (by defending his father in the hospital and later taking
revenge on Vito's would-be assassins). The link is complex. The dissolve,
the music, Michael with his mother, Vito buying fruit, all suggest warmth
and sentiment; but the darkness surrounding Michael, his statement that
things are changing (in the context of his mother dying, Kay leaving him,
his having his own brother Fredo killed), suggest the coldness and emotional
emptiness that is beginning to engulf him. The music too is initially quiet
and, with the dissolve to Vito, heard on solo oboe, a cold, lonely sound,
although, on a long, sepia-tinged shot of the street, this gives way to mandolins and the recovery of the warmth of the Vito episodes. At the moment
of the link, though, it is the coldness of Vito's legacy to Michael that is
uppermost, not the warmth that gave rise to it.

Godfather II: Michael (Al
Pacino) in the 1950s; his
father Vito (Robert de Niro)
in the 1920s

   The brief snatch of the immigrant motif as Vito makes his getaway after
murdering Don Ciccio uses only the first, tentative part of the motif and is
played quite differently, on low strings, slightly altered to create more of a
downward turn to the melody, and it is soon eclipsed by the sound of bells.
There is no release into the lyrical melody that usually follows this introduction. Music here performs a standard movie music function, underlining
the dark drama of the situation, but it also marks the darkening of the motif
itself and what it has been redolent of, a darkening made all the more intense
by its not giving way as hitherto to the full and soaring melody.

   The use of the Michael/fate and the Vito/immigrant motifs in the Sicily
sequence work in opposite directions. The former, brooding and doom-
laden in the rest of the film, is here childlike and pretty; the latter, mainly
warm and optimistic, is here dark and dramatic. Both, however, affectively
connect warmth and doom, affection and monstrosity, cradling and violence, the former incubating the latter. This is what the overall narrative trajectory of the *Godfather* films demonstrates, Vito becoming a source of
power and violence in defence of his family and neighbours, Michael drawn
down the same path for love of his father.

   The sequence ends with a shot of the train leaving Corleone, Vito holding Michael at one of the windows, telling him to say goodbye. This is

accompanied by the *Godfather* waltz, the main theme of the films. It is heard at the very start of *The Godfather* on a billowy unaccompanied trumpet and similarly at the start of *II*, where it is slightly extended with a sombre string accompaniment; in both cases, it introduces scenes of men paying court to the Godfather, Vito in *The Godfather*, Michael in *II*. It is, like the hold of the Godfather himself, extremely pervasive, in various guises. For instance, in *The Godfather*: at Connie's wedding; accompanying the famous horse's head sequence, in a very complex arrangement moving from echoey, far-off trumpet via a music-box effect to cacophony; coming in softly when Michael assures Vito in the hospital, after the assassination attempt, 'I'm with you now pop'; after the killing of Carlo, Connie's husband who has betrayed the family; over the last shots of the film, men coming to Michael after Vito's death and Kay having the door closed on her, excluding her from their meeting. In *II*: at Anthony's first communion and the party following it; covering a dissolve from Michael looking at his first born, Anthony, asleep in bed, to Vito looking at his, Sonny, in his pen; when Fredo runs away from Michael in Cuba, conscious that Michael knows Fredo has betrayed him; sung by a man on the steps sitting behind the family, after Vito has killed Don Fanucci; accompanying Frank Pentangeli, one of the senior Corleone henchmen who has turned state's witness for the Kefauver hearings, talking to Tom Hagen about the Corleones being like emperors. This is only a selection of its occurrences: no other motif runs so repeatedly and, whether on slow melancholy trumpet or with the oom-pah-pah waltz rhythm emphasised, so insinuatingly.

When Vito tells Michael to say goodbye as the train leaves Corleone, the motif can only just be heard within the sound of the train itself. It is played on a high solo instrument, perhaps a flute or recorder, melancholy, without warmth, and the melody is not completed, ending on a long held note before its end, fading away as the film dissolves quickly to the exterior of the family home in Nevada and Mama Corleone's funeral. The dissolve is a transition from the literal and metaphorical warmth of Sicily to the literal and metaphorical coldness of snow-covered Nevada, and one from being cradled by one's father to confronting the death of one's mother. The music is not warm at all, there is none of the dreamy echoey trumpet or the smile-inducing oom-pah-pah that the motif sometimes has in the films. Earlier in *II*, an even younger Michael is cradled by Vito after the killing of Fanucci, telling him 'Your father loves you very much', sitting on the steps behind them is a man playing a guitar and singing the *Godfather* waltz melody as a lullaby. The voice is that of the kind of semi-trained tenor of Italian song in the first part of the twentieth century, pre-crooning and pre-rock, popular bel canto. Although the man is seen strumming a guitar, it cannot be heard; only at the end do non-diegetic violins and then mandolins play briefly the oom-pah-pah section of the motif, taking it in a slightly different direction towards resolution, before giving way, over a blank screen, to the Michael/fate motif, bringing the first half of the film to an end. Here Michael's cradling by Vito, as if, despite being the youngest, he is all along

Godfather II: Vito cradles baby Michael after the killing of Fantucci, as a man on the step behind sings the *Godfather* waltz

to be the special son who will become the Godfather, is warm in sound, emanating from the community itself. Only at the fade-out is the connection with what Michael will become suggested musically. In the brief, semi-eclipsed, unresolved statement of the motif at the end of the Sicily sequence, though we have seen Vito cradling Michael, there is nothing left in the music of the warmth of such cradling. Perhaps it is simply too late in the unfolding of both films to evoke cradling with unequivocal warmth; cradling is now clearly the incubation of atavistic loyalty, an intimacy leading inexorably to monstrosity. Young Michael is saying goodbye to Sicily, although a notion of Sicilian values will keep its hold on him; middle-aged Michael is saying goodbye to his mother, whose death allows him, as he sees it, to arrange the death of his brother Fredo for his betrayal. The seeds of such behaviour were already there in that moment of paternal love.

At the very end of *Godfather II*, there is a flashback, signalled as Michael's memory, to the moment in the early 1940s when Michael announces to his family that he has joined up for the war effort, an act symbolising his choice of country over family, of wider, chosen bonds of loyalty. The return from this to Michael, sitting in Nevada remembering, consists of two dissolves: from him sitting alone in the 1940s at the dining table having made his announcement, while off-screen everyone else is greeting Vito on his birthday, via the shot of Vito and the child Michael at

Godfather II: Michael in New York early 1940s; Vito telling young Michael to wave goodbye to Corleone; Michael in Nevada late 1950s

the train window leaving Corleone, to Michael alone in the garden in Nevada. This is accompanied by the *Godfather* waltz picked out on flute over a mandolin sostenuto, the melody, as before, not completed, the promise of resolution withheld. The 1940s was the moment when Michael might have broken with the family, with 'this Sicilian thing'; the dissolve at the end of the Sicily sequence, with the uncomforting instrumentation and the lack of melodic closure, raises the question of whether such a break was ever emotionally possible. It is the question at the heart of the *Godfather* films.

The Sicily sequence in *Godfather II* illustrates in an especially condensed form Rota's use of motif. Connections are made with the rest of the film, so that, for instance, the folkloric loveliness of Sicily, the cradling of Michael and the hold of Sicilian values over the immigrant Vito, elements established in relation to these motifs elsewhere in the film, are all made available through the use of the motifs here. Yet the motifs are also musically altered, with further suggestiveness – there is a moment of melancholy in the playing of the love motif, of childlikeness in the Michael/fate motif, of menace in the immigrant theme, and the waltz is musically unresolved. All these alterations complicate and illuminate the meanings carried in their reference back to their significance elsewhere in the film, melding warmth and foreboding, affection and menace. At the same time, and this is very characteristic of Rota, none of this is insisted upon. The motifs do other standard jobs – scene setting (the love motif), individuating characters (the Michael theme, indicating which this particular child is), providing dramatic reinforcement (the immigrant theme as Vito makes his getaway) – so that they do not exist only to provide thematic echoes. They are also reticent: if the love theme is poured inescapably over the image, perhaps suggesting the inexorable sweep of the romantic idea of Sicily, the other themes are fleeting, barely audible.

Motifs do in Rota's work what they do in other composers' scores: they set a tone, they articulate characters and themes. They may also permit reflection on the cultural sources of emotion and the implications of this: café concert sassiness (*Zazà*), popular balladry (*È primavera*, *Sotto il sole di Roma*), folkishness (*Rocco*, *Godfather*), tourist Orientalism (*Death on the Nile*). In their sometime reticence, shifts of allegiance, changes of instrumentation, rhythm and melodic shape, they may also try to keep us from attending to a film solely by following characters or narrative development, cutting across these to wider affective associations.

REFERENCE

Rota's scores make copious use of musical reference. They use both citation, quoting actual pieces of music, and imitation, writing in a given style, whether compositorial or generic. This may be for standard functional purposes of scene setting or generic tone,[15] but sometimes a light signalling of the musical element, indicating that reference is being made, highlights its provenance and history.

Rota uses both citation and imitation as forms of reference. He quite often explicitly quotes a given piece of music.[16] Songs of national belonging are often used, for instance, to contrast the Germans ('Deutschland über alles') and the Americans (Sousa, 'Anchors Aweigh'[17]) in postwar films such as *Come scopersi l'America*, *L'eroe della strada*, *Napoli milionaria* and *Vivere in pace*. The various citations in *Mio figlio professore* chart changing times: 'Come chioveva',[18] a Neapolitan classic, 'Bombolo'[19] and 'Pippo non lo sa',[20] two popular songs of the fascist period taken to be making fun of leading regime figures (Borgna, 1992: 132, 164), 'Lili Marlene' and 'It's a Long Way to Tipperary', tunes of occupation and liberation; in *Il brigante* (1961) the Calabrian song, 'Fiuri, fiuri, fiurite tutto l'anno', 'runs through the depiction of the rural setting but also serves to bring out sociological aspects' (Comuzio, 1986a: 23);[21] *Film d'amore e d'anarchia* (1973) uses over a dozen songs popular in the early 1930s, when the film is set, their titles supplied in the end credits; the music for *Waterloo* is based on carefully researched military music of the period.[22]

More still, Rota uses various forms of imitation, music that is like other music without actually quoting it. This includes music that evokes specific pieces of music: Beethoven's Sixth 'Pastoral' Symphony, Dvořák's Ninth 'New World' Symphony and George Gershwin's *Rhapsody in Blue* (*Vivere in pace*), Wagner's *Tristan und Isolde* and Debussy's piano prelude 'Footsteps in the Snow' (*Le notti bianche*),[23] Prokofiev's opera *War and Peace* (*War and Peace*).[24] Equally, scores may simply work within a given musical style: generic (musical and filmic), period, national and regional.

Signalling reference

Citation and imitation do not of themselves imply reference in any strong or signalled sense, but still the very fact of them deployed so abundantly may itself bring the practice to the fore and thus make what is primarily representational also referentially evident. The score of *La regina di Saba* draws on the biblical musical palette established by Victor Young for *Samson and Delilah* (1949) and Miklós Rózsa for such films as *Quo Vadis?* (1951) for the credits and scenes of political manoeuvrings, Rimsky-Korsakov's *Scheherazade* for romantic encounters, standard adventure movie horns and orchestral pounding for galloping off and adventure and quasi Latin-American music for a dance entertainment at the Queen of Sheba's court with images of women playing zither-type instruments (and some attempt in the score to reproduce the sound these might make). Though the main function of this is to evoke or reinforce certain moods and spaces, still there is a sense of the composer having fun with the conventions at his disposal rather than just doing a very professional job of producing a genre score. *Città di notte* and *Caro Michele* (1976) suggest other things such multiple referentiality may do. *Città di notte* centres on fifteen-year-old Marina, at once prey to adolescent exaggeration and genuinely vulnerable, wandering the streets of Rome one night. The film opens with a rather sleazy scene between a man and a younger, wary woman, complete with expressionist lighting and creepy music, which turns out to be a rehearsal for a play; later a play with the farcical title of 'Rientra nei ranghi James' ('Get Back in Line James') is read in a tone of high seriousness by its author, the improbably named Achille Caldixon, played, uncredited, by the film's director, the beloved character actor Leopoldo Trieste, who had memorably played a pretentious young playwright in *I vitelloni* (1953) three years earlier. The motif that will chart Marina's night is first heard on a merry-go-round, then a little later played by a band at the Spanish Steps in Rome, linking it and her to childish pleasures and tourist-oriented performance. The opening music and the introduction of Marina's motif provide a context of false impressions, errors of aesthetic judgment and an immature disposition for Marina's picaresque night in Rome, which also involves a number of musical styles: mandolins – classic catering folklorism – in a restaurant where Lidia meets Alberto and others from the theatre group; atonal contemporary music, reminiscent in a film context of Giovanni Fusco's scores for Michelangelo Antonioni[25] and Hanns Eisler's for *Nuit et brouillard* (1955), when Marina wanders round a modern art gallery; mute trumpet, piano and brushed percussion playing dance band jazz over Marina in darkness by the Tiber, perhaps initially thinking of

La Regina di Saba: Balkis, Queen of Sheba (Leonora Ruffo), and King Solomon's son, Prince Roboam (Gino Leurini)

La Regina di Saba:
the Queen's court

throwing herself in: there is no diegetic source but the music Americanises – movie-ises? – her situation; mute trumpet over a slow boogie woogie vamp, more moderne than the previous music, but at moments slurred to the point of burping, for a scene at the bohemian Adriana's (another member of the theatre group); reflective guitar accompanying someone reading poetry speaking of love and agony; a mazurka on violin, with a xylophone middle section, accompanying an elderly dancing Polish couple at a cultural association, the tune then given a music-box quality as they are seen leaving afterwards by car.

Apart perhaps from the music at Adriana's, none of this music is of itself pointed, that is, pastiched, but, taken together in the context of the film's hints about misleading impressions and adolescent impressionability, their combination begins to hold up each one as a particular kind of playing.

Caro Michele is a film of connection and disconnection. All the characters are in a chain of connections, although some do not know of each other at all. The eponymous Michele never appears in the film (except briefly as a child in a flashback) and dies two-thirds of the way through; his mother Adriana writes to him but he writes to his sister Angelica; the mother's letters are heard in her voiceover but his letters in his sister's; Adriana is separated from Michele's father, but still sees him regularly (in the opening sequence sitting not talking in a deserted café in Rome); the father, who has lost touch with Michele, dies early on in the film; vagabond Mara claims that her child is Michele's, then that she is not sure, later that he definitely isn't, then that she doesn't know; Michele's friend Osvaldo, who helps her, may also have been his lover and hers. The music reinforces the senses of connection and disconnection, music as a bond between people, music as something that separates them, partly because of the various levels of reference in it. The main non-diegetic music is a piano quintet, dedicated to Rota's composer grandfather Giovanni Rinaldi;[26] it is primarily associated with Adriana, attached to the past in her memories and her discontinuous relationship with her husband. The latter sings the Republican Spanish Civil War song 'Ay Carmela' to himself, which is then picked up non-diegetically in ways that connect him and Michele, despite the fact that they have no contact in the film and are entirely (Michele) or soon (the father) absent from it. The father was a left-wing sympathiser, Michele is an activist: at the very moment his father dies, Angelica gets a letter from Michele asking her to dispose of a machine gun he's left in his flat; the letter and her doing as he requests are accompanied by 'Ay Carmela' sung by a male choir with guitar accompaniment. The same music is heard when Angelica identifies Michele's body after he is killed in student actions in Amsterdam and also as Adriana reminisces about Michele and her one-time lover Filippo singing it together. Towards the end of the film, in modified form, the tune is also heard over shots of Mara, perhaps simply reminding us of her personal connection to Michele, possibly suggesting that her lifestyle, free-spirited, unconventional, on the road, not remotely hidebound (unlike almost everyone else in the film), is rebellious in its own way. Her character is highlighted by the contrast with Fabio, the learned bachelor publisher who briefly takes up with her before dropping her in embarrassment, and who plays the slow movement from a Mozart piano concerto, isolating him culturally from Mara and suggesting the hypocrisy of refinement. Mara herself is associated with an almost Straussian waltz that suddenly bursts out when she gives Fabio a cup of Nescafé, with terrific lilt and drive, suggesting her energy and sense of fun. Yet this is purely non-diegetic and only heard in relation to her; there is no suggestion of connection to anyone else, reflecting the way Mara is caught up in her own world, self-centred, a little crazy. The film ends with her pushing the baby in a pram loaded with bags down a motorway in Sicily, where a taxi has finally dumped her after she has rowed with the driver; the Straussian energy and fun of the music gives those qualities to an ending which is yet also an image of Mara's utter disconnection, not only from the characters in the film but from the world itself. In sum: the Rinaldian quintet relates to a character connecting primarily with the past, 'Ay Carmela' with connections made from the past to the present, across seemingly dead relationships (Michele and his father, Adriana and Filippo), the Mozart piano concerto with a sealed-off high-bourgeois culture, the Straussian waltz with a no less sealed-off bohemian, more or less Lumpenproletarian lifestyle. Connections and disconnections.

Such examples signal reference mainly by virtue of combination and juxtaposition. However, many scores are also often more evidently signalled as imitation, that is to say, they deploy pastiche.

It is not always easy to decide whether something is meant to be taken as pastiche. This is partly a characteristic of the mode itself: pastiche is very close to what it imitates, sometimes to the point of being mistaken for it; part of the point of it is not taking a distance, which is in turn why it is so central to the production of ironic attachment. For *Le due orfanelle* (1954) Rota composed a song 'alla francese',[27] in other words, in conscious imitation of a certain period and nationality of song. The film tells of two girls, Henriette and Louise, a foundling, who grow up together as sisters. When, in their teens, their father dies and they travel to Paris, Henriette is carried off by a Marquis, leaving Louise, who has become blind, at the mercy of a beggar woman, who puts her to work in the streets of Paris, singing a song her mother sung to her in the cradle, Rota's song 'alla francese'. This then recurs at various telling points in the story. When an honourable aristocrat, Ruggero, tells Henriette that he loves her, there is a cut to Louise singing in the street, providing a contrast of the sisters' fates. When the Countess de Linières gives Louise money outside a church, the theme played non-dieget-ically suggests a connection between them, of piety but also (unbeknownst to either of them or, unless we already know the story, to us) of in fact mother and daughter. Later in the street the Countess passes a house and hears Louise singing the song inside and realises that she must be her daugh-ter, but she is prevented from making contact with her. Later still Henriette, now imprisoned, hears the song and thinks she has found her long lost sister, but it is only another prisoner who has learnt the song from Louise. The song then does a great deal of affective work, but, though the mode of period melodrama was already unfashionable,[28] the film (including its score) does not condescend to its material: we are not supposed to think that the song is a pastiche but rather to treat it straightforwardly as a song of the period with this role in these characters' lives.

The matter of whether something is a pastiche also relates to another use of the term: an imitation that traduces its object. Some of Rota's scores may stand accused of this. The music for Katherine Dunham's dance company in *Mambo* is described on the soundtrack album of the film as a pastiche of the kind of music Dunham used for her ballets. This is itself a 'stylized imita-tion' of African-American elements within the art music forms of its time,[29] pastiche in the sense of both combining different elements and the selfcon-scious imitation of forms. The opening number consists of a wordless sung call, suggestive of Caribbean (and perhaps specifically Haitian[30]) tradition, which gives way to bongos and phrases on guitar and brass (in other words, combining instruments from different parts of the world), sometimes keep-ing an Afro-Caribbean feeling going, sometimes coming closer to bebop; for sections focusing on Giovanna (Silvana Mangano), there is greater use of clarinet, oboe and violin, all in a much less jazzy mode, while the number ends in a big-band style. This combinatory musical style might be under-stood as a conscious signalling of the hybridity of black American music (and Mangano's dancing, so exciting in *Riso amaro* (1949), so wooden beside Dunham, may be felt to contribute to the pastiche sense of putting on a style). However, all of this is contained within a discourse of authenticity. Giovanna is a young Italian woman who is drawn irresistibly to Dunham's company by the sound of the bongos; the number that demonstrates, at least to the satisfaction of the characters, including Dunham, that Giovanna has got what it takes as a dancer, is called 'Black Night'; the Caribbean or jungle visual and musical *mises en scène* of the numbers contrast with Latin-American dance music and songs, seen here as sedate in comparison. Thus, while one might judge the music to be conscious and signalled imitation in its hybridity, this is not really recognised by the film, which treats it as authentic (accurately black) and, as is common in contrasts of black and white cultures, as more authentic (in touch with the physical well springs of the human) than anything whiteness has to offer.

This sense, that when it comes to non-white music the notion of authenticity rules, is evident in a number of other films. In *Senza pietà*, 'Nobody Knows the Trouble I Seen' and other Negro spirituals, sung by black GIs and incorporated into the non-diegetic score, express depths of feeling and hope otherwise lacking in the white female characters' lives. For *This Angry Age* (1956), the director, René Clément, went on a field trip to Indo-China and collected musical materials for Rota to work up into the score; they are used to provide local colour and to contrast to the Western music favoured by plantation owner Madame Forrestier (light classics she plays on the piano) and her children (rock 'n' roll). The music seems at its most Indo-Chinese – that is, at its least familiar to a Western audience in terms of instrumentation, rhythm and harmonics – when two characters (Michael and Suzanne) make love after a picnic, a sequence signalled as the moment of truest feeling in the film. The score of *Hurricane* combines Western instruments with Polynesian elements (strong, complex rhythms, whistling and chants, Hawaiian guitar, wooden drums) that Rota studied on recordings that he had of 'ethnic' music put out by the Ocora and Bärenreiter companies (Lombardi, 2001: 176). The latter are predominantly used diegetically, the Western elements non-diegetically, and this division perhaps reflects the structure of the story, centred on Charlotte, daughter of the white Governor of a Samoan island, who falls in love, much to her father's revulsion, with the local Chief, Matangi. She finds more in the local culture (the music, the ceremonies, Matangi) than merely local colour, something resonant with the usual notion of the truth of the primitive, but the music that carries the narration non-diegetically is

Senza pietà: Jerry (John Kitzmiller) and Angela (Carla Del Poggio) in hope and despair

Western, indicating the perspective from which everything is seen and heard. Indigenous music is an authentic but inert backdrop, narrativity is white.

Something may come to be perceived as pastiche – by virtue of a mode falling into desuetude (a period melodrama like *Le due orfanelle*) or changing perceptions (post-colonial critique and *This Angry Age* and *Hurricane*) – but may not have been intended as such. However, much of Rota's music is more purposefully pastiche. This may be discerned in the formal properties of the music itself and also in the relation of the music to the other elements of the film.

Pastiche as a formal property of works is conveyed in the high degree of similarity between the pastiching work and that to which it refers (always allowing for changing perceptions of the latter) together with elements that deform (select, accentuate, exaggerate, concentrate) or are discrepant from that referent (Dyer, 2007a: 52–63).

The main theme of the *Godfather* films and various examples of salon music in Rota's work are examples of musical deformation. The former, established at the very beginning of each part, is played on a rather blowsy trumpet with a very slight echo, suggesting something at once inexpert and far away, not fully grasped, remembered, imagined. Although the theme goes through many variations, from time to time the underlying waltz rhythm is emphasised, most notably at the very end of the long credits of *II*, where,

This Angry Age: brother and sister Suzanne (Silvana Mangano) and Joseph (Anthony Perkins) dance to rock 'n' roll

after all the films' other themes, the main theme is rounded off with a delicate exaggeration of the underlying rhythm, broken up and interrupted:

    oom-pah-pah
    [pause]
    oom-pah
    [pause]
    oom.

The effect is almost comic, something playful and charming at the end of all this carnage and sorrow, bringing out a formal property of the music and, in the context, a surprising one, namely, that it is a waltz. It is the charm that makes it so insidious, so drawing in, although the smile elicited here may also be Rota saying that it is after all only a film.

Something similar is achieved in Rota's forays into genteel salon music, including the *Concerto Soirée* in which he pastiches, with the most gentle of deformations, the waltzes, polkas and other dances of nineteenth-century bourgeois popular music. Examples in film include a brief moment of Totò in paradise towards the end of *Totò e i re di Roma* (1951), the motif for signora De Ritis in *Un eroe dei nostri tempi*, discussed in the 'Comedy' chapter, and 'Pendolin' (*Cento anni d'amore*), where the high violin pastiche is in accord with the phoney quality of the performances of Vittorio De Sica and Nadia Gray as the uncommitted, playing-at-it adulterous couple Giovanni and Mariella. In *Death on the Nile*, a trio in the ship's restaurant plays rather waveringly with uncertain rhythms; in *Film d'amore e d'anarchia*, there is a wonky all-female quartet playing on the terrace café visited by the couple Tunin and Tripolina. In both these cases, the music one hears is clearly, as evidenced by the instrumentation and fingering, not emanating from the players on-screen, which may just be continuity carelessness but may also remind us of the deliberateness of the musical quality here. The humour derives from the 'off' playing, but also from the supposed incongruity and insecure competence of, respectively, Arab and women players.

If the *Godfather* waltz and the salon music of 'Pendolin' or *Death on the Nile* achieve pastiche by virtue of musical deformation, pastiche in *Film d'amore e d'anarchia* and *Zazà* relies more on discrepancy. In the former, the basic music for the sequence of Tunin and Tripolina's time together sounds, in its preparatory phrases, as if it is going to be, more or less, the Barcarolle from Offenbach's *Tales of Hoffmann*, a piece redolent, whether or not you know the operetta, of young lovers or honeymooners on holiday. In the event a different melody comes in, but the underlying barcarolle figure and lilt is retained: the discrepancy between what these set up and maintain and the new melody casts the music as pastiche, heightened because the Barcarolle is a classic piece of tourists' Venice music (supposedly sung by gondoliers) whereas here the couple are effectively tourists in Rome. All this is highly appropriate for the rather unreal quality of these two days, playing at courtship or honeymooning in the face of his certain imprisonment or death.

In this case, the discrepancy arises from an expectation not fulfilled; in the case of *Zazà* it is a discrepancy with regard to the referent. Zazà's two songs, 'Zazà' and 'Canta con me', may sound to us now as accurate evocations (or may even be mistaken for actual café chantant songs from the early twentieth century), but their pasticheness is evident if one compares them to recordings of the songs and performers they are based on, recordings that were to the original audience for the film from only twenty years earlier and still in circulation. Zazà's/Isa Miranda's soft, crooning voice and delivery is utterly different from the sharp, nasal qualities of the singers the music references, such as Maria Campi or Zara 1ª. We get a glimpse of something closer to the style of the period in the delivery, and the plump appearance (compared to Miranda's svelte glamour), of the woman who appears before Zazà on the bill. The songs themselves are entirely correct in their verse and chorus structure, in the content of their lyrics (the celebration of the singer's desirability) and the space for an all-male audience to join in, but not in their pacing (slower, more plodding, less syncopated). These elements of closeness and discrepancy produce a pastiche of the look-at-me-I'm-sexy song of the period; this is the basis of Zazà's confidence in herself and Alberto's fascination with her as well as the reason she cannot become a respectable married woman. Doing this through pastiche enables a sense of both of them being caught up in the cultural construction and social placing of sexy femininity, not making a point so much as conveying the way construction and placing are felt and lived.

The pasticheness discussed in the last few paragraphs is already in the music, but in other instances it is a potential in the music only brought out by its place in the film. In *Il maestro di Vigevano*, Antonio and Ada watch, on television in a local café, a programme about getting married called 'Sogni per due' ('Dreams for Two'). Over images of a couple being in love and planning marriage, accompanied by a female voiceover, there is a slow melody on strings, not quite romantic, not excessively sentimental. Although already used in the credits, initially this appears to be music emanating from the television. However, when the camera tracks in on Ada, cutting Antonio out of the frame, and she leans against the wall with a faraway look, the music – and the idea of 'Sogni per due' – becomes associated with her; when the film then cuts to Antonio and Ada walking home, the same music continues, uninterrupted in its flow from the previous shot. Already, in the transfer from television programme to Ada and from diegetic to non-diegetic, the sense of the music as a type is suggested. This becomes more evident as the film progresses, because of the discrepancies between the music's associations and what is on-screen. When Antonio says to Ada that he wishes he could be rich for her sake, he imagines her in a fur coat, tiara and jewels vamping towards him, to the accompaniment of the 'Sogni per due' theme. Later, Antonio and his friend Nannini, out together for a walk, talk of wanting a better world, of loftier ideals, but then notice a cuddling couple, whom they spy on making love. Here the introduction of 'Sogni per due' contrasts both with the lusty couple and the voyeuristic middle-aged men. Agreeing with Nannini that the sight of the couple is beautiful, Antonio immediately adds that he must go home, where, as we know, such 'paradise on earth' (as Nannini describes it) no longer characterises his marriage. The television tune, though always played in exactly the same way, seems more saccharine with every use. It occurs again when Ada, snuggling up to Antonio in bed to persuade him to give up his teaching post, fantasises about how life could be, going to night clubs, Sunday trips to the lakes in the car, holidays in Riccione, in other words really rather modest, petit-bourgeois fantasies, pitched at the level adumbrated by the television programme. When later Ada, who has embarked on an affair, speaks kindly to Antonio, saying she should have understood how important the teaching was to him, 'Sogni per due' now accompanies this enactment of the ideal wife (contrite, knowing her place, privileging the husband) at the very moment she is in fact destroying the marriage. The last use of it occurs after Antonio has found out about the affair and is heard over him playing cards with his men friends; here the music no longer directly relates to Ada, but this is perhaps about another stage in the story of marriage and the dreams that inspire it, husbands and wives drifting apart. One could hear the 'Sogni per due' tune straight, but, anchored as it is initially, albeit ambiguously, in a television programme, it gradually acquires the sense of a culturally constructed, and contested, affect.

There is something similar going on by the end of 'L'ora di punta' (*Oggi, domani, dopodomani*, 1965), even though this is based melodically on citation. The first part of the film uses one of Rota's characteristic comic modes, perky, bustling, occasionally squeaky woodwinds, but interpolates every so often phrases from the Wagner and Mendelssohn Wedding Marches,[31] all to accompany Michele's visit to his old friend Arturo and his wife Dorotea, and the couple's excessively cute mutual endearments; when a row develops between them and Arturo draws a gun, the music becomes more dramatic but still drops in phrases from the archetypal marriage music. Arturo shoots at Dorotea and she collapses; when a little later she comes round, this is heralded by a bassoon playing the Wagner, with occasional brass flourishes. Arturo explains to Michele that he uses the gun to keep Dorotea in order, using blanks but occasionally substituting real bullets so that she doesn't become complacent. It transpires that neighbouring husbands have taken up the idea and the next morning, at the 'ora di punta' (rush hour), as Michele and Arturo drive off together, the neighbourhood resounds to guns going off. At this point the film cuts suddenly to a bride, groom and wedding party leaving a church and now we have at last Mendelssohn's Wedding March in full orchestral arrangement, stately and sweet, pretty much as he wrote it. However, given all the mischief that has been done to it before this, both musically and in relation to the depiction of a marriage, it is liable to sound, even if now being played at its most straight, quoted, even pastiched. A little boy hands the groom a pistol, and then all the men in the party start firing pistols into the air (cross-cut with Michele looking delighted at this way of handling marriage), all the while to Mendelssohn's majestic strains. The Wedding March is pressed into the service of a peculiarly stark fantasy of male domination within marriage, revealing – though in my judgment uncritically – what the march would surely normally be taken to conceal.

Reference and subject matter of film

Sometimes the function of reference may just be fun, a sense of a film enjoying itself, neither taking itself too seriously nor, all the same, wishing to undermine the generic pleasures it offers. *Femmine di lusso* (1960), a light-hearted story of romance and misunderstanding on a yacht cruise in the Mediterranean (a popular formula in the period), uses a big swirling theme with Latin-American underbeat for the many panoramas and shots of lovers within them; it also uses 'Casta Diva', listened to in its operatic version by one of the characters, but then used non-diegetically in a swung Latin-American version – fun and, in keeping with the film, blandly vulgar. The jolly swashbuckling shifts in the fortunes of the female pirate *Jolanda la figlia del Corsaro Nero* are variously accompanied: for the entry of the British into Maracaibo by warm Elgarian marching music, for Jolanda having her hair cut like a man's by Spanish guitar music and for a dance in a castle a pavane owing more to Fauré and Ravel[32] than to the putative sixteenth-century setting (which of course Fauré and Ravel were themselves referencing). The same may be said of the minuet in *La nave delle donne maladette* (set initially in Spain) and the court dances in *I pirati di Capri* (though these also sound rather like parts of Prokofiev's *Classical Symphony*,[33] thus suggesting a pastiche of a pastiche).The sense of having fun chimes especially well with *I pirati di Capri*, which plays on the idea of the theatricality of swashbuckling. Its basic premise, the foppish Count of Amalfi at the royal court in eighteenth-century Naples who is also the daredevil Captain Scirocco leading the proletarian rebellion, is heightened in set pieces, with appropriate music to match: in the opening sequence, some of Scirocco's followers, posing as entertainers, perform daring acrobatics among a ship's masts and sails as a sign to the rest of his followers to board and commandeer the ship; Amalfi's staging of a court ballet culminates in a masked man, supposedly danced by Amalfi, rescuing women from the gallows, followed by a duel between a corps of swordsmen, during which Amalfi's (that is, Scirocco's) arch enemy, the Baron von Holstein, realising it is not Amalfi onstage, pursues Amalfi's stand-in backstage, to the same music, only to be foiled at the last moment by Amalfi taking his stand-in's place; finally, there is a real duel between Amalfi and, first, von Holstein's men, then a little later von Holstein himself, each time the duel ending up on stage to the tune of, now, non-diegetic music. Swashbuckling music accompanies the action, regardless of whether it is staged or for real (and sometimes it is both) and always with a sense of fun.

I pirati di Capri: the Count
of Amalfi, alias Captain
Scirocco (Louis Hayward),
commandeers a ship

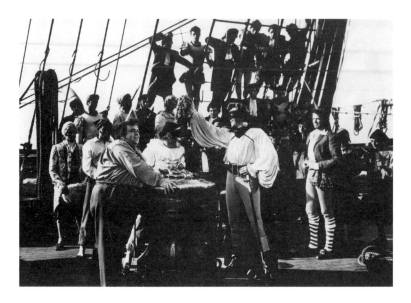

However, as the examples of *Il maestro di Vigevano*, 'L'ora di punta' and
even *Jolanda la figlia del Corsaro Nero* suggest, pastiche may also serve to
provide a sense of the social and historical specificity of the music, and the
attendant and disputable culture and sensibility involved.

It might, for instance, register a sense of cultural difference. *Un americano in vacanza* tells of Dick, a GI who has a week's break in Rome and
meets an Italian woman, Maria, who, after being initially wary, falls for him
as he has for her; the film is about mixed feelings, romantic and national, that
become harmonious. The credits opens with a fanfare over a shot of St
Peter's and a snatch of 'Anchors Aweigh' which then gives way to a very
Italian-sounding melody (by Rota). When Dick sets off from the army
camp in a jeep with a fellow GI they sing a song (also by Rota), the words of
which speak of some of the drawbacks of Rome but then have the refrain,
'But when I kissed her, I said "Bella, bella Rome"'. Both the Italianate
melody of the credits and 'Bella Roma' are pastiche Italian, the first sweeter,
more of a ballad, the second closer to tarantella. On the way to Rome, they
encounter Maria and give her a lift, and now the ballad melody is played
again, but on saxophone, suggesting an integration of the American with the
Italian. From then on the melody becomes the motif for their relationship,
perhaps suggesting the real enchantment of a furlough romance, perhaps
still keeping it within a notion of Italian for foreigners (this being a point-
edly Italian tune in a film made by Italians, which nonetheless centres on a
US protagonist). The idea of mixing culturally different musical themes in
the context of heterosexual romance is also present in *È primavera*. For
Beppe's relationship with Maria Antonia, his theme, based on the eponymous song, is intertwined with a genteel, minuet-style tune, anachronistic,
but suggesting the sweet old-fashionedness of the girl, especially in contrast
to Beppe's wide-boy character. When, on his transferral to Milan, the pair

part at Catania station, the two elements are counterpointed, charmingly but not harmonised as one, leaving open (at this half-way point in the film) the compatibility of his modernity and her old-fashionedness, of Sicily and the North, perhaps even of masculinity and femininity.

Pastiche may acknowledge and throw into relief the fact of construction. An interlude in Malaga in the Second World War film *Londra chiama Polo Nord* (1955) depicts a holiday affair between Mary and Bernes, with visits to a bullfight, a mantilla and fan shop, a variety show with 'Spanish dancers' and a Spanish guitarist's performance. As if the selection were not hackneyed enough, the first has music clearly referencing the 'Toreador' aria from Bizet's *Carmen*, 1875, a by-word for foreign constructions of Spanishness and a show which Mary had earlier enquired about trying to see in Malaga; the Spanish dancers in fact mambo, a Latin-American dance. All these insistently clichéd backdrops to foreign romance convey the delightfulness of it but also relate to a further ambiguity, namely, that, as both characters are spies, on different sides, they are also playing at being lovers for strategic ends. Though it would be wrong to make too much of the sequence, much of its interest comes from the fact that there is a sense of a real attraction between the pair (and a real sense of regret when later the truth comes out), with the cod Spanish music for tourists poised precisely on a recognition of the seductiveness of foreign affairs and their superficial bases.

The use of markedly Venetian music in *La mano dello straniero* (1953) in a film set in Venice in which none of the main characters is Italian, leave alone Venetian, highlights the sense of dislocation in the events: an English boy comes to visit his father, who doesn't turn up; he is befriended by a Yugoslavian woman and her American boyfriend who help him track down his father's Slav kidnappers. The music has both a melody reminiscent of Tchaikovsky's *Capriccio italien*, 1880, itself based on songs supposedly collected by him during a visit to Italy, and a rippling bass figure reminiscent of the Barcarolle music from *Tales of Hoffmann*, another foreign construction of Venetianness. The sense of the latter is especially emphasised when the boy opens the windows of his hotel onto the Grand Canal, as if letting in a sudden surge of Venetianness, powerful for him (and no doubt us), no less strong for being vaguely pointed as factitious. The use of foreigners' takes on Venetian music, signalled as pastiche, emphasises the sense of all the characters being outsiders to the city.

Perhaps the most sustained instance of mobilising a cultural musical perspective is to be found in Rota's Neapolitan music. Neapolitan song has a presence in Italian culture comparable to the French chanson and the Broadway show tune: commercially produced popular traditions that have taken on the status of national song, occupying a position with almost as much cultural capital as both classical and folk music, yet also still a presence and reference point in mainstream popular culture. There are other traditions of regional song in Italy but none has attained the presence of the Neapolitan.

In addition to Rota's own Neapolitan songs and music, actual Neapolitan songs are scattered throughout his films, including 'A cammesella' (*Fuga in Francia*, 1948), 'Simmo' e Napule, paisa' (*Proibito rubare*, 1948), 'O sole mio' (*Totò al giro d'Italia*), 'Dicitencello vuje' (*È più facile che un cammello*, 1950) and the football supporters' song in *La domenica della buona gente*.[34] The scores for the Eduardo De Filippo films are full of traditional Neapolitan songs: *Quei figuri di tanti anni fa* is entirely based on them, while *Napoli milionaria* features 'Funiculì funiculà', 'Chist'è 'o mese de rosa', 'Munasterio 'e Santa Chiari' and 'Marcher'.[35]

Perhaps because he was not Neapolitan and/or because by the time he was writing, Neapolitan song was already an historical mode of music, little of this music is straightforwardly scene setting. *Un ladro in paradiso* (1952), a vehicle for the Neapolitan comic actor Nino Taranto, opens on a bustling Neapolitan street scene full of Neapolitan music, where each level of cliché seems merely to confirm the others' rightness (Taranto's image, the teeming street, the music); but the whole sequence is about Vincenzo (Taranto) as a con man, so that the Neapolitan overload (star, street, music), though it may be meant to suggest nothing more than that entertaining conning is part of Neapolitan reality, also associates the latter with falsity. On the other hand, in *Proibito rubare* 'Simmo' e Napule, paisa' contrasts with boogie woogie in an opposition of popular tastes, Italian/American, autochthonous/commercial, characteristic of neo-realism (even though the Neapolitan song here was a recent composition[36] and Neapolitan song has always been commercial). Such ambiguity – affirmed cliché, the falsity of reality, commercially produced autochthonicity – is a key trope in Rota's Neapolitan films.

It is explored in *Le notti di Cabiria* through a song, 'Lla rì lla rà', composed by Rota with words by the Neapolitan lyricist Enzo Bonagura. As a new song in an old-fashioned mould, this functions like a pastiche. At the very beginning of the film Cabiria tra-las a snatch of it, just before current boyfriend Giorgio pushes her into the river and steals her bag. At the end, when Cabiria and Oscar go on their honeymoon to Naples (itself a cliché), they have lunch in a trattoria overlooking the Bay of Naples, with, seated behind them, a man playing a guitar and singing the song; Cabiria hums along to it, smiling and swaying her head. An idyllic scene: marriage at last to a respectable man, sunshine, the bay of Naples, 'Lla rì lla rà'. Yet minutes later Oscar seems on the point of murdering her and, when his nerve fails for that, he steals her bag with all her life savings in it. Twice then, with Giorgio, with Oscar, Cabiria expresses her happiness through the song and twice that happiness is shown to be based on an illusion. The song itself, its lilting refrain, is thus associated with a chimera of happiness through love, while the fact that it is a pastiche of the mode of Neapolitan song generalises the point, suggesting the mode itself as inextricable from illusion. Yet at the end of the film, after Oscar has run off and much later Cabiria has dragged herself to her feet and started to walk back to Naples, she is surrounded by young people, one playing a guitar and singing, wordlessly and somewhat faster, 'Lla rì lla rà'. It gradually works a kind of magic, restoring her spirits, at last bringing a smile to her face. There is hope in the readiness of the young people and Cabiria herself to respond to the idea of happiness embodied in the song, to pluck a real feeling from facticity. Neapolitan song is an exemplar of the way popular music is used more generally in Fellini and Rota's collaboration, but the particular standing of the Neapolitan mode, at once a product yet felt as a tradition, gives special force to the perception of it in *Cabiria*.

Elsewhere their attitude to it is more teasing. In *Lo sceicco bianco* (1952), Ivan is eating with his relations in a restaurant, desperate to keep from them the fact that his new bride Wanda has apparently run off. A singer sings the classic Neapolitan song 'Passione',[37] but sung with cliché words, 'o mare, o cielo, o sole' repeated over and over to a particularly pealing mandolin, the singer slightly exaggerating the bel canto delivery and holding onto the high notes, coming up close to Ivan following Ivan's attempt to recite a clichéd poem which is interrupted by the arrival of the fettuccine. There is then a sudden cut to the shore where a photo-romance is being shot (and where Wanda has been taken), where there is indeed, as per the song, sea, sky and sun, and wind. In *I vitelloni*, Fausto and Sandra bring back from their honeymoon a record of a tune that they say is from a revue they saw in Rome, and Fausto and Alberto dance to it in the street. It is a syncopated version of perhaps the most famous of all Neapolitan songs, 'O sole mio'.[38]

Quel bandito sono io opens with a Neapolitan song that highlights the characteristics of the form: the opening part of the melody slowish, with pauses on high notes and then vertiginous drops down, giving way to a tarantella second part; the words an amalgam of clichés about the sea and the moon, with the word 'Napoli' (pronounced in the Neapolitan way, that is, 'Na-poo-lay') repeated over and over again; sung by a bel canto tenor accompanying himself on mandolin. The singer not only exaggerates the lingering over the high notes but also pulls faces at the camera, in case there is any doubt as to the fun that is being made. He is singing it in the gangster Leo's flat, and Pietro, one of Leo's henchmen, tells him to stop his caterwauling. At the end of the film, the melody is played again, first with souped-up strings, then as a furious tarantella.

Nowhere does Rota parody Neapolitan song quite so strongly as here,[39] but the teasing and the ambiguities already discussed also inform his work with Eduardo de Filippo, the person more responsible than any other for the production of the idea of Naples in the twentieth century.[40] Though a quintessential man of the theatre (playwright, director, producer, actor), Eduardo was also a prolific film-maker (including many adaptations of his theatre works), eight with scores by Rota,[41] who also wrote for him incidental music for the theatre, for television adaptations of plays (by Eduardo himself and his natural father Eduardo Scarpetta) and two operas, one based on *Napoli milionaria* (which draws substantially on all his work for Eduardo). Eduardo's works are for the major part set in and around Naples and consistently retailed, and perhaps had a large role in strengthening and even inventing, the image of Naples and its inhabitants: teeming streets, people living on top of each other, homes spilling out onto narrow alley-ways, misery and nobility cheek by jowl,[42] sexually confident women and sexually eager men, matriarchs and hen-pecked husbands, a population ener-getic, noisy, constantly arguing and trying to out-do one another but always banding together against the powers-that-be, endlessly seeking ways round the law, often by means of clever tricks and verbal brilliance, and every-where song and dance, and all of this lovable, above all in its cunning and corruption, saved from the banality of folklore by a vein of bitterness, despair and madness that often spills over into a kind of magical realism. According to view, Eduardo has captured the truth about Naples or prom-ulgated a stereotype about it. Rota's music has the effect of highlighting this ambiguity.

In *Napoli milionaria* an American official observes 'molto piacere Napoli, tutto canzoni, tutto musica' (sic) ('Naples very nice, all songs, all music'), an observation made all the more comic by his revealing that he is a good singer and then, this white officer, bursting rotundly into the Negro spiritual 'Go Down Moses'. This is the foreign perspective. But in *Filumena Marturano* (1951), when Domenico gets Filumena's grown sons to sing a classic Neapolitan song 'Santa Chiara', to see if this will reveal which is also his son, and they all sing together, badly, Domenico laments 'How can you be Neapolitans if you don't know how sing?' The local perspective confirms the foreigners', affirming the cliché that Naples and song are indissoluble.

In the 'Gennareniello' episode of *Marito e moglie* (1952) a classic Neapolitan song, 'Uocchie c'arraggiunate',[43] is heard as the camera tracks over roof tops at the beginning of the film. Later the character played by Eduardo, Gennarino, sings it to Anna Maria, the young neighbour he is making a bit of a fool of himself over. It is evident that his was not the voice heard singing it at beginning: there it was sung smoothly and confidently, whereas Eduardo has to strain. When he goes to the balcony to cross over to Anna Maria's balcony to receive a kiss, he looks down and a piano is heard playing the tune; it carries on over his making his way across to her. A piano plays on and off throughout the film, as if coming from a nearby apartment. When Gennarino makes up with his wife Concetta after his little dalliance, the tune comes in again on the piano. Finally, she sings it as she wrings out the washing (on an invention of Gennarino's), the camera tracking across her, her voice augmented by piano and, now, orchestra. The song is known to the characters and used by them, but it is also literally in the air, in the piano somewhere in the building, in the disembodied voice at the beginning. Music is everywhere in Naples.

At the dinner to celebrate Gennaro's return in *Napoli milionaria*, a hand-some young man appears and sings in bel canto style 'Chist'è 'o de rosa'. The singer is Giacomo Rondinella, one of the best-known Neapolitan song stars of the day in his sixth film appearance; his character is given no name, not because he is Rondinella playing himself, a nationally famous singer, but rather because he is just a local boy with a good voice who of course comes along to the party. As he sings a series of shots picks out different characters and little actions, uniting them under the aegis of his song. A sense of community is produced, even including Gennaro's daughter Maria Rosaria, conscious of being illegitimately pregnant by a departed GI, having to turn away from a nice young man who wants to court her correctly (and who in fact comes as a friend of Rondinella): her distress runs counter to the cheer of the party, but she is still included in the spirit of community, embraced by the song.

These two examples affirm the image of Naples and song. They also involve rather little intervention from Rota. Where the latter occurs, in the use of known Neapolitan songs and in Rota's pastiches of them, the affirmation is less straightforward.

In one of the dream-cum-vision sequences in *Spara forte, più forte, non capisco* (1967), Alberto enters the Cimmarutas' apartment, where he suspects a murder has taken place, and Rosa Cimmaruta, who opens the door to him, opens a further one into a room in which some kind of awards ceremony is taking place. As a man receives an award, Rosa says, 'How wonderful he is! Neapolitan song – he is reworking it!'.[44] This is accompanied in snatches by the refrain to 'Funiculì Funiculà',[45] one of the most famous of all Neapolitan songs, to the point of cliché. In this strange sequence the idea of Neapolitan song and of reworking it is explicitly invoked in the context of its most well-established representative. Reworking the cliché characterises Rota's use of Neapolitan song, and specifically 'Funiculì Funiculà'.

'Funiculì Funiculà'

In *Spara forte* it is used every so often throughout the film, usually just in snatches of the refrain. When Alberto wakes one morning and marvels at the sunrise over the Bay of Naples, his eyes finally lighting on Tania posing in a bikini, the camera gives us his point of view in slow pans before zooming in on Tania, and the refrain is played repeatedly in mounting steps: the music expresses a sense of wonder at the beauty of sunrise, Naples and women, but it also links them to the most hackneyed of Neapolitan songs, risking the perception that all these wonders are standard issue. In a later sequence, in which Pasquale Cimmaruta tries to drown Alberto, the tune is played lower, slower, suggesting perhaps, in line with Eduardo's work, the sinister undertow to Neapolitan high spirits. (As the Cimmaruta family drive with Alberto to the spot he is to be murdered, they sing nonchalantly another Neapolitan standard, 'Anema e cuore'.[46])

Napoli milionaria uses 'Funiculì Funiculà' even more extensively. Near the beginning, the neighbourhood gets together to outwit the authorities, who, in an affront to Neapolitan custom, have forbidden all domestic activity in the street: police load stoves, laundry, mattresses, furniture, hens in cages onto a lorry, but people put a series of obstacles in its way, such as a baby and a burning basket; as the driver stops to sort these out, the people unload the lorry, a little bit each time, so that by the time the lorry reaches the police station it is completely empty. 'Funiculì Funiculà' comes in the moment the thwarting starts, evoking spontaneous coming together in a spirit of energy, fun, ingenuity and big-hearted illegality – the action and the music are in perfect accord in retailing this quintessential image of Naples and Neapolitans, though the arrangement is stylised, extending the pauses in the melody, having the winds squeal a little. At the end of the film Gennaro and his son start rowing politically, family and bystanders join in and it turns into a brawl, all of which is rendered cheerful by perky music that erupts into 'Funiculì Funiculà' as they all make their way, quarrelling, down the street. Elsewhere though the tune is also used dramatically, mixed in as an underlying figure to the film's main theme for an air raid, and the refrain repeated with increasing urgency over Gennaro being arrested and deported as a prisoner-of-war (for stealing apples); in other words, the cliché of 'Funiculì Funiculà' is nonetheless true enough to be used for other emotions than its own energy and fun. The music confirms the truth of the stereotype – and yet the very resort to such an almost absurdly familiar stereotype must at the least raise the issue of the truthfulness of what is depicted. Stereotypes when they work as stereotypes affirm the truth of what they represent, but when a stereotype is seen as a stereotype it is apt to call that truth into question: Rota's music risks making possible in the audience's mind the second move to the stereotype seen as stereotype.

As well as using existing Neapolitan songs, Rota also writes Neapolitan-style melodies for Eduardo. The main theme of *Spara forte, più forte, non capisco* is a tune whose contours follow closely 'I' te vurria vasà',[47] one of the most beloved of Neapolitan songs, still in the standard repertoire. There are many, sometimes surprising variations. It is first heard in the credits on sweet violins but then giving way to a swing jazz version; when Alberto gets into Tania's car on his way to report Aniello's murder to the police, he finds its inside decked out like a pink bordello and then discovers a bloody glove in the glove compartment, all to the accompaniment of the tune first on Theremin, then electric organ with piano decorations, then violins and piano; later, in his seaside studio, there is a jazzy version over Tania in a series of provocative poses and then, when she comes to his door, the theme comes in on full, gloupy violins; when Uncle Nicola blows himself up with fireworks, the tune, tinklingly high on piano, sounding like a music box, accompanies the magical images of chairs flying through air; finally, the tune is played on full violins over the end, Tania and Alberto driving off away from Naples but the camera tracking back from them and towards the city.

Once again a Neapolitan tune – this time a pastiche of one rather than a known standard-cum-cliché – is shown to be able to be able to express a range of feelings, yet in the context of the sheer weirdness of the film it's hard to decide if this confirms the reality of the magic of Naples or draws attention to it as fantasy.

The music for the credits for *Napoli milionaria* includes neither 'Funiculì Funiculà' nor 'Chist'è 'o de rosa', that is, the songs known by tradition or in the text of the film itself as Neapolitan. It does though combine three of the musical modes associated with Naples: first a big Rota tune, then pipe and tambour, then a religious chant sung in rather a sharp, nasal timbre by predominantly women's voices. The last two are seen as rooted in Naples itself, with documentary footage of street life (the drumming seeming to accord with close-ups of nails being hammered into shoes) and a religious procession, and a credit telling us that the local people seen in the film are 'genuine inhabitants of the Vicolo Pallonetto in Santa Lucia'. However, the religious music does not reoccur in the body of the film, while the pipe and tambour instrumentation, but not their melody, is confined to sequences showcasing the indelibly Neapolitan Totò. The big tune does more work in the film: used nobly and dramatically for an air raid; mixed in with swing music, the tune itself half played traditionally, half swung, for the Americans in the streets of Naples after the war, fitting in with the cheerful chaos of the streets; in a sad arrangement for Gennaro returning from prison camp, which becomes more strongly plaintive as makes his way into the city; and so on. It is the kind of tune teased as Neapolitan in *Quel bandito sono io* and *Le Notti di Cabiria*, with a swoop down from a high note and a little twiddle of notes in the course of a long-noted melody. However, outside of the context of the film, its Neapolitanness might be less obvious; notably, it eschews mandolins or modality. In a montage sequence after the credits of panoramic shots across the city, street singing and calls are mixed in with the big tune, rooting the latter – by Rota, within a commercial tradition – in the autochthonous former.

The big tune in *Napoli milionaria*, Neapolitan but not wholly, represents a coming together of two sensibilities. Eduardo's insistent Neapolitanness was at the same time understood to be much more widely representative. As Renzo Tian put it in *Il messagero* on the occasion of Eduardo being awarded the Premio Feltrinelli:[48] 'The Neapolitanness of Eduardo as a writer moves outwards towards its Italianness, even if the choice between the two terms is never definitive. This Neapolitanness is transformed into a universal theatricality.' Puppa (1990: 144) discusses the 'compromise between local intensity and wider accessibility' in the language of Eduardo's work, such that, 'the dialect is diluted, filtered, disguised and adapted to the underlying structures of high discourse, in the process siphoning off the communicative weight and expressive immediacy, leaving … those rhythms, traces of vocabulary, a patina of sound'.[49] The ambivalent result of this project may have been heightened in film, where Eduardo had less control over production and compromises had to be made with the demands of studios and producers. *Filumena Marturano* was released in Italy in two versions, one with the language 'more Italianised'.[50] Paola Quarenghi reports that, while *Napoli milionaria* had considerable success in Italy, it also 'provoked very lively polemics in Naples, where it was accused of providing a distorted image of the city, one veined with racism, which, not coincidentally, pleased Northern audiences because it confirmed them in their preconceptions about Southerners'.[51] The passage from the local to the national and universal is liable to entail compromise in the presentation of the former with the consequent risk of being embraced as stereotype and cliché. Rota's referential procedures habitually recognise cultural forms as forms, of which stereotype and cliché are only the most blatant declaration. The meeting between Eduardo and Rota – everywhere, but condensed in the big tune for *Napoli milionaria* – is at an overlap between a local culture perceived as authentic packaging itself, dangerously, for wider consumption and a practice of pastiche that never quite takes anything as authentic anyway. Rota's music accords with a notion of what might be called the natural theatricality of the Neapolitans, but it also leaves room for a sense of this as, rather, a theatricalisation of them in cultural tradition and in Eduardo. The big tune is thus poised on the cusp of local specificity and wider digestibility and that of unconscious and conscious stereotypification.

This is the delicate position to which all Rota's deployment of reference tends. It does help to paint the picture, identify time and space, roll out the generic coordinates, but time and again it reminds one, gently, not insistently, certainly not alienatingly, that it is doing so. If it denaturalises, it does so only on the assumption that there is nothing natural anyway. Where it destabilises – which it perhaps comes near to doing with Eduardo – it is where the film to which it contributes itself has something invested in the affirmation of the natural.

DIEGETIC AND NON-DIEGETIC

In *The Taming of the Shrew*, Petruchio and his servant Grumio return home a little drunk from the former's wedding. A lively, knockabout theme on full orchestra accompanies them, although there is no orchestra anywhere in their vicinity; as they rollick about, they start to sing 'diddle dum' along with this non-existent music, delighting especially in coming in with the cute little phrase at the end of each section of the melody. The tune that they sing along to is first heard as a goliardo[52] earlier in the film, back in Padua, it's a tune they could know or have picked up there, but all the same it's not playing now in their world, and yet they join in with it.[53]

Film-makers and audiences alike know the difference between music evidently produced in the world of a film, music that characters can and/or do hear, diegetic music, and music evidently not, music that is and could not be heard by the characters, non-diegetic.[54] Petruchio and Grumio diddle-dumming along with music that they cannot hear is a gag that depends on the (here transgressed) distinction between diegetic and non-diegetic being familiar and accepted. Much of the time the distinction is perfectly clear.

However, in practice, and in a considerable variety of ways, the distinction is more complicated and muddled up and therein lie many of its expressive possibilities.[55]

Rota was perhaps more promiscuous than most in playing about with the distinction. It is one of the key strategies in producing ironic attachment, since it constantly plays on the borderline between the illusion of an autonomous world going on in a film and acknowledgment of the means not just of constructing that world but having a view of it, an attitude towards it. In what follows I trace some of the forms of this play in Rota's practice. For much of the time, the films adhere to the diegetic/non-diegetic distinction but there are some which don't at some point or other, or complicate it, and it is these that I discuss: diegetic music manipulated in the service of narration, movement between diegetic and non-diegetic music, interaction between them, and cases where what is diegetic and what is not are hard to determine.

Manipulation of the diegetic

At a minimum, diegetic music contributes to establishing the world in which characters live and have their being, which forms them and with which they have to interact. *Londra chiama Polo Nord*, for instance, makes more use of diegetic than non-diegetic music: fairground organ, accordion, mouth organ, music box, sometimes played by characters, sometimes by people in the scene; although this does sometimes have narrational connections, for much of the time it merely contributes to setting the scene in which the film's quite complicated spy story unfolds, if anything bringing out the patina of everyday life under cover of which the characters must conduct their business. However, many of the uses of diegetic music in Rota films go beyond this naturalism in standard ways, contributing to narration, to telling the film.

Characters may consciously use or respond to diegetic music.

> *LA NAVE DELLE DONNE MALADETTE* The song 'Malatierra', sung by one of the women in the prison hold of the boat, expresses the misfortune and wretchedness of all of them.
>
> *WAR AND PEACE* Natasha is intoxicated by being at her first ball and, as was common, by the waltz, an intoxication that Anatol uses to ensnare her.
>
> *GODFATHER II* At the opening party by Lake Tahoe, Frank Pentangeli cannot get the band to play, or the crowd to sing, the song 'Luna mezz' 'o mare'[56] that had been sung with such gusto in the party that opens *The Godfather*; his and their failure indicates the family's loss of their Sicilian roots by the time of the move to Nevada.

Music may be broadly in sympathy with the characters' feelings.

> *CAMPANE A MARTELLO* At the opening of the film in Livorno, there is the sound of church bells and military fanfares, scene setting but also symbolising the two institutions that the two prostitute protagonists, Agostina and Australia, find themselves caught between in the rest of the film.

War and Peace: the joy and the danger of the waltz, Natasha (Audrey Hepburn) and Pierre (Henry Fonda), Natasha and Anatol (Vittorio Gassman)

CITTÀ DI NOTTE Marina and Lidia go to a fairground and a merry-go-round tune in the background first expresses the jollity of being at the fair, but then, behind Marina telling Lidia she is in love with Alberto, it expresses both her delight in being in love and also her naivety (she is only fifteen, Alberto is obviously a womaniser and Lidia is already involved with him).

It may make a comment on what is happening in the narrative.

ROCCO E I SUOI FRATELLI Nadia, having moved in with Simone in his mother's flat, listens to Tchaikovsky's Fourth Symphony on a transistor radio. This is the work whose 'Fate' motif Visconti asked Rota to take as inspiration for the main theme of the film; Nadia, dandling the radio from her hand, is not listening to it for its fatalism but nonetheless it connects her and the situation to this notion.
THE GODFATHER In the opening party, the singers sing sexually suggestive verses to 'Luna mezz' 'o mare', much to everyone's amusement. Sexual suggestiveness is common in the context of a wedding, but here it cross-cuts with the eldest Corleone son, Sonny, taking a woman upstairs for sex, in other words, literalising the lewdness of the words with a woman who, however, is not his wife.

It may be anempathetic (Gorbman, 1987: 24),[57] the music at odds with a character's feelings in ways which make the latter all the more poignant.

SENZA PIETÀ In a sleazy bar, a client, a South American general, has the very lively, up-tempo song 'Brazil' put on the juke box; when one of the girls,

Dina, is killed by a van, the music stops momentarily; as it comes back in, brassy, driving, full of joie de vivre, the film's central character, Angela, weeps at her situation and says that she must go, but the pimp Pierluigi will not let her. 'Brazil' makes a mockery of her anguish, not least because it embodies the world of commercial sex that she is caught in.

IL GATTOPARDO The dances at the ball in the last third in their liveliness and youthfulness, and the sense of the dance going on and on, contrast with Don Fabrizio, and his increasing sense of mortality. The contrast is particularly poignant when he looks in a mirror and starts to weep, just at the point that the 'valzer del commiato' comes in, the melody perhaps a little melancholic but also graceful and charming, the world carrying on without the gattopardo.

Narrational use of diegetic music may go further than this, the music itself manipulated in response to the story. This sometimes means augmenting the diegetic musical forces used.

VIVERE IN PACE Grandfather and Joe, the black GI hiding out at the farm, both play the trumpet, creating a bond between them despite differences of culture, politics and wartime allegiance; when Grandfather plays a tune rather waveringly, a (non-diegetic) brass band oom-pah-pah comes in as accompaniment; when, moments later, Joe plays, a double bass figure and eventually a jazz band come in; each accompaniment emphasises the different musical roots of the players; finally, Grandfather takes back the trumpet and plays the bersaglieri fanfare,[58] but the (non-diegetic) jazz band continues as accompaniment, thus integrating the two kinds of music – and politics.

Vivere in pace: trumpeters Grandfather (Ernesto Almirante) and GI Joe (John Kitzmiller)

MOLTI SOGNI PER LE STRADE As Paolo slinks off, leaving his wife
and little son on a roundabout, the fairground music gets gradually louder and
more dissonant as they realise what is happening.

More commonly, there is a wholesale organisation of music and image track
to produce a narrative coordination.

UN AMERICANO IN VACANZA Maria and Dick are sitting on a bench
outside a party; he suggests they might kiss and, as he speaks and she listens,
smiling and anxious, swoony big-band music emanates from the party; but she
says that, much as she likes him, all the same she 'isn't going to lose her head'
and the music at the party changes to something faster, more jivey, as the
romantic moment passes.

ANNA When Anna goes to visit Vittorio in his flat, symphonic music plays on
the radio (the film insists on its diegeticness, having her turn the radio off and
him turn it back on). The music's emotional quality intensifies as the scene
between them develops, she telling him that Andrea has proposed marriage to
her, he expressing indifference and confidence in his own attractiveness. With
melodramatic irony, the music shifts harmonic gears and becomes louder (that
is, wholly losing any sense of the sound perspective of its source) exactly
when, in reply to his saying 'So it's over between us?' she says 'I think so' and
turns over suggestively on the bed.

LA DOMENICA DELLA BUONA GENTE Bruno, once a champion
footballer but now out of work, goes to join his wife and daughter in a little
park after the Sunday match; his wife, Gisella, impatient with his
unemployment, has decided to leave him, taking the little girl with her. When
Bruno arrives at the park, a radio announcer, via a loudspeaker, is giving the
football results, but then, as he moves towards his wife and daughter, a
symphony concert is announced and starts: though it sounds like an unfamiliar
work in a nineteenth-century symphonic mode, the melodic basis is in fact the
motif established as Bruno's in this particularly motific film. Non-diegetic has
become diegetic using a theme associated with the central character in the
sequence. As he moves forward, his daughter runs towards him, but then
pauses, realising she is thereby running away from her mother, and the music
too pauses, expectantly, dramatically. When she calls out to him, it swells. He
goes to her and together they go to Gisella, all three holding hands, as the
music swells again. The diegetic music underscores the emotional development
of the scene in the manner of non-diegetic music, and this diegetic music is
itself derived from the film's non-diegetic score.

WAR AND PEACE A soldier sings the plaintive love song, 'The Maid of
Novgorod', at night during the retreat from Moscow, while Natasha is looking
for Andrei. The singing stops just when she reaches the threshold of where he
is lying wounded; then, as she swiftly pulls herself together emotionally, the
tune starts up again, but just on balalaika; when he says 'I love you', the male
voice, singing of love, comes back in.

Movement between diegetic and non-diegetic and vice versa

As the example of *La domenica della buona gente* indicates, a musical element established non-diegetically may be taken up diegetically. Even more common is take-up in the opposite direction, diegetic to non-diegetic. I give next examples of both of these, before considering cases where the transition from one to the other occurs within the course of a sequence and ending with a consideration of some of the implications of such movements between levels.

Movement from non-diegetic to diegetic status include the following.

FUGA IN FRANCIA Gino, on his way to France to find work, stops with a group of other men in the station at Oulx, where Pierina works in the buffet. There is singing, and Pierina joins in with the men; when Gino follows her into the kitchen, a romantic theme is heard non-diegetically in counterpoint to the theme associated with another of the men, Riccardo. He is an ex-fascist and criminal on the run, whom Pierina recognises, having previously worked for him, a fact that he realises endangers his incognito. The newly introduced romantic theme for Gino and Pierina is then set against the established one for the menacing Riccardo; however, in the course of the scene between Pierina and Gino, as they clearly begin to fall in love, their melody becomes stronger. Later, in her bedroom, Pierina picks up a piece of sheet music and the pair sing together, to their melody, 'Ma quando tornerà' ('But when you return'). When they kiss, the melody is taken up non-diegetically again on strings. 'I'll be

Fuga in Francia: Pierina (Rosina Mirafiori) and Gino (Mario Vercellone)

back,' he says, 'I swear'. After he has left, the melody plays over her fondly folding his scarf and putting it in a drawer as a keepsake, but stops suddenly when she realises Riccardo has come into the room. To ensure that she doesn't expose him, he kills her. He picks up the song sheet and stuffs it in his pocket when he hears Gino whistling outside. Later it falls out of his pocket and Gino picks it up; Riccardo implies that he slept with Pierina and not for the first time, snuffing out Gino's love. The sheet music is present but the melody no longer is.

QUEL BANDITO SONO IO A non-diegetic comically menacing theme behind the setting up of the situation (Leo's mob threatening the family of Leo's lookalike Antonio) becomes a wild diegetic samba at Catoni's villa in Sorrento (where the family have gone into hiding). Catoni is a somewhat shady lawyer with underworld connections and Antonio, incognito as a waiter, is soon recognised by one of the mob: the gap between the two worlds was never secure and, in this farce, the menace readily becomes a manic dance.

APPASSIONATAMENTE Rulli's eponymous waltz, heard and listed in the credits, is heard non-diegetically on and off throughout the film, usually in snatches, charting the ups and downs of Andrea and Elena's relationship. About a third of the way through, they dance to a (different) waltz at the ball that she has organised and they seem reconciled. Later in the evening, Elena asks the orchestra to play 'a waltz' and they play 'Appassionatamente'. When she sees him, she says expectantly, 'It's a waltz!', but he has since learnt of Carlo's love letter and rejects her, saying that they have done their social duty as far as dancing is concerned. This is the only time the title melody is used diegetically and it is at a moment when their hopes of reconciliation seem destroyed. Because it is a known tune as well as appearing diegetically, the non-diegetic snatches suggest moments of love flaring up, unrequited or quickly dashed, as if the promise of the melody in the film's world is a deceptive one, only for it to be triumphantly vindicated in its full statement over the couple's final reconciliation and embrace.

'Appassionatamente'

THE GODFATHER/ GODFATHER II The main theme announced in the credits in both films and used non-diegetically throughout is also heard diegetically near the beginning of each: when Don Vito leads his just married daughter Connie in a dance in the first, as Michael and Kay dance in the party for their son Anthony's first communion in the second. In both cases, the characters are, literally and metaphorically, dancing to the

The Godfather: Don Vito (Marlon Brando) dances to the *Godfather* waltz with his daughter Connie (Talia Shire) on her wedding day

godfather's tune. In the first case, however, the tune is one of a string of other Sicilian tunes played by the orchestra, with both mandolins and the waltz rhythm to the fore, and the film cuts immediately to Los Angeles and slick, smooth jazz music,[59] the antithesis of the Corleone's old-world culture. The second is more ambiguous. It has already been heard buried in the organ music accompanying Anthony taking communion. At the party, Michael and Kay initially dance to another tune, as Michael reassures Kay that he is trying to dissociate himself from the family's 'business'; as the camera moves back from them, the *Godfather* theme, on trumpet (as at the beginning of the films) comes in, the other tune fading out but not the hi-hat rhythm accompaniment, so that the tune is integrated with the dance-band style. In both cases in the second film, the tune infiltrates respectability, of official Catholicism and middle-class, middle-American popular culture; it does not in either case wholly dominate respectability (as the Sicilian version does when Vito and Connie dance), but it is inescapably present, insinuating itself into the texture of American life.

Examples of diegetic musical material being picked up non-diegetically in Rota's work include the following.[60]

LA NAVE DELLE DONNE MALADETTE 'Malatierra', sung, as noted above, by one of the women prisoners about their collective lot, a theme already established in the credits, is taken up non-diegetically in relation to the specific vicissitudes of the other main female characters.

THIS ANGRY AGE Joseph sings 'One Kiss Away from Here' in a heartfelt manner to Claude, but later, when his mother sees them together, the tune is played non-diegetically in a twangy, overblown way, suggesting either the actual sleaziness of their relationship (a young man with an older married woman) or the mother's perception of it.

UN ETTARO DI CIELO The melodramatic song 'M'hai detto una bugia' ('You Lied to Me') is sung at the fairground dance, already appropriate over shots of Severino and Marina dancing (he is a mountebank and untrustworthy with women); it recurs later non-diegetically, in scenes between the two of them (when, for instance, he promises to take her with him to Milan, obviously with no intention of doing so) and also at the end, when he does drive off with her, but after telling the village menfolk how stupid they were to believe his story about buying a hectare of the sky.

THE TAMING OF THE SHREW Two of the student songs established in opening sequences become motifs. 'Let me tell, gentle maiden', sung by one of students when they all catch sight of Bianca in street, is thereafter associated with the love of Lucentio and Bianca. The rumbustious goliardo tune touched on above characterises and perhaps, by association with boisterous students, lightly mocks middle-aged Petruchio; when he sings along with it, he is having fun and maybe even being self-aware; later he sings to this tune the speech 'Where is the life that late I led?', lamenting having got married and putting behind him his youthful and perhaps exaggerated rowdiness.

In most of the above examples the diegetic theme is used non-diegetically some time after its diegetic appearance (or vice versa). The transition can though occur within a sequence. In some cases this simply means allowing the music to continue playing after the space of its diegetic source has been left.

> *CITTÀ DI NOTTE* The modern jazz that Adriana plays on her LP player carries on over her going out into the night to join the man hanging about in the streets below her flat, she thinks for her; he, however, runs off when she appears and she sits down on some steps. The music gets louder as she sits there and only when the record comes to an end does the scene do so.

Here there is no lapse of diegetic time, but there can be.

> *MAMBO* Although in love with the croupier Mario, Giovanna has married the Venetian prince, Enrico; she is discontented, not least because of the hostility of Enrico's mother, who considers Giovanna beneath him; disconsolate, she turns on the radio which is playing a romantic violin concerto; this continues on behind Enrico explaining to her that he is fatally ill and also over a dissolve to the next day, the music's emotional turbulence only brought to end when Enrico's mother interrupts her trying to make a phone call to Mario.
> *IL MAESTRO DI VIGEVANO* Antonio and Ada watch 'Sogni per due' on the television in the local café and the music from it plays on as the camera tracks in on Ada looking dreamy. When there is a cut to her and Antonio walking home afterwards, the melody is still playing, with no jump, Ada still in her reverie.

Sometimes the non-diegetic version takes off from the diegetic, as in the return of the love theme to the non-diegetic in *Fuga in Francia* or the bleeding of the eponymous waltz back into the non-diegetic in *Godfather II*, or the following examples.

> *SENZA PIETÀ* For the first half hour, there is no non-diegetic music, but quite a lot of diegetic, including from the radio. Then black GI Jerry and white Italian Angela kiss for the first time and Jerry bursts out spontaneously with 'All God's Chillun Gotta Row'; this is then immediately supported by non-diegetic strings which develop the tune after he has stopped singing and continue with it as they meet Angela's friend Marcella, at which point another Negro spiritual, 'Nobody Knows the Trouble I Seen', is interpolated non-diegetically, the two themes alternating and intertwined as they encounter the pimp Pierluigi, suggesting the twin poles of hope and despair that subtend their relationship. The white commercial music provided by the radio cannot be made into non-diegetic music that expresses the white women's destinies, it has to come from the natural source of the Negro spiritual. All the soundtrack of their love and tragedy is then derived from this, albeit in symphonic form.
> *WAR AND PEACE* Flustered by her response to waltzing with him, Natasha leaves Anatol on the ballroom floor before the dance is over and goes into a

side room; he follows her and shuts the door and the sound level of the waltz
drops accordingly and naturalistically; however, when he approaches her,
turned away from him looking in a mirror, and he kisses her bare shoulder, the
music swells unnaturalistically, louder and also very slightly dissonant, to
signal her surrender and the danger of it. Thereafter, in the whole section of
the film devoted to the relationship, as his deceitfulness becomes more obvious
to us but not to her, this theme is used non-diegetically, maintaining the poise
of that musical transition in the side room: it conveys at once the deliciousness
of her feelings and its perils.

An especially elaborated example of the move from diegetic to non-
diegetic, which also involves a return to the diegetic, occurs in the first
meeting of Romeo and Juliet at the Capulet ball.[61] At a break in the dancing, the song 'What is a Youth?' is heralded by a solo flute (whose sound
level would suggest it is non-diegetic although we do later see a recorder or
old-fashioned flute that could be taken as its source); it is then sung, well
but not classically pitched, with just a few instruments as accompaniment
(visible in the background, though they may not be producing the sound
we hear, which is probably more modern);[62] the singer (Glen Weston)
stands in the middle of the floor with the other guests grouped round him
in a circle, as if he might be one of them – in short, singing style, instrumentation and placing all integrate the song into the fabric of the ball rather
than making it a spectacular number. This already paves the way for the use
of the song non-diegetically, as something that is already part of the aural
texture of the scene. The song has three elements: a main melody (that, to
different words, became the hit song 'A Time for Us'), a bridge passage and
a faster, pavane-like section. During the singing, there are shots of Romeo
looking for Juliet; after it has been sung all through, it is repeated instrumentally and the first statement of the main melody continues diegetically
behind Romeo taking Juliet's hand, leading her aside into the shadows and
beginning to court her. The music only starts to be more clearly non-
diegetic when a solo violin takes up the bridge passage; this is in its spare-
ness enough like the Elizabethan instrumentation we have seen so far to
arise seamlessly from it, but it is also a modern violin playing in classic
romantic vibrato style and broken down, as in classic Hollywood practice,[63]
into smaller phrases to limn the development of the pair's conversation.
The pavane element is also used, slowed down, especially when there is an
element of tension between the pair; the big statement of the main tune
only comes in on full violins when at last they kiss. On their second kiss, the
film cuts back to the singer, a much more rapid transition back from non-
diegetic to diegetic, almost as if they are snatched back to the riskiness of
their situation, while the words of the song also remind us that love is brief.
The non-diegetic music arises then almost imperceptibly out of the world
of the film, on the one hand emphasising the couple's embeddedness in it
(as lovers in tune with the sentiment of the song but also implicated in its
melancholy), but, on the other, their temporary, fleeting separateness from

it. One might even say that, just as their tryst in the shadows gives them only a temporary and fragile cover, so too the music that accompanies them is only a few steps away from its source in a public realm that condemns their love.

The move between diegetic and non-diegetic is especially able to articulate a sense of the cultural world of the film as it shapes or invades the lives and feelings of the characters. The progress of a relationship and the role of (musical) culture in shaping this is indicated whether the relationship is true but doomed (*Fuga in Francia*, *Senza pietà*, *Romeo and Juliet*) or false from the start (*War and Peace*) or even eventually successful (*Appassionatamente*); the influence of nostalgic Siciliana pervades the family life of the American Mafia and then beyond it (the *Godfather* films).

There can also be an effect of irony. Severino, in *Un ettaro di cielo*, does, as the song says, tell lies to Marina; on the other hand, Gino and Pierina in *Fuga in Francia*, are not able, as their song says, to return to one another. 'Sogni per due' (*Il maestro di Vigevano*), a song to celebrate marriage, mocks the progress of the actual marriage in the film. The rumbustious goliardo song that becomes Petruchio's motif teases his ageing laddishness. Adriana's modern jazz (*Città di notte*) is a sign of her sophistication, somewhat undermined when she misreads the motive of the man hanging about outside and is left sitting about on her own.

An especially strong version of the irony involved when, in this case, a diegetic theme is picked up non-diegetically occurs in *Waterloo*. Most of the non-diegetic music for this film is reminiscent of the nationalistic, even militaristic Tchaikovsky of the fourth and fifth symphonies, operas like *Mazeppa* and *Iolanta* and, of course, the *1812 Overture*. However, at the point of maximum set-back for the British, when the battle seems to be lost, the music becomes much more atonal than anything to be found in Tchaikovsky; then, as one of the soldiers cries out in despair at the slaughter, there are skimming overhead shots of troops, fire and smoke, accompanied by a violin playing vibrato, slowed down, one of tunes used (diegetically) at Wellington's ball earlier in the film, becoming ever more acidic in the arrangement. This picks up on an exchange between Wellington and his daughter Sarah at the ball, when she is piqued by a disparaging comment made by General Picton to her new beau, Richard:

SARAH	General Picton doesn't even know how to walk in a ballroom.
WELLINGTON	But he's very good when he's dancing with the French.
SARAH	But one dances with them in a field.

The music and camera might now be said to be dancing in a field with the French, emphasised by the skimming camera movement and the ball tune; but the camera movement, in its smooth trajectory and flamboyance (in a film characterised by epic pans and overhead shots), and the eerie tone of the music turn Sarah's light-hearted remark to bitterness: this dancing is carnage and defeat.

Interaction between diegetic and non-diegetic

Using diegetic music narrationally as well as moving between diegetic and
non-diegetic bring the world and its framing very close together, the told
and the telling, making possible a degree of commentary, of cultural awareness and irony. Sometimes, however, a play on the difference can, even while
connecting the two sides, also draw attention to the difference and have fun
with it.

A character may, for instance, appear to respond to the music which in
principle she or he cannot hear (Petruchio and Grumio 'diddle dumming'
along to the goliardo theme in *The Taming of the Shrew*). In *Roma città libera*,
the 'distinguished gentleman who has lost his memory' finally learns who he
is, namely, a leading senator; he looks in the mirror, as one of themes of the
film, a slightly halting march, comes in; straightening himself up, he marches
off to the parliament in time to the music. In *Un ettaro di cielo*, as several of
the village men are sitting around chatting at night, the film's big main theme
comes in and one of them looks up and around, as if to say 'Where's that
coming from?'. This might be like similar moments of characters registering
with a double-take that they're in a movie (e.g., *Hellzapoppin'*, the Marx
brothers, Jerry Lewis), but he then looks up and there is a cut to a shot of the
moon emerging full from behind the clouds. This gives the moment an air of
magic, precisely (as elsewhere in the film) in the moment of acknowledging
its fabrication. Later a similar effect is achieved when the poacher Nicola is
sitting among the reeds and looks up in surprise when music suddenly starts
up; the film then cuts to the arrival of the villagers to the spot. The music is
the lightly comic music that often accompanies them in the film and so its
occurrence here makes non-diegetic, motific sense – but it doesn't make sense
to Nicola, who, unlike us, isn't watching a film.

In these examples, characters become aware of non-diegetic music,
although only in the case of *Un ettaro di cielo* registering that this is an
impossibility. It is also possible to have a character interact with the music as
it were unconsciously, as in the opening sequence of *È primavera*. Here the
cheeky protagonist, Beppe, sings the title song as he cycles along on his
bread delivery round, slightly out of tune and slightly out of synch with a
non-diegetic accompaniment, which is played on a small band with high
winds to the fore and a plinkety-plunkety rhythm reminiscent of an old
barrel organ; there is then a section where he whistles the tune and then lets
off from time to time, at which point trumpets and other winds take up the
tune; in the block of flats where he flirts with all the young women, there are
brief stretches (especially when bounding up the stairs) where he sings unaccompanied, stretches which alternate with the opening phrase of the tune
used as a basis for variations on low winds (to accompany his interactions
with the women). Beppe's singing and whistling interplay in a slightly off-
kilter way with the non-diegetic music, which itself takes off from the tune
he is producing and is often itself all over the place – just like Beppe.

In *This Angry Age*, Joseph sits next to Claude and her male companion in
a cinema. As hyperdramatic music comes from the screen, there is a close-up

of Joseph's fingers touching Claude's; they abruptly separate hands when sounds of gunshot on-screen waken Claude's companion. The gunshot from the film they are watching has a direct effect, but did the earlier the music also induce, or at any rate facilitate, an effect, stimulate the pick-up, or is it just the film-makers having fun with the coincidence?

Where the distinction seems impossible to make

Although the examples above mix up and play about with the diegetic and the non-diegetic, they work by virtue of the distinction. Petruchio and Grumio diddle-dumming along is only fun if you know they shouldn't be able to; the dramatic irony of Natasha's infatuation only works if you know the source of the music that moulds her feelings; the bitterness of Andrea and Elena not dancing to 'Appassionatamente' is only meaningful if you know what it has been used to indicate up to that point. In some cases, however, diegetic and non-diegetic are so fused that they are hard to disentangle. This may be because the music has become subjective, or because the film is representing a world utterly pervaded by music, or because ambiguity is the point.

Music may be considered to be subjective, not so much playing in the film's world as being what the character literally hears. Most examples of the latter are of characters hearing music that is also clearly playing in their world. It is when it is a question of memory or imagination – characters hearing the music in their mind's ear – that the matter can be more uncertain.

In *Anna*, Anna has to decide whether she will stick to her vows as a nun working in a hospital or renounce them and rejoin Andrea to whom she was once engaged; at night she walks past the hospital chapel which is in darkness; there is the sound of a choir singing, at first sounding as it has in the film in regular services, but then, as she begins to weep, becoming more celestial, sweet angelic female close harmony. The music is appropriate to a space we see on-screen, the chapel, but that space is itself at present unoccupied; it is something related to that space but not directly of it (that is, it remains sacred but becomes celestial, the music of angels rather than a congregation); it also relates to Anna's state of mind – as it becomes more celestial, the intensity of her feeling increases so that she weeps – but it also anticipates her decision, which is to stick with her vows and renounce her fiancé.

In this example, it is not at all clear whether one should consider the music to be diegetic or non-diegetic. It is not coming from the chapel at that moment (though that is where it has been heard to emanate from earlier in the film) and the music may be telling us how Anna is feeling, conveying her turmoil. However, the music may literally be in Anna's mind, music she remembers as she looks at the chapel, or it might even be celestial, actually heavenly music. Since Anna, or God, are actually in the world of the film, then, if we think she is literally hearing this music, it must be considered diegetic. This is different from a moment near the beginning of

Appassionatamente, when Andrea looks at a portrait of Elena and 'Appassionatamente' begins to play. Andrea clearly lives in a culture of portraits and orchestral waltzes, but there is no reason here to suppose he actually hears this music at this point in the film. This is reinforced by the fact that we do not get a direct point of view of the portrait; rather, the camera cranes over him, in sympathy with the direction and intensity of his gaze but not substituting for it. Camera movement and music present what he is feeling to us but not in the exact mode in which he is experiencing it.

In *Via Padova 46* (1955), Arduino is taking an ice cream by himself in the Caffè Italia and, as it is very crowded, the waiter asks him to allow an attractive young women, Jolanda, to share his table. When she sits down, the music, supplied by a small group, changes from an upbeat Spanish number to a well-known romantic ballad, 'Un ora sola ti vorrei',[64] sung by the popular singer Flo Sandon's. Arduino, however, appears not to notice the song and merely to be flustered by his glamorous companion. That night, however, he cannot sleep. He looks across at his wife and thinks he sees Jolanda in her place, smiling provocatively at him. The song from the café is heard. Sandon's sings just the first line, then the tune is taken up by a female chorus, much more ethereal in sound than at the café, with electric organ; as it develops, the music rises in tones, with perhaps male voices under and bit of brass towards end, to suggest an epiphany as she turns and looks at him with delight in her eyes. It stops suddenly when he touches Jolanda and she turns into his wife. In the next sequence, Arduino is at work, helping his boss take files down from the stacks; he looks at his boss standing on the ladder and again sees in his place Jolanda, the camera tracking up from her stockings and suspenders to her inviting face, with first Sandon's voice then choir and this time still more and yet more brass, a triumphant overflow of desire.

In both these sequences, the music is clearly not literally playing in Arduino's bedroom or the office stacks. Even so, it is also clear, by means of standard point-of-view editing, that he does see Jolanda (even though she is not there) and so it is perfectly possible to consider that he does also actually hear this music (worked up from what he heard unconsciously at the Caffè Italia). However, the sequences are also comic, especially the second, where Arduino gazes at his boss's trousers and sees silk stockings and suspenders peeking out from under a skirt. The exaggerations of the music, parodies of paradisiacal evocations of adoration, may be what he actually hears but they also signal to us the absurdity of this desire. They indicate the way he has worked up an unconscious response to a standard form of balladeering and connected it to his response to Jolanda, all the more striking for her evident (to us) indifference to him and the discrepancy between her and the music's romantic clichés. In other words, the scoring of the music does narrational work even while the music can be taken to be diegetic; it comments on what he hears even as it gives us what he hears.

When Maria returns home after the party in *Un americano in vacanza*, she dances dreamily by herself and a waltz is heard on the soundtrack. This is the waltz to which she had earlier danced with Dick, in a sequence affirming their

love for one another.[65] She looks in the
mirror and there is a dissolve from her reflection to her as she was dressed at the ball, in a
glamorous borrowed gown; if she can see
herself as she was at ball, perhaps she is also
hearing the music, the special music, that she
danced to there. The camera is positioned up
high above her, that is, quite some way from
an over the shoulder shot that would by convention pass for a virtual point-of-view shot;
however, it is still reasonable to consider that
she is seeing and hearing the party in her
mind's eye and ear.

However, the waltz tune starts in the
sequence as she is walking into the room;
maybe the tune is already echoing in her
mind now that she is on her own (for other,
clearly non-diegetic music was behind her
carriage ride home with Dick), maybe the
music is at first simply indicating to us the
kind of feeling Maria is wrapped up in at this
point, without necessarily indicating that she
is literally (albeit mentally) hearing it.
Moreover, when she hears a knock on the
door, she rushes from the mirror to the bed
(to give the impression that she has long
been in it) and the music, by means of a little
woodwind flourish based on a phrase of the
music and ending on a shriek-like sound,
immediately expresses the break in her
reverie and her fear of being found out. This
last snatch of music cannot be conceived of
as even mentally diegetic, yet it is seamless
with, and founded in, the music to which
Maria has been dancing (even though it is
not playing in the room) and of course it
expresses her feelings.

As in *Fuga in Francia*, *Senza pietà*, *Romeo
and Juliet*, *War and Peace*, *Appassionatamente*

Un americano in vacanza:
Maria (Valentina Cortese) in
front of the mirror after the
ball

(eventually) and the *Godfather* films, all these cases – Anna and sacred
music, Arduino and a ballad standard, Maria and an old-fashioned waltz –
suggest the way the musical environment fashions characters' imaginative
lives. They allow especially strong access to a character's consciousness and
imagination, not just by conveying the feelings they are having but also by
suggesting the very (musical) mode in which they are feeling it. However,
by not keeping that unambiguous, by not undoubtedly showing us what the

character is hearing, the films also refuse complete identification with Anna, Arduino or Maria, making all the clearer the sense of the fashioning of their feelings and even suggesting the sense that they are performing these feelings, performing the cultural scripts available to them in music, rather than presenting feelings as spontaneous and wholly inner emanations.

An uncertainty about the diegetic or non-diegetic place of music may also derive from the presentation of an environment as utterly pervaded with music. This often means that the source of the music is not necessarily shown or precisely handled.[66] In *Treno popolare*, the crowds taking the day trip from Rome to Orvieto sing along together, on the train, after a picnic lunch, humming on the train coming back. Yet we don't always see them singing and sometimes it might be coming from a portable gramophone. It expresses a kind of fantasy of collectivity through music that transcends the individuals producing the sound, and although in *Treno popolare* this has fascistic overtones, the fantasy is a recurrent feature of films of the 1930s, including the Marxist *Kuhle Wampe* (1932) and the Gracie Fields vehicle *Sing As We Go!* (1934).

Such films, and their musical collectivity, reinvent a folk paradigm for an urban people. Where a more conventionally understood folk is presented, the trope of pervasiveness is almost inevitable. There is no felt need to source precisely in the image the Polynesian music and singing in *Hurricane*, it's just there. An end credit to *Proibito* indicates that the peasant song deployed throughout the film comes from 'ethnographic' sources. Sometimes we see where it is coming from, more often not, and there is no care over sound perspective or location (whether in the small town or the countryside): peasant song permeates the film's world beyond the bit of it to which the film gives us access. This is all the more telling in that the only other music in the film, used rigorously non-diegetically, is from Brahms' Fourth Symphony. This does not belong to the world of the film although it does contribute to establishing the film's (tragic) perspective on that world. The contrast is between a tradition of music seen as having attained the condition of abstraction and universality and one that remains doggedly, and literally, grounded and local (cf. Mangini, 2001: 148).

Such notions of musical pervasiveness are especially common in the representation of Naples, itself, as argued in the previous section, poised perilously on the brink of folklorism. In movies set in Naples, music plays from loudspeakers or radios pointed out into the streets, characters keep singing snatches of song, people live so close to one another, and so much in the streets, that music played anywhere can be heard everywhere. In *Proibito rubare*, one of Rota's most neo-realist films, there is a constant flow of Neapolitan music in the background (drawing on classic Partenopean song) and one assumes it is diegetic, but, just as with *Treno popolare*, *Hurricane* or *Proibito*, this is not clearly shown, it is as if Naples is assumed to be so full of song that it is there all the time, regardless of whether anyone is actually playing and singing. The opening sequence of *Un ladro in paradiso* pullulates with street performers and musicians, hawkers selling their wares by means of improvised, rhythmic speech and passers-by and crowds giving as good as they get in terms of vocal expressivity. This representation of everyday Neapolitan life as a continuous street performance lays the ground for the use of a comic Neapolitan tune that is played sometimes on-screen on barrel organ, sometimes on mandolin that might be off-screen or non-diegetic, and sometimes more clearly non-diegetically by other instruments. The uncertainty of where the mandolin is coming from (it makes sense to think of one playing in the environment, it is a cliché of Neapolitan musical mores, but we never see anyone playing or even possessing one) effectively dissolves the boundary between diegetic and non-diegetic, affirming a notion of Neapolitan culture so saturated with the principle of song that it needs no precisely delineated material grounding.

In the opening of the first episode of *Marito e moglie*, set in a village near Naples, we see men returning from work in the country. One of them passes a man seated in a doorway playing on a mandolin a tune already stated behind the credits. The playing carries on behind scenes of village life, including the voice of Donna Rosalia wailing and villagers thinking this means that her husband Don Matteo is dead (when in fact she is only lamenting the failure of her hen to lay eggs); sometimes the music is drowned by the voices but there is never any alteration of sound perspective depending upon how near or far the characters are in relation to the player. The source has been clearly signalled, but, on the one hand, its use does not remain anchored to that source and, on the other, it does not simply become non-diegetic. Moreover, if the source of the mandolin has been clearly signalled, the source of the tune has been equally clearly signalled in the credits sequence as different, namely, Nino Rota. This is then lightly commented upon when the mandolin player, who is the local barber, whistles the tune briefly while shaving Don Matteo and says that it is his own composition. In episode two, there is on and off throughout the sound of a piano playing, romantic in character although still with a Neapolitan flavour. It makes sense to think of this is someone playing the piano somewhere nearby (the blocks of flats are piled up next to one another, much action takes place on the balcony, doors and windows are always open), but the credits explicitly tell us it is Rota playing the piano. Towards the end it is heard as Gennaro and his friend Michele are walking along the sea front, Gennaro reading a poem; it could not possibly be heard so far from the flats, but once again the sense of music always being around, no matter where technically it comes from, means that this is not just straightforwardly non-diegetic. What complicates the case in both episodes is the reminder from the credits that the source is Rota: if both films participate in the notion of pervasiveness, signalling Rota's involvement also hints at the construction of this and thus of the very notion of pervasiveness. As suggested in the previous section, Rota is often liable to destabilise the Neapolitan, and perhaps even more the Eduardian, myth.

The folklore paradigm fuses diegetic and non-diegetic music and provides a justification for doing so. Elsewhere ambiguity about the distinction can be more unsettling.

LA DOMENICA DELLA BUONA GENTE Towards the end, Ines, the young woman who has come to Rome to confront the older, married man who has made her pregnant, goes back to the station, having failed to track him down, but then catches sight of him and searches in her bag for the revolver with which she now plans to kill him; she does not know that the young man who befriended her earlier removed it from her bag to prevent her from using it. At the station jazzy music blares forth, music of the kind associated with gangsters and used with negative implications in the films of the period. There is no other music like this in the rest of the film, putting it out of step with the extensive non-diegetic score, and it might be coming from loudspeakers; however, this diegetic source is not actually indicated and it comes and goes, sometimes, but only temporarily, eclipsed by the non-diegetic, tragic theme associated with Ines. It seems to acknowledge a certain kind of narrative (the crime story) and its presence in the popular culture that the characters inhabit, and the fact that Ines has a gun shows that she thinks that she lives by this. Yet the coming and going also signals that this is not that kind of story, but rather one of everyday life, the kind in which women don't in the end get to kill the man who done them wrong.

PLEIN SOLEIL Marge, Philippe and Tom are a few days into their rather tense yacht trip (she resents Tom's intrusive presence, Philippe is uneasy about Tom's interest in him). After a bit of a row, Philippe holds a 45 rpm record in his hand, smiling after Tom; there is then a sequence of all three lazing about on deck, Philippe and Marge making love. The music that accompanies them could be what Philippe has just put on the record player, but it is also one of the film's themes and carries on playing over what the cutting suggests is a longish period of time. It is languorous, played on Hawaiian guitar, and evokes the hedonistic, who-cares-what-time-it-is atmosphere, but also perhaps the lack of a sense of coordinates, the kind of drifting that will enable Tom to realise his perhaps barely formed plan (of killing and becoming Philippe). Something of the amoral quality of life produced by the characters at the same time provides a perspective on it.

The opening shot of *Anni facili* provides an especially complex example with which to end this section. It consists of a single camera movement, tilting down the façade of a massive baroque church, tracking left and circling to move past a bust on a plinth commemorating 'Agesilao Palermo, Patriota', the inscription briefly filling the screen, but the camera continuing on round to show the no less imposing, colonnaded façade of the Scuola Magistrale Matteo Raeli (named for another nineteenth-century patriot); it is accompanied by solemn organ music and a voiceover announcing that this is the centenary of the death of Agesilao Palermo, who died in the name of liberty at the hands of a Bourbon executioner. It could be documentary: it follows a single shot behind the credits taken from the back of a moving vehicle along the long central artery of Palermo and the opening shot of the film proper, just described, is also showing a famous Palermitian location; moreover, not only the fact of it being accompanied by a voiceover giving information but also the tone of voice of the speaker suggest documentary. Even though anyone going to see *Anni facili* would know that it is a fiction film (and a comedy at that), still such documentary-style openings were common in postwar cinema (*Vivere in pace*, *Molti sogni per le strade*, *Napoli milionaria*), even in comedies (notably *Totò cerca casa* (1949)). In the context of being a documentary, the organ music could actually emanate from the church, or be the sort of music that would be played there, or simply be appropriate to the solemnity of the voiceover. In the most rigorous conception of documentary, it makes a considerable difference which of these it is, and the fudging here suggests an element of manipulation, documentary as, in this case, propaganda for the assertion of values that all sides claim: patriotism, liberty. However, two things suggest that the film is also signalling this shot as adopting the documentary mode: the fact that many might recognise the voice as belonging to Nino Taranto, a very well-established star and announced already in the credits and the promotion of the film, and, even were one not to recognise the voice, the fact that the organ is playing the same tune as was heard moments earlier behind the credits (a tune written for the film, not an established piece of church music). This already unsettles what nonetheless still appears plausible, that the music is coming from the church. However, the tune that it plays has already been given in two very different versions in the credits sequence: first in a very Rota-esque, perky arrangement, woodwinds over a quite fast, bouncy rhythm, becoming a little brasher, orchestra with brass to the fore, a second time through, and then, considerably transformed, slowed down, desyncopated, played on massed, plunging strings. The fact that it is basically the same tune catches precisely the tone of the film, at once comic and bitter. So, when it is next played solemnly on an organ in a documentary-style sequence, the spirit in which it is intended and in which we are supposed to take it is deeply ambiguous. Nothing is straightforward here and this is then compounded when the voiceover is revealed to be Taranto's character, Luigi De Francesco, talking to his pupils in the school whose façade we have just seen. Here we have a shift from one possible diegesis, with its own rules and claims, the documentary, to another, the film's fictional narrative. The music, however, precisely because of its multiple ambiguities (of tone as well as of diegetic belonging) refuses any simple shift. The music was, after all, not from the church, nor, as it seemed for a moment, part of a documentary opening, but non-diegetic accompaniment to what Luigi is saying, which itself is the giving out of information characteristic of documentary and pedagogy alike. Luigi is a complex figure: a rigorously honest man and thus a fish out of water in the corrupt Italian society the film depicts, but also pompous and naive. The music – comic/bitter from the word go, then fake (it turns out) solemn or documentary, but not entirely out of synch with the kind of person delivering the lines – provides a range of possibilities for attending to his character.

The distinction between the diegetic and the non-diegetic is not one that we typically have problems with. We know the difference. We know that there is a world going on which has music in it and also that that world is told, including by means of music, means that are not in that world. We also know that to go along with this we have temporarily to suspend disbelief, to treat the diegetic world as if it is just there, going on regardless of the film-makers' and our activity, and to treat the apparatus of telling as if it were not there. What Rota's practice touches on is what we temporarily disbelieve. It keeps in play the bases of disbelief but never so much as to undermine the willing suspension of it.

Shifts from diegetic to non-diegetic allow acknowledgment of the fact that the diegetic world is itself constructed in the service of the telling of the story: Petruchio's goliardo, the waltz in *War and Peace*, the merry-go-round music in *Città di notte*, 'Luna mezz' 'o mare' in the *Godfather* films, the 45 rpm record in *Plein soleil*. Shifts may indicate that the characters' subjectivity is itself constructed in the diegetic: Anna and the sacred music, Arduino and 'Un ora sola ti vorrei', Maria after the ball in *Un americano in vacanza*. The especially rich use of reference in Rota's work further allows for an acknowledgment that the construction of the diegetic world is itself based on what is available in the musical culture of those who produce it and the (real) world they inhabit.

Remaining poised on the cusp of the supposed diegetic/non-diegetic divide allows a film to acknowledge the perspective that is brought to bear on the world and the characters that it appears to disclose, without seeking to disrupt interest, engagement and access, that is, attachment. We can share in Anna, Arduino's and Maria's musical imagination without forgetting the sources of them. We can sense the film's view of the Corleone godfathers' influence in the dancing to the *Godfather* waltz, of Adriana and her modern jazz in *Città di notte*, of the fate of Gino and Pierina ('Ma quando tornerà') in *Fuga in Francia*, of Romeo and Juliet ('What Is a Youth?') and of Andrea and Elena ('It's a waltz!') in *Appassionatamente*. If something of the idea of Naples is upheld by the fusion of diegetic and non-diegetic music, the fact of its fabrication is touched on by the acknowledgment of Rota's presence in the barber's composition and the piano playing in *Marito e moglie*. *La domenica della buona gente* acknowledges the appropriateness of the melodramatic mode (Bruno and his wife and daughter and symphonic music) and the inappropriateness of the gangster mode (Ines and her gun and flashy jazz) for this story of everyday life. *Anni facili* simultaneously acknowledges and throws into relief the truth-telling claims of the modes of documentary and satire that subtend its socially critical comedy. All of these are made possible by remaining poised on the brink of the purely non-diegetic; yet, just because it is the brink, they also allow the fiction of the diegetic world to carry on. The film is neither wholly within nor wholly without the world of the film, attached but knowing and indicating its role in producing it in the first place.

SCORING: UNDER, OVER AND ALONGSIDE
A film's non-diegetic score (which in this section I shall simply call the score) may underpin events on-screen, unobtrusively but in detail, or it may be

intrusive to the point that the events seem to be performed to them rather than vice versa, or it may be neither, carrying on alongside the events, neither unobtrusive nor intrusive, neither following nor leading. If the first is underscoring, an industry term to describe the characteristic practice of mainstream cinema up to, say, the 1970s, the second is overscoring, not an industry term, but becoming a more common practice since the 1970s. There are copious examples of both in Rota's work and I deal with these first. However, Rota himself identified the third approach as what he aimed at: 'to produce music for film that keeps itself apart as music, which runs alongside the film and doesn't submit itself to it, only adapts itself materially'.[67] I end this section with an exploration of this alongside method, itself the most conducive to the construction of ironic attachment.

Underscoring

Few composers, leave alone Rota, have produced scores with quite the detailed, precise and copious underscoring of the literal and affective movement within a sequence characteristic of the supreme exemplar of classical Hollywood scoring, Max Steiner.[68] However, Rota could, if need be, come close to it.

He does, for instance, sometimes have music mimic on-screen movement: in *Molti sogni per le strade*, on the family's uneasy day out in the country, music picks up pace as their car does and stops when it does (with even more acceleration when Paolo starts speeding to try to get away from the police); during a parachute training sequence in *Divisione folgare*, when one after another the men leap out of a plane, there are a series of plink-plunk falling notes, and then a repeated spiralling descending figure on strings reflecting their floating, twisting, down to the ground. This is Mickey Mousing, sound movement precisely coordinated to visual ones, a procedure often used for comic effect, but here more straightforwardly underlining the element of the mechanical in the on-screen movement. As obvious as this is the stinger, the sudden burst of music that comes in on an especially intense moment. A couple of examples from Rota films: *Senza pietà*, a crash of music when Angela is told that the brother she has come to find, and who seems to be her only hope of finding a way out of a life of prostitution, is dead (the music here having no African-American colouring, which is reserved in the film for what seem like avenues and persons of hope in the film); *Sotto il sole di Roma*, when the young hero Ciro kisses his neighbour Iris for the first time, a long kiss celebrated with a violin trill. Both these examples are moments of melodrama, in the second case in a film that is not itself mainly melodramatic.

Mickey Mousing and stingers, standard procedures in Hollywood and Steiner, nonetheless run counter to the prevailing wisdom in classical Hollywoodian scoring, namely, that music should be unobtrusive, unnoticed, as it were unheard. Claudia Gorbman has extrapolated some of the unwritten rules that were followed in order for this unobtrusiveness to obtain. It is possible to find examples of them all in Rota's work, and one, in many ways the most interesting, seems quite common, namely that music may come in, cease or change 'with a decisive rhythmic or emotional change in mood' (Gorbman, 1987: 78).

SENZA PIETÀ Marcella is looking after Angela, after the latter has tried to drown herself on learning that her brother is dead. The (non-diegetic) music is initially wandering, in doom-laden orchestral colours, as Marcella explains to another of the girls, Dina, what has happened, and the latter says that she too has thought of killing herself. Marcella tries to change the tenor of the conversation, talking of her GI, Jack, who is going to take her away; at this point the music changes, incorporating the upbeat Negro spiritual 'All God's Chillun Gotta Row (to Get to Heaven)'. Angela stirs in her sleep and calls out for Marcella, and the earlier, dramatic music returns. Marcella again turns the conversation to her and Jack and 'All God's Chillun' returns, but in a slower, saxophone version, less affirmative than moments earlier. This continues, ending with the saxophone picking up speed on what would be the words 'Heaven! Heaven!', somewhat harshly played, over a rather disquieting image of Marcella almost stabbing her lipstick on.

LE BOULANGER DE VALORGUE (1953) A slow, sweet melody accompanies a scene of the main character, Felice, doing the early morning baking, which, however, pauses before returning in a louder, more plaintive version as Felice begins to speak of how distressed he is at the thought that his son Giustino is about to go off to do his military service. The next day, another, equally saddish melody on strings accompanies Giustino leaving home: when his mother embraces him, there is a little fanfare (celebrating mother love? reminding us of where he is headed?); as he walks to the bus that will take him away, the music reaches a climax, then quietens as he speaks with his sweetheart Françoise, and then flourishes up again for him going off in bus and them waving to each other; it then diminishes as his parents start to go about business again, the sequence brought to an end by a reveille call.

Music may be coordinated with telling cuts.

UN AMERICANO IN VACANZA When GI Dick catches sight of Maria outside St Peter's in Rome, having thought he'd lost her, the film cuts to his point of view of her and with the cut a romantic theme comes in. A little later, in St Peter's, they are talking; on a cut to an extreme close-up of them, him telling her that she is the one for him, the theme returns on a throbbing cello, less sweet, more ardent.

GIORNO DI NOZZE (1942) Here, comic music becomes less so on a cut to a different angle. Mariano and Amalia are taking their daughter Mariella home to the flat that she has not seen, having been away at boarding school; she does not realise that, because of the sacrifices they have made to send her to school, the flat is very much less grand than the homes of her school-mates. As the three climb the stairs, shot from above, the music has a trudging quality, vaguely Mickey Mousing their walk, suggesting the effort of climbing the stairs

(even while Mariano and Amalia reassure Mariella that 'adesso tutti preferiscono di stare in alto' ('nowadays everyone prefers to be up high')); this, with its comical flavour, sets up the potential gag of the discrepancy between the flat itself and both what Mariella anticipates and how the parents are talking it up. But then there is a cut to the three of them seen from below at the door of the flat and the music becomes sadder, more solemn, as if reflecting Mariella's disappointment. The high angle lessens the characters' dignity, the low one increases it, and the music performs the same function, the indignity of comedy, the dignity of pathos.

Giorno di nozze: Mariano (Armando Falconi) and Amalia (Amelia Chellini) introduce their daughter Mariella (Anna Vivaldi [Anna Proclemer]) to their top-floor flat

In *La grande speranza* music responds to cuts, positioning and gender. The film tells of a group of survivors of mixed nationalities from an Allied ship during the Second World War, who are rescued by the Italian submarine that has torpedoed their ship; one of the survivors is a nurse, Lily Donald, the only woman in the film. There is sailing music, sombre dramatic music for scenes of tension, no music for action sequences, triumphant, major mode music for arrival at safety, and, in appropriate interludes, comic music; there is also a sentimental theme. This is heard first as the survivors are being taken on board the submarine; there is no music as each, in mid-shot, comes on board, until a cut to a mid-close-up of Lily and the sentimental theme, the first time we realise there is a woman among them. It next occurs in a sequence when the survivors are taking a turn on deck; a couple of the men indulge in horseplay with comic music behind; Lily is sitting unobtrusively in the background; when the men break up, Lily stands up and walks towards the camera until she is centre screen; there is no cut or change of camera position, but nonetheless the sentimental theme comes in as Lily in effect displaces the chaps' boisterousness.

The sentimental theme is associated with the default locus of sentiment in any film, a woman. In both cases, though, the theme carries on beyond the initial foregrounding of Lily, in the first case over a shivering wounded man who is helped along the prow of the submarine by a couple of the Italian sailors, in the second case behind Lily falling into conversation with one of the other survivors, Robert Steiner, a playwright, signalled by the film as

La grande speranza:
the men spar, Lily (Lois
Maxwell) comes forward,
the music changes

manly but also, like Lily, sensitive and reflective. Thus the film identifies, partly through the music, the elements of femininity in men: in wounded-ness, in artistic refinement. The theme is used again later in connection with her developing relation with the captain of the submarine. It comes in on a cut to a long-held shot of a conventionally beautiful sunset; Lily and the Captain watch it, a moment of rapprochement (earlier she has been hostile because her fiancé had been killed in the war by Italians), the sunset as well as the music also hinting at the possibility of a feeling of romance between them that circumstances cannot allow to blossom; a little later both are seen lying awake in their bunks, the theme playing continuously across cross-cutting between them, each presumably thinking of the other. Here it is not only the association of femininity with romantic love that is affirmed; it is also that he is a man of high moral sensibility (confirmed by his humanitar-ian treatment of the survivors and correct delivery of them to neutral terri-tory, rather than treating them as prisoners of war). (Later in the film there is another quite long sequence of cross-cutting, using a different, more fully sorrowful theme, showing the Captain returning to his berth after a suc-cessful attack on an enemy ship and shots of the latter in flames; the music, that does not alter whether showing the Captain or the ship, suggests the pain felt by this honourable man at the bloodshed he must execute.)

In keeping with the principles of underscoring, all of the above (bar the Mickey Mousing and stingers) are unobtrusive. Indeed, on the whole, Rota's scores are even more unobtrusive than classical Hollywood practice. For one thing, they are probably never as detailed and sustained in their submission to what's taking place on-screen: most often they are only broadly in line with it and just occasionally precisely coordinated. For another, they are often simply rather quiet (perhaps as a means of backing off from the sense in classical underscoring of being led by the plot and of promoting identifi-catory relations), a tendency much lamented by Rota's mother in her diary.[69]

Overscoring
In *Le notti bianche*, Mario, recently transferred to Livorno and on his own, encounters a young woman, Natalia, in the street and they chat tentatively.

After he chases away some boys on a motorbike who are teasing Natalia and shouts after them, he turns and she seems to have disappeared, but he retraces his steps and catches sight of her. He puts his head down, as if uncertain how to proceed, and then raises his eyes, smiles very slightly and moves forward, and exactly on the moment of raising his eyes, some music comes in, a gently, unemphatically romantic theme, which continues up to the point where she closes her bag (in which she has put the handkerchief she was wiping her tears with). This follows Gorbman's 'decisive rhythmic or emotional change in mood' rule, for the music comes in and ends at points that indicate shifts of feeling within the scene, but these are also microscopic in terms of both the actual performance gestures and also what they signify at this very early stage in the relationship. The music, in a way characteristic of the whole film, gives a kind of presence and pregnancy to what is happening. The Gorbman rule is followed but in excess of what directly calls the music forth, so that it risks being more rather than less noticeable, teetering on the brink of overscoring.

I am using the term overscoring, which is not used either professionally or critically, to identify uses of music that not only do not subordinate them-selves to what the rest of the film proposes, but also seem to lead or at any rate to be an equal partner with those other elements. The most obvious, and widespread, form of overscoring is the use of pop music, usually existing prior to the film, the film working on the assumption of the music being already known, anticipated and noticeable. Yet modes of scoring can be obtrusive even when not familiar, by virtue, for instance, of strongly accented rhythm, easily grasped and fully played melodies (not broken down into snatches[70]) and volume.

Given the sense of reticence and irony, the lack of insistence, even the quietness, in Rota's approach, it would seem evident that overscoring (even had he lived into the period in which it became a dominant mode) is not characteristic of his work. The clearest exception is also his first film, *Treno popolare*. A contemporary review noted that the music was 'aderente all'azione' ('stuck to the action')[71] and this is especially noticeable in the long opening sequence of the train's departure from Rome and journey to Orvieto. At the station the music is onomatopoeic, imitating buzzing kids, slamming doors and hissing steam. Once the journey is underway, the music accelerates as the train picks up speed (and slows down as it reaches Orvieto), using a thumping rhythm that mimics the sound and movement of pistons and wheel cranks (rather than the clickety-clack over-the-tracks music that became the standard musical representation of train travel). Brighter music is used later to reflect the movement of the bikes hired by the central romantic triangle of Carlo, Lina and Giovanni. The approach is characteristic of the period. Some of the most immediate parallels are with, in Italy in the same year, Gianfranco Malipiero's music for *Acciaio* (1933, lots of bicycles as well as steel production), as well as, elsewhere, Hanns Eisler's for *Kuhle Wampe* (especially the opening bicycling sequences), and Benjamin Britten's for *Coalface* (1935, cranks, wheels, lifts) and *Night Mail*

(1936, pistons as well as clickety-clack). *Treno popolare* was a flop, Rota did not compose another score for eight years and there is little similar anywhere else in his work, at any rate in a sustained form, though we might note the train rhythm in *Zaʒà* and the pumping chords for the departure of the steamer in *Death on the Nile*.

However, while *Treno popolare* is an exceptional score for Rota, it might be argued that the two genres in which he worked most fully, comedy and melodrama, almost by definition entail overscoring, no less in Rota's case than any other. Overt, indiscreet scoring is naturalised in both genres. I discuss the implications of this for Rota and comedy in the next chapter. Melodrama advertises the involvement of music in its very name (melodrama = music plus drama), and if its etymology might not be known to all audiences (even if they might unconsciously make the connection with melody), in Italy the word *melodramma* also means opera, where the musical connection is unmissable. In any event, being moved by stirring, touching, passionate and heart-rending music is a basic expectation of melodrama, and Rota (who also wrote operas) seems to have felt entirely at home in the genre, as if the strong musical presence was too natural, too taken for granted a part of it to constitute an offence against discretion.

Much of Rota's melodrama scoring is consummate but nonetheless straightforward. In *Divisione folgare* one soldier is about to kill another and then realises he is not enemy but his own brother, and at that moment an astonishingly sentimental melody comes in on solo violin, and then clarinet; it is at times drowned by the off-screen sounds of bombs, adding to poignancy as the melody struggles to be heard in the surrounding carnage. The emotionally graduated multiple climaxes of, for instance, *Zaʒà*, *La donna della montagna*, *Senʒa pietà*, *Anna* and *Appassionatamente* do not hold back from wringing the heart strings.

With Rota's scores for Visconti there is still at times reticence (Bruckner's Seventh Symphony bleeds in unobtrusively as Livia and Franz take their first walk through Venice in *Senso*, 'Paese mio' begins barely perceptibly within the word 'Rocco' when Rocco is talking with Cecchi about his training alongside Simone) and, as we shall see, music alongside. Yet Rota's Visconti scores also work at times through overscoring in relation to the selfconsciousness of Visconti's use of *melodramma* (of which the creation in *Rocco e i suoi fratelli* of a Marxist melodrama is but one version).

Just after the moment near the beginning of *Le notti bianche* described above, Mario tries to comfort Natalia and she to shake him off; he says that he only approached her because he could see she was crying, which then makes her start crying again. A prostitute hangs about unobtrusively in the square behind them but at a certain point she moves forward. As Mario is trying to explain himself, his good intentions, and as the prostitute draws nearer to them, music comes in, the series of separated, as it were dropping phrases, strange, perhaps even sinister, established already in the credits. The moment it comes in, Natalia and then Mario turn to look at the prostitute, almost as if hearing the notes as much as becoming aware of her. The music then continues with the camera panning right to follow the prostitute over the bridge, and thus away from Mario and Natalia (although we still hear him explaining himself); the pan and the music come to an end when the prostitute, who has already glanced back once at them, stops at the entrance to the café, looks back at them again and then pushes the door to go in. The prostitute (she is given no other name by the film) has no precise narrative role in the film but she is a recurrent, disquieting presence.[72] What is curious about this shot is that the film chooses so to emphasise that presence, to the point of partially taking attention away from the central couple, something emphasised still more by the sudden dropping in of the music, the way it seems to interrupt Mario and Natalia and is dovetailed to the prostitute's walk across the bridge.

Like the figure of the prostitute itself, the music is a very deliberate intervention in the strange affective texture of the film. *Le notti bianche* takes place in a Livorno filmed entirely on a meticulously recreated set that, by virtue of its difference from the texture that had become familiar from neo-realist location shooting, looks like a set. It includes strangely handled transitions to and from flashbacks, such that characters seem to be directly watching events from the past. The transposition to Livorno from the St Petersburg of the Dostoyevsky story on which the film is based makes the arrival of the snow towards the end (even if no doubt it does snow sometimes in Livorno) seem magical, and this is how the characters respond to it. All of this – and the disquieting presence of the prostitute – relates to the story of the girl whom Mario befriends, Natalia, who tells him she comes every night at ten o'clock to wait for a man she fell in love with, a lodger in her grandmother's house who told her that he needed to go away for a year but would then return for her if she will wait for him. Everything about the story, and not least Maria Schell's fey performance, suggests she is deluding herself; yet at the very end, the lodger does turn up and take her with him. The artifice, the disquiet, the uncertain emotional tone of the film all conspire to make this ending seem as if a willed, even wilful, happy end.

A further musical contribution to the unsettling unclassifiable tone of *Le notti bianche* is its melodramatic character. I have already touched on the strong use of music in relation to tiny details of action and performance in the film, suggesting or supplying an emotional intensity that is not otherwise evident. Elsewhere, when there is more emotional intensity – as Natalia tells the story of her great love, as Mario tears up the letter she has given him to give to her love (who she has learnt has returned to Livorno) and later when he tells her that he has done so, as they seem to achieve a rapprochement in the magic of the snow, when at the end Natalia sees her love waiting on the bridge and runs to him – there is very strong, searing, loud, unequivocally melodramatic music. Given what for much of the time seem to be delusions on Natalia's part, given the often desultory sequences of hanging about the square or dancing in the bar, given the patina of evidently created naturalism, the music seems a paradigm of excess, artificially hyperemotional.

One might compare it with *Senso*, Rota's previous film with Visconti, for which he selected and arranged parts of Bruckner's Seventh Symphony. The film opens with an opera, *Il trovatore*, which is the occasion for the married Countess Livia to tell the Austrian lieutenant Franz that she only enjoys opera, which is to say melodrama, on stage; yet there are moments in the development of her affair with him when the score behaves in a shriekingly melodramatic way. When, unable to find Franz, she gets a note from, she supposes, him, she blurts out to her husband that she has a lover; there is a cut from a two-shot to a high overhead shot and at the same time a crash of dramatically discordant music, as Livia rushes off to join Franz. This under-lines the sense that Livia, for all her earlier protestation to the contrary, is all too prone to being melodramatic. Such melodramatic sound and fury is all the more savagely ironic in that Franz obviously treats her as just one con-quest among many, with the added advantage of her having money and position; in the name of this falsely based love she is prepared to betray a cause in which she says she believes, the Risorgimento.[73] The object of her love is wretched (if, in the shape of Farley Granger, meltingly handsome), her passion deluded, and it causes her to betray her ideals. In the moment of rushing off described above, the irony is ratcheted up even some more – the note is not from Franz, but from Roberto; she has needlessly given herself away to her husband, in her and the music's outburst of hysteria. *Le notti bianche* plays a similar game for much of the time, except that it turns out that Natalia's love is genuine. It is as if at the end Livia's Franz turns out really to have loved her all along.

Alongside

Daniele Cortis mainly uses one theme, restricted to the sequences of high emotion (Elena and Daniele in love, then picking up again after her marriage to someone else, she realising she must renounce Daniele, she in the carriage beside her unloved husband on their way to America and away from Daniele for ever) with no music in most of the rest of the film (Elena at school, the marriage, her husband's gambling and scamming, Daniele's political career). When the big theme is used it is played over and over again, on full orchestra, sometimes with strings sweepingly, turbulently to the fore, some-times on melancholy or desolate winds.[74] The music is symphonic, yet it is also mainly played rather quietly (the final big statement over Elena in the carriage being the exception) and the melody plays over and over in tonal accord with what is on-screen but not in any precise coordination with it.

In an interoffice memorandum in March 1940, Max Steiner spoke of two schools of composition:

> 'Mickey Mouse' and 'over-all' scoring. The 'Mickey Mouse' scoring (my way of scoring) ... fits a picture like a glove. In other words, if I want to underline a love scene in a parlour and we were to cut away to a boat on the water, I would try and write my music so that the love theme would modulate into some kind of water music or what have you, as naturally the love theme would have

nothing to do with the boat as the locale would be changed and probably would indicate time elapse. The 'over-all' school … would keep right on playing regardless what happens.[75]

If sometimes Rota's scores fit like a (loose) glove in the way Steiner intends, it is much more characteristic of them to keep right on playing, not exactly regardless of what is happening, but often just alongside it, often in broad sympathy, but sometimes more oblique, ironic or indifferent. Francesco Lombardi (2000: xvii) writes of Rota's 'distinct detachment … from the filmic events, the story',[76] while Rota himself speaks, in the context of working with Fellini, Visconti and Zeffirelli, of music that 'expresses above all the spirit of the film rather than the materiality of the succession of images'.[77]

We may account for this practice by circumstance. First, sound, including dialogue and ambient elements, was until very recently always post-synchronised in Italian cinema, and Chion (1994: 64–5) speaks of the habit of 'loose synchronisation' of sound and image in Italian cinema. The sense then of sound not quite emanating from the image and the possibility of it being thought through after filming make a slightly less conjoined conception of sound–image relations possible. Second, Rota, not least because he was always busy, worked very quickly, telling Sergio Miceli that he often kept quiet about it because people might criticise him: 'If you knew how long it took me to write the music for [one of Fellini's most important films], you wouldn't believe me. … But do you know how long it took Mozart to compose *The Marriage of Figaro*?'.[78] Moreover, his practice was to write a score after the film was made, usually without reading the script or being on set, leave alone watching the finished cut first.

> In fact Rota worked mainly from notes; usually he saw the film on the editing table, having already composed the major part of the music, and only in order to sort out technical problems (length, gaps, orchestration). He hardly ever saw the film in its entirety, in its definitive version, not even after it had come out.[79]

No wonder that the scores fell into an 'overall' approach.

One way of describing Rota's procedure in many of his films is to say that the music, while always relevant to what is on-screen, is allowed to have its own musical agenda. I look at some instances of this next before turning to consider further the aesthetic implications of his practice. Music running alongside may have been a product of circumstances and of Rota's quietly stubborn desire to protect the integrity of the music, but it also has formal and expressive consequences, making possible a range of affect from homogeneity to heterogeneity, from affirmation to misgiving, affects wholly in line with his overall aesthetic inclinations.

Rota wanted his scores to be 'a sé stante come musica' ('to keep themselves apart as music').[80] This is not a bid to create music that can exist as concert works independently of the film: there is always a relationship, albeit one that works in terms of tangency. Nor is it deliberate, antagonistic counterpoint of the kind canvassed by Theodor Adorno and Hanns Eisler, nor random juxtaposition of the kind associated with John Cage: the music is always broadly speaking appropriate to the matter in hand. Nevertheless, much of what a Rota score does may be driven by internal musical logic as much as, sometimes more than, filmic (visual, editing, dialogue, sound) ones. Much of the score of *Mio figlio professore* subjects 'Come chioveva' to a set of authentic variations, comparable in approach to such popular classics as Brahms' *St Anthony* or Elgar's *Enigma Variations* (in other words, not just replaying the theme with different instruments, but bending it, altering its harmonic and rhythmic base, inverting it and so on). The opening of *Fantasmi a Roma* is a monologue about life by the ageing Annibale, accompanied, as if for an aria, by a set of variations, which, however, go their own way rather than underlining Annibale's words. The last ten minutes of *Senza pietà* constitute a kind of symphony on Negro spirituals that, with a bass solo voice and full choir and orchestra, intertwining 'No-body Knows the Trouble I Seen' and 'Deep River', takes its cue from the development of the spirituals as a concert-hall music and the work of the Harlem Renaissance composers.

In 'Il lavoro' (in *Boccaccio '70*), Ottavio, whose photograph in the company of prostitutes has just been splashed across the newspapers, goes to speak with his wife Pupe. She is playing jazz on her record player, a Miles Davis-style piece (as far as I can ascertain written nevertheless by Rota) already heard over the credits. They squabble and she tells him that she is planning to get a job, to keep herself from boredom. At a certain point the jazz stops, naturalistically (that is, when the record finishes). It comes back in, without anyone having apparently put it on, when Ottavio asks one of their menservants, Antonio, to confirm that having a job is a pain; Pupe approaches him and, with the appearance of real concern, says that surely it is not that awful, not a source of anxiety. As she says this the jazz gives way to a solo violin, and the music for the rest of the scene is for a small ensemble, playing music that has elements of the sentimental (melodic phrases, the violin played with vibrato) but that is also harmonically spare and astringent, with no developed melody, in many ways a concert music equivalent of the jazz, perhaps an andante movement of a chamber piece. There is a further musical element: when Pupe says to Antonio that surely he only has little worries, he understands her to mean his wages, taking the opportunity to remind her of her promise to give him a raise, at which point she cuts him short, revealing the true level of her concern, saying that this not the time, and on this last remark there are four little squeaking notes in the music in a downward pattern like comic exclamation marks. The pattern for the music for the rest of this scene is then a kind of contemporary chamber music, serious but not solemn, astringent but not radically atonal, leave alone dodecaphonic, with occasional comic decorations, and one that one could imagine Rota writing independently of the film, combining as it does his trademark sentiment and humour in a clearly modern, but not avant-garde, setting. This perhaps catches the tone of the sequence and indeed the film: a modern

young couple with problems, which nonetheless has its funny side. What it does not relate to is the development of the scene. Ottavio and Pupe's quarrelling becomes more heated (he becoming more agitated than she) but the music doesn't. The music stops briefly when Pupe answers the phone, but returns as she speaks on the phone with the lawyer Zacchi about what to do about the scandal in the papers, of which she is dismissive, all the while taking off her clothes down to her slip. Here there are more of the squeaking notes, but while one might see the sequence as comic there are no gags to occasion these notes. The music stops again when the maid comes in and Pupe asks her to run a bath, and then it returns, as she is telling Zacchi she has no money and so must go out to work; there is a cut to a choker close-up of her, as she agrees with Zacchi that a certain physical attraction is not enough for a marriage, and as she says goodbye to him a tear appears – and here the music does get a bit louder, but without changing substantially, even for this moment of emotional revelation and intensification (the extreme close-up, the tear). In the music's lack of connection to anger that gives way to chat and then to grief, it is almost as if the record that has been put on is of some unknown contemporary chamber piece following its own, faintly lyrical, occasionally witty but somewhat dry trajectory.

In a sequence a little later when Pupe is preparing to go out to meet a friend at La Scala, there is, as it were, a second movement of the chamber piece, perhaps allegretto, with often a gay lilt. When she decides to change, because she realises she is too smartly dressed for someone looking for work, and the music stops, she puts on the radio, which is playing some light jazz on xylophone. This is almost a reverse of the procedure with the first movement, which seemed to grow out of the jazz, whereas here the chamber piece points towards the jazz to come on the radio. The third movement – when Ottavio has agreed to pay her for sex – is lento, and, while it uses some phrases from the first movement, is much more mournful, with mainly oboe, bassoon, cellos. By the end he is cheerful, writing her a cheque for services already rendered, she is in tears, but the music is neither, until the very end when it does come to a keenly plaintive climax over an extreme close-up of her mouth as tears wash down onto it.

'Il lavoro' illustrates the way that a piece of music may accompany a sequence in a self-contained manner, following its own musical progression, but it also suggests the way the music for a whole film may be seen to organised along musical lines, in this case the three movements of a piece for chamber orchestra. There are other such examples in Rota's work. The music for *Un americano in vacanza*, for instance, is in two halves, with the second recapitulating the material from the first half, working variations on it but moderating it only slightly to fit with the length of the scenes and only once introducing an entirely new musical element, the old-fashioned waltz. This is not done in total disregard of the rest of the film. The break point between the two musical halves occurs with the break that until even very recently was standard for screenings in Italy, forcing an interval between a *primo* and *secondo tempo*. Moreover, the boy-and-girl narrative of the second half pretty well repeats that of the first: postwar contextualisation, pursuit, misunderstanding, falling in love, the intervention of religion, regretful parting. This, however, is submerged in the visual patina of (neo-)realist convention, whereas Rota's score tends to suggest the formal structures of the narrative peripeteia. It also plays on the potential for both comedy and pathos in repetition itself, although the introduction of the new element – a very Rota-ish sweetly melancholic waltz – perhaps finally inflects the recapitulation more towards gentle pathos.[81]

An especially complex example is provided by *Campane a martello*. A number of original themes are gradually introduced, which we might characterise as a descending melancholic/tragic melody, a *meridionale*[82] tune, a love theme and comic material. These are then variously combined, sometimes with new melodic material (e.g., the descending theme with one reminiscent of the second subject of the second movement of Dvořák's Ninth Symphony, acting in *Campane a martello* as in the symphony as a quickening that offsets the solemnity of the first theme), sometimes using only already-established material (e.g., the descending theme punctuated by the comic material). The last six minutes of the film interweave all the elements, although all taking their tone from the descending theme, thus bringing the score to an affective musical resolution. While the score of *Campane a martello* would probably not stand alone as a concert piece, it can be described, as I have just tried to show, in purely musical terms. All the above is relevant to the story of two reformed prostitutes, Agostina and Australia, obliged to return to the former's native Ischia, much to the pleasure of her abandoned fiancé but the disapproval of the local dignitaries. However, the score is neither subordinate to the actions and details of the narrative nor is it in dialectical counterpoint to it; rather, it provides a set of colours, flavours or tones to the film. It offers us keys within which to attend to the story. If in *Campane a martello* stars, plot situations, character types and conventions of entering and identifying within the diegesis may all pull us towards direct emotional engagement, the music offers a perspective on it (plaintive but not downcast) that is no less engaging or affective and provides a counterweight partly by virtue of its own inner musical coherence.

Whether or not driven by a musical more than a filmic agenda, music that runs alongside can work in different ways with the events on-screen. It may simply affirm, and participate in the production of, the emotion of a scene or a whole film; that is, it produces an effect of emotional homogeneity. However, the emotion of the scene may be much less straightforward and Rota is particularly inclined to write music that perceives and brings out mixed or contrary emotions. In other cases, Rota's music runs somewhat counter to the emotions otherwise constructed by the scene or film. These three possibilities structure what follows.

Rota's running alongside music may confirm the dominant emotional tone of a scene (while not altering in relation to the detail of the narrative and emotional development).

> *SOTTO IL SOLE DI ROMA* A descending theme accompanies without variation a central section in which the protagonist returns home from escapades in the wartime countryside, learns that his mother is ill, goes to the hospital, talks with his neighbour (and would-be sweetheart) Iris and, finally, is told his mother has died. Melancholy pervades the scene but there is no alteration of intensity or timbre.
>
> *LA NAVE DELLE DONNE MALADETTE* The climax of the film is a series of connected scenes, each with appropriate music but without more precise character-oriented underscoring. The women are whooping it up after they have broken free from the prison hold, with a bare torsoed black male dancer dancing for them to the accompaniment of jungle rhythms; these disappear behind the love theme for a close-up of the central couple, Consuelo and Paolo, which then gives way to tempestuous music as a storm develops and the women carry on partying despite the danger it poses; then there is loud dramatic music for a fire on board and an eventual wreck, and at last solemn music as the women come to understand the situation in which they find themselves and all pray.
>
> *IL GATTOPARDO* Here the film is cut loosely to Rota's pre-existing *Sinfonia sopra una canzone d'amore* (see Chapter 1), shifts in the film roughly coinciding with the subjects and variations of the symphony itself. Thus the stately andante sostenuto comes in on Tancredi saying goodbye to his uncle

Fabrizio, after a brief altercation between them concerning Tancredi's
allegiance to Garibaldi, and continues behind his going through the house,
bidding farewell to members of the family; when the theme is abandoned by
the symphony for a short, less melodic bridge passage, the film shows us
Fabrizio giving Tancredi money and then the latter speaking with Concetta
(who is in love with him), quieter moments of more complex emotions; the
andante returns on Tancredi leaving the house, leaping into his gig and driving
off to join Garibaldi. What is on-screen is embraced by the overall sweep of
the melody and its Romantic character and the perspective this gives to the
events and characters. Similarly, the tumultuous allegro impetuoso, with
leaping violins and clashing cymbals, comes in towards the end of the sequence
of fighting in Palermo, just after the battle has been won but not on any
obvious moment; when the symphony gives way to a second subject, a slower,
mounting melody on horns, the film cuts to the carriages carrying Don
Fabrizio and the family to Donnafugata. The tumult of battle in the music
occurs after the battle is over, so that what carries over to the second subject
and the carriages in flight is a sense of tumult and turmoil, even though the
image does not itself convey this. The clashing subject returns at the point that
Tancredi uses both his role as a heroically wounded Garibaldini and the
prestige of his uncle to force soldiers to dismantle a road block to let the
carriage through. The action is momentous in terms of what it means (the
persistence of hierarchy in the context of democratisation, one of the film's
themes, as well as Tancredi's forceful impetuousness) and it is this that warrants
it being set to the tumult of the allegro, but not the actual actions on-screen.

The above examples concern music broadly sympathetic to the overall tenor
of a scene or sequence within a film, but the same may be true of the score
for a whole film.

JOLANDA LA FIGLIA DEL CORSARO NERO Fun music throughout this cross-dressing swashbuckler.

MELODIE IMMORTALI Mascagni's music accompanies the events in this biopic of his life, in a 'life and works' spirit; that is, the music is always with him because he is a composer, and the music makes his life appear in musically generic (though not, despite his being most famous as an opera composer, operatic) terms.

DIVISIONE FOLGARE Standard war film music, suffering, epic. At the end, there is a male voice choir over the men crossing the desert, becoming louder and more confident over the end credits (mainly crediting those who advised on film), wrapping the film up.

All the above scenes or films produce a unified emotion. However, the effect of music running alongside may be to bring out the complexity or variability of an emotional tone. A signature tone may be set in the opening credits. *Molti sogni per le strade* opens with a rumbustious tune followed by a sadder one, but still with a rumbustious underscoring; there is then a third, much more plaintive melody, but at the end of each phrase in it there are little comic flourishes. *Molti sogni per le strade* is a film hard to classify generically, part comedy, part realism, part sentimental melodrama, among other things; the music establishes this shifting tone, not as something uncertain but as something agreeably mixed.

Music in the film itself may similarly bring out the mix of feelings in a scene.

UN AMERICANO IN VACANZA Dick and Maria, who met by chance on the road to Rome, have bumped into one another outside St Peter's and talk; there is a pretty theme behind them, romantic but not ardent, played on violins and then cello. She tells him though that she is not the kind of girl he is looking for on his week off and then says she must go; she walks off past a splendid fountain as Dick returns to his fellow GI, Tom. On this shot of her and the fountain, phrases on woodwind and strings seem to echo the arc and fall of the fountain, its loveliness, but they alternate with phrases from the pretty theme just adumbrated, on cello, an instrument tending towards melancholy. The emotions in play – the exuberance of being in Rome (the fountain music), having met Maria again (the pretty theme), the regret at the immediate parting (the cello) – are caught, glancingly, together, by the music, and this combination continues for a while behind Dick's going back to Tom: élan, glow, disappointment.

LE MISERIE DEL SIGNOR TRAVET There is a main theme associated with the protagonist, Ignazio Travet, a modest clerk, humiliated equally by his fellow workers and his wife. The affective potential of the theme is doleful, in keeping with the eponymous miseries, and often realised through the use of violins and woodwinds, but plaintiveness is frequently offset by a bouncing cello phrase or repetition of the theme's opening phrase on comically quivering violins or else the theme played on low trombone immediately followed by high sweet violin. The sense of woe is never far away, but Travet (played by, Carlo Campanini, an actor more famous for comedy) is also a figure of fun, very much so for the characters in the film, and not entirely not so for us too.[83] The music captures this ambivalence on and off throughout the first two-thirds of the film. There is very little music in the last third, perhaps because there is more dialogue, but perhaps too because the film becomes much more melodramatic, takes Travet's misery much more seriously (as he finally stands up to his odious boss and to his wife) – the affective ambivalence of the music would now be out of synch with the unequivocal feelings of the film. *SOTTO IL SOLE DI ROMA* A very intricate intertwining of melodies in the opening sequence conveys at once a general sense of youth and liveliness (chirpy tunes with woodwind decorations) and a little melancholy (one of Rota's characteristic sad little spirally descending melodies), setting the tone for the rest of the film (larking about but learning to grow up in the last years of the war and the first years of the peace).

Two films, the English thriller *Obsession* and the commedia all'italiana *Anni facili*, are especially complex in their deployment of a contrary musical tone in keeping with the tone established also by other means by the two films.

Obsession is about a successful psychiatrist, Clive, who decides to murder Bill, the latest in his wife Storm's string of lovers. He keeps him locked up for several weeks, until the interest in his apparent disappearance has died down, planning then to poison him and dissolve the body in a bath of acid. In the end he is thwarted partly by Bill befriending Storm's dog, who has found his way into the secret prison, and training him to pull the plug from the acid bath (which is inaccessible to Bill himself), and partly through the efforts of a local policeman, Superintendent Finsbury. The tone of the film is really very English, at once morbid (the film stays close to Clive's obsession throughout) and macabre (the acid bath) and yet comic (the role of the dog and, as we shall see, Finsbury). It is heir to Agatha Christie and Alfred Hitchcock, to that sense of the crime story as fun. Perhaps the sense of this is heightened by the involvement of two foreigners, themselves of remarkably different artistic temperaments, Edward Dmytryk, acrid and cruelly violent,[84] and Rota, ironic and serene.

The mixed tone is achieved by many things besides the music. The basic plot is driven by festering, methodically executed revenge, but there is also much that is comic in the film. Sometimes this is incidental: we come in on the end of a consultation with one of Clive's patients, a Mrs Humphries, who is talking about the distress of her husband's doing it every night and it being a bit much; it turns out that she is speaking of his going to play with boats on a pond; as she leaves, reassured, she turns to Clive with, 'As you say, doctor, it could have been worse – it could have been kites.' The humour runs alongside the thriller elements. Clive has a line in dry humour, notably when discussing organisational matters with Bill in his prison, matters that are the organisation of Bill's death; Bill responds with somewhat feistier humour. There is the cute dog, a poodle, whose name Monty may

Obsession: Clive (Robert Newton), Monty (Monty the Dog) and Bill (Phil Brown)

itself be a little gag (for Field-Marshal Montgomery, commander of the British troops during the Second World War and still head of the army), and Superintendent Finsbury, played, with much whimsy, by the well-known comic actor Naunton Wayne (one of the humorous elements in *The Lady Vanishes* (1938), a canonical example of the comically toned thriller). The elements of the comic and the macabre come closely together towards the end. Finsbury is closing in on Clive (and hence Bill), but chats calmly with Storm, as she paces hysterically up and down, him saying what a clever plan it was (to keep Bill alive until police have stopped looking for him): 'Most original – and ingenious' and 'I wonder what he proposed to do with the body when the time came.' Moments later, Bill asks Clive what he is doing, putting bricks under the legs of the table in the room, and Clive replies, 'Bloodstains you know, an awful give-away – and dismemberment is an awfully messy business,' going on to explain how one can avoid 'the menace of bloodstains', as if discussing domestic arrangements (rather than how he is going to dismember Bill). Perhaps the detail that most catches the tone of the film is Clive's methodically pouring acid into hot water bottles, the ne plus ultra of comfy cosiness, every time he goes to see Bill and gradually filling up the bath with it.

The music is perfectly in accord with this tone. There are two main elements. One is a bland dance orchestra ballad-like theme; quite early on we learn, when Bill puts it on the record player for Storm (spied on by Clive), that this is 'their tune', but it is also used non-diegetically throughout. The other theme consists of busy, spiky phrases in high woodwind, music that is intended to make one smile, even laugh. Neither element is left alone, however, constantly being nudged in contrary directions. The dance music is

Obsession: Clive, with a hot
water bottle full of acid,
and Bill

played very dramatically near the beginning, when Clive returns home and
spies on the house from basement entry (at a point when we do not know
what he is up to), but when he goes up the stairs, the tune is played slightly
staccato on low strings, hinting in its near Mickey Mouseness at a comic perception; later when he speaks to his manservant, the tune is on bassoon, an
instrument commonly used to suggest the comic. All this is only faintly
comic, but it is exactly that suspicion of the comic within the serious that
contributes to the tone of the film. The spiky woodwind phrases, that
already come with a comic overtone, are sometimes used alongside events
that could be taken seriously (Clive hiding behind the drapes to spy on
Storm and Bill), sometimes in more straightforwardly comic or jolly situations (especially in connection with the poodle Monty, accompanying him
finding his way to Bill's prison, then again at the end when he visits Bill
recovering in hospital from Clive's attempt to poison him), and sometimes
yet more ambivalently: when Clive leaves his surgery with one of his hot
water bottles full of acid to go to the prison, the spiky tune responds to the
macabre absurdity of what is going on, but dark sostenuto violins beneath it
(a classic suspense technique) also suggest the tension and horribleness of
the situation. The elements are brought together at various points. There is,
for instance, a sudden very dramatic drum roll followed by loud violin
phrases taken from the dance-band tune, an interjection of music that is tan-
tamount to a stinger or overscoring, when Clive puts down the phone extension by means of which he has eavesdropped on Storm making an
appointment to meet a man (some weeks after Bill's disappearance). The
sudden interjection is not in itself comic, lest it be by virtue of the film's
music suddenly behaving in such an obvious, excessive thriller mode,
although it does constitute dramatic irony, since Clive assumes the man in

question is Storm's new beau, whereas it is in fact Superintendent Finsbury: Clive is getting worked up about the wrong thing, jealousy towards his wife (the right one is that Finsbury suspects that Bill is still alive and wants to discuss this with Storm). The theme then modifies into a very slightly wonky saxophone treatment as he hears Storm coming downstairs and goes and sits down to surprise her before she leaves the house, catching the cat-and-mouse quality of the game he is playing with her. Then it gives way in turn to the spiky woodwinds, as, sitting in the darkness of the sitting room, he calls out her name just as she is about to sneak out of the house and confronts her with her misdemeanour. The music moves then from the melodramatic via the ironically sinister to the comically morbid. All of these shades are in the sequence; the music brings out now one, now another, or the two together (the wonky saxophone) as it proceeds along.

Anni facili produces a similar complexity of tone, coming from, as it were, the opposite direction. Here the generic assumption is that the film is comic, although like much commedia all'italiana, one would not necessarily be able to tell this from its story of a decent, incorrupt school-teacher, Luigi, who, reduced to desperate financial straits, finally gives in and, at the insistence of his head-teacher, accepts a bribe to give a rich man's dim-witted son a pass in his examination, only to find himself hauled up in court and sent to prison. Luigi is played by a noted comic star, Nino Taranto, and there is much incidental comic detail, gags and business throughout the film, although it never loses a sense of bitterness and even, by the end, tragedy. Notably, Luigi is not the kind of self-important, self-deceiving comic male figure common in Italian comedy, so that his anxieties and humiliations seem unfair, with no overtone of comeuppance. The credits establish two themes, a characteristic Rota ploy in that one is cheerful, perky, over a regular, quite fast, tarantella-like figure, while the other is keenly emotional. Unusual, and apposite in the context of the film, is the way that each tune is in fact a variation on the other, so that the comic is always implicated in the plaintive and vice versa. The arrangement, especially in the credits sequence, is sufficiently different for this not be strongly evident, but it enables the score throughout to suggest the funny side of the tragic and the tragic of the funny. Sometimes the comic is to the fore, as in the longish sequence of Luigi going from office to office, ministry to ministry, to try to get a licence for the drug Virilon (a job he has taken on in an attempt to supplement his meagre salary); the arrangement echoes the scurrying from place to place and the absurdity of bureaucracies. Yet even here other qualities are brought out: there is a remorseless underlying treading (rather than bouncing) movement to the rhythm, sometimes slightly dissonant harmonies and occasional squeaking, slurred, downward phrases on woodwind at his being passed on to yet another office, a sort of 'oh dear' effect, that, with accumulation, may also feel heart-rending.

Two sequences are especially notable for their deployment of disquietingly comic/bitter music. The film opens in Palermo, but soon after Luigi is transferred to Rome, much to his concern, given the expense of living in

Rome, but to the delight of his wife and especially his daughter Teresa, in love with Luigi's nephew in Rome, Piero. The family's journey from the station in Rome to their accommodation consists of a series of shots of Rome, initially of familiar streets and monuments, but shot from low, often skewed angles, and accompanied by very slightly sinister or 'off' music, low winds, unexpected rhythms and sudden, perhaps comic low brass flourishes, and with the more emotional variant of the theme coming in, not here plaintively but also never completed – all unsettling, even if also tinged with the comic; image and music combined suggest the threat of the new life in the big city, even though the characters are all full of excitement and wonder at being there. When monumental Rome gives way to low-angle shots of new blocks of flats, there is blaring, brassy, slightly cacophonously jazzy music (reminiscent of Gershwin at his more dramatic), continuing this comic tone that is not so funny.

The film ends in the Stazione Termini in Rome. One group of well-wishers bids farewell to Larina, the official who took a bribe of several million lire to grant the licence for Virilon that Luigi's diligent, exhausting scurrying from office to office could not obtain; Larina has been removed from his position in Rome, but only to be transferred to another in Milan. At the same time, Luigi's family come to say goodbye as he is taken off to prison (for accepting the small bribe to pass the dim-wit). As Luigi's train pulls out, what was initially the perky tune is introduced, briefly in a melancholic version, but then played at the faster speed, but a little more forcefully, giving it a hard edge. This comes to an end, in slightly dissonant final chords, but still with the (albeit much diminished) tarantella figure carrying on, over a shot showing both trains (the one with Larina, the other with Luigi) pulling out, the film's bitter comparison of the two men. As the family walk away, the more plaintive variant of the theme comes in, but the camera comes to a halt at two men sitting together on a bench; behind their cynical exchange about the corruption of all governments, the theme continues on solo oboe. When they finish, there is a fade to black, with the end credit accompanied by an unequivocally plaintive statement of the theme on full strings – the comedy ends with the tragic to the fore.

All the examples of running alongside discussed above are aligned, with greater or lesser precision, to the emotional tenor of the sequence or film, sometimes creating an emotional homogeneity, sometimes a more complex or contrary timbre. In other instances the music may suggest an emotional dimension that does not seem to be otherwise indicated by what's on-screen.

Some short examples.

MOLTI SOGNI PER LE STRADE A little way into the film, there is a sequence of Linda getting up in the morning, making breakfast, talking commonsensically to her son Rigoletto who is playing with his toy gun. This kind of sequence is common in neo-realism, canonically in *Umberto D.* (1952, the wordless scene of the maid Maria's early morning routine is often taken as a textbook – and in fact rare – instance of neo-realism's interest in the ordinary lives of ordinary people), prefigured in *Quattro passi fra le nuvole* (1942), parodied in *Totò cerca casa*. *Molti sogni* has, moreover, established its neo-realist credentials with an opening sequence, in which, over shots of a city, a voiceover tells us that this is a city like any other with people like any other, to the accompaniment of rather grand 'theme for a city' music. The sequence of Linda and Rigoletto getting up is accompanied by a lovely melody, sweet sorrow, with harmonic shifts reminiscent of Samuel Barber. Nothing in what has gone before (Linda and Paolo have a row and Linda says she's leaving, but everything suggests this is a regular occurrence) and nothing here in Linda's behaviour (or Anna Magnani's performance), leave alone the pace of her and Rigoletto's actions and the film's standard issue neo-realism, call forth this prettily melancholic, and previously unheard, music. Yet the sequence ends with her shouting through to her husband Paolo that she is going and not coming back, not knowing, as we do, that he has already left to look for work (his lack of it being a source of the tension between them). The music anticipates the sadness of splitting up, but its gentleness also prefigures the fact that they are not going to split up or even reminds us that this is not that kind of film.

ANNI FACILI When sweethearts Teresa and Piero are about to kiss on the balcony, shortly after she and the family have arrived in Rome from Palermo, the theme song for *Sotto il sole di Roma* comes in instrumentally and non-diegetically; they are interrupted by Luigi and Rosolo (her and his father respectively), who then stay on the balcony, with Rosolo explaining the class layout of the view (they live where salaried people live, further out is where the proletarians live); behind them the building of a huge apartment block is in progress; all the while 'Sotto il sole di Roma' carries on behind. The song, familiar from the film of only six years before, is redolent of the beauties of Rome as a backdrop for l'amore; this association seems appropriate for the sweethearts, but they are interrupted, and the Rome that is spoken of and shown (class divisions, brutalist architecture) is anything but that celebrated by the song – though, certainly, the sun is shining.

L'ENNEMI PUBLIC NO 1 (1953) Cheap and cheerful trumpet and banjo B-Western music accompanies the first shots of Joe, that is, more importantly, Fernandel, as a cowboy in some prairie scrub. This is the first gag, Fernandel as a cowboy, but it is then revealed that he is only dressed as a cowboy on a set in a big store (gag #2), selling air-conditioning (#3), by means of the slogan 'Du beau, du bon, du bon air' (#4, a play on the contemporaneous slogan for the sweet aperitif Dubonnet), work hampered by his short-sightedness (#5), for which he needs his, Fernandel's, trademark glasses (#6). Throughout this routine, the music does not change at all; apart from being cowboy music, it does not participate in the gags (as Rota's comedy music often does). The effect is the same even if one takes the music as being diegetic, that is, piped in as ambiently appropriate by the store (though Joe's stand is only one among many). Later Joe goes to the movies and sees a B-Western, which is accompanied (parodically and anachronistically) by banjo silent-movie music; this music shows no response to the various actions on-screen (galloping, a hold-up, a brawl and so on); it too carries on alongside.

WAR AND PEACE Sinister music accompanies Pierre and Hélène on the morning after the first night of their marriage. Both are content (he with her gorgeousness, she with his money and position) but the music prefigures the unhappy future of their marriage.

A scene near the beginning of *Vita da cani* is one of the most exquisite examples of this kind of procedure. The film tells of a number of young women who join a variety show. One, Franca (Tamara Lees), is at the start of the film engaged to be married to a garage mechanic, Carlo (Marcello Mastroianni). The young couple visit the flat they are to move into after they marry. Franca looks round balefully at the sparsely furnished rooms, the dust and the beetles; Carlo talks eagerly of his new invention to improve petrol consumption. She is indifferent, but to his surprise ('You always said we should wait'), she invites him to join her on the bed. The scene ends.

The scene is in its subject matter typical of that strand in neo-realism dealing with ordinary people in ordinary settings without marked socio-political significance (e.g., *Molti sogni per le strade*, *Una domenica d'agosto* (1949), *Le ragazze di Piazza di Spagna* (1952)). However, three things give it a very particular feeling. One is the casting of Tamara Lees. Mastroianni was an already established minor star, playing to perfection, as here, the classic *ragazzo perbene* (the nice young man), but Lees, with only a couple of

Vita da cani: Franca (Tamara Lees) and Carlo (Marcello Mastroianni) visit the flat they are to live in; she looks at the dust and insects, he shows her his invention; she invites him to join him on the bed

movies behind her, suggested something much less familiar. Of considerable but distinctly Nordic beauty (she was, in fact, of English and Russian parentage), her almond-shaped eyes and slim figure suggest a melancholy and refinement at odds with the earthily Italian beauties so much part of postwar and quasi-neo-realist culture: Gina Lollobrigida, Sophia Loren, Silvana Mangano, Franca Marzi.[85] Second, the cinematography, by Mario Bava, creates evidently crafted and slightly mysterious patterns of clearly delineated chiaroscuro. Third, there is the music, a delicate, non-diegetic waltz. These three elements create a disjunction between the banality and relative cheerfulness of the scene and their affective qualities: melancholy, mystery, delicacy.

The use of a waltz was already an anachronistic choice in 1949. The melody has basically an AABA structure, but each of the As is subtly different so that it might more properly be rendered as $A_1A_2BA_3$. The basic line of each A mounts up and down in a series of little spiralling phrases. A_1 is on violins; A_2 uses woodwind and both goes higher and ends lower; A_3 uses lower strings, predominantly cellos, goes even higher but is slower, with a clear rallentando at the end. Each A ends with more separated notes, emphasising the waltz rhythm. Thus the melody repeatedly soars a little and sinks back, but not back into the stillness or calm of sadness but rather to the charm of the gently suggested underlying rhythm. This off-setting of upward against sinking phrases and both against an endearing rhythm suggests an affective register that encompasses yearning rather than keen longing, aspiration rather than ambition, melancholy rather than tragedy, ruefulness rather than self-pity. All of this is very different from the dull, drab apartment and Carlo's banal conversation.

The music occupies the length of the scene and is dovetailed to its beginning and end. In the previous scene, Carlo picks Franca up on his bicycle from outside the factory where she works; the first spiralling phrase accompanies the movement of the bicycle off-screen, the movement of music and bicycle alike feeling as if they are at the same pace. At the end of the scene, the music slows right down as Carlo moves towards Franca on the bed and fades as they start to kiss. Yet despite this care over the beginning and end, in between the music does not follow Carlo and Franca's movements about the flat or the shifts in feeling between them.

It would be possible to interpret the music as expressing her feelings. In the previous scene, her dissatisfaction with the prospect of a safe marriage to a nice young man on the outskirts of Milan has been indicated, and the romantic tenor of the music could be taken to express what she is feeling in the face of the dreary prospect of living with poor old Carlo in this characterless flat. Later in the film, the theme is reprised. Franca has had a brief career in the variety show and entered a loveless marriage to a rich man; Carlo has become a successful engineer, who works for her husband; Franca meets him the day after her wedding; realising her love for him and the emptiness of her choices in life, she kills herself. In both sequences you could take the music as expressing what she is feeling, but it seems to me too ironic and melancholic, not whole-hearted or passionate enough, for that. Rather it suggests a relationship to her character, sympathetic, feeling, affectionate, but also aware of the limitations of her dreams, the music indicating their anachronistic prettiness and melancholy undertow.

If in *Vita da cani* music alongside suggests a relation of affection towards but not identification with sympathetic characters and events, in *Plein soleil* it suggests a kind of amused indifference to appalling (though perhaps glamorous) characters and events.

There are moments, notably at the very beginning of the credits, when there is very loud, dramatic, intrusive music. There are even a couple of stingers, each time using the very dramatic four-note phrase on brass that opens the credits: when Marge, Philippe's girlfriend, fed up with Philippe and his and Tom's boysy behaviour, asks to be put off the yacht at Taormina, and Tom says to Philippe (here's the stinger) that of course if he'd like him to leave rather than Marge ...; a little later, as Marge walks off down the quay and the boys set sail again. These stingers are all the more surprising, because they are occasioned by not especially dramatic or sinister events (while the scenes of murder do not have this music). They contribute though to the tone of the film: they come in at moments that are important in the development of Tom's malevolent plans and yet their obtrusiveness seems jokey, just as the film is, and their very exceptionality throws into relief the casualness of the rest of the music.

The opening sequence of *Plein soleil*, as friends Tom and Philippe kid about on the Via Veneto in Rome, is accompanied by very quiet, modern night-club music, on xylophone, clarinet and muted trumpet (very much in the mode of *La dolce vita*, made the following year and in which the Via Veneto is a signature setting). It remains unchanged when they are joined briefly by Freddie, who makes clear his distrust of Tom, and then when, having paid a blind man for his stick, they play at being blind. Even when a car screeches to a halt because it nearly runs over Tom crossing the road as if blind, the music does not alter at all.

The score works like this throughout the film. Whenever the film returns to the Sicilian seaside village of Mongibello (notably the first time on a cut from Tom laughing uproariously having just stolen the earring of a girl they have picked up), there is a cod, tourist-friendly Mediterranean theme on mandolins, regardless of how deep the story has got into deception, treachery and murder. There is also a main theme, stated in the credits, but this too is used in an alongside manner. For instance, when Tom returns to Mongibello after killing Philippe, and Marge helps him pack Philippe's things, believing, as Tom has told her, that Philippe simply doesn't want to see her any more, the main theme of the film is played on accordion, alternating with a slow, lazy, jazzy saxophone variant of it. The accordion echoes the music that accompanied Marge leaving the yacht at Taormina, suggesting sadness, while the sax, on the other hand, is redolent of a low-key casual sexiness. The alternation is not connected to who is on-screen at any moment or what is being done, it is rather as if each emotion, present throughout the scene, is allowed by the music to come to the fore at one moment rather than another, in the process stemming any sympathy or excitement that might be in play or any privileging of Tom or Marge's perspective. Much later in the film, when Tom is back in Mongibello in Philippe's flat, making it look as if Philippe has until recently been living in it (putting ash in the ashtrays, rumpling the bed and so on), and then typing Philippe's suicide note to his mother, the music is at first cool jazz, which then incorporates the main theme in a slightly staccato version. The music is moody, but not mysterious, suspenseful, dramatic, sinister or any of the other feelings one might expect, just urbane and modern, at once restless and casual.

Diegetic music too acts with the same sort of telling indifference. In Rome, after Tom has killed Freddie (because the latter has discovered that Tom is living as Philippe), there is a piano playing quietly somewhere in the block of flats where Tom is living. After the tension and focus of killing Freddie, it could signify the return of a sense of the surrounding world, but it continues on unperturbed behind Tom taking a chicken out of the oven and eating, while Freddie's body lies dead in the next room; when Tom begins walking Freddie's corpse down the stairs of the block as if Freddie were drunk and incapable, initially there is silence but then the piano starts up again, continuing notably alongside a low-angle shot of Freddie's arm bouncing along the curving banister – the piano comes in and out in a way one could consider naturalistic, yet at the same time it produces both a slightly comic quality (the dead man's arm bouncing to music) and a reinforcement of the indifference of the world, and perhaps the film, to Tom's goings-on. In an earlier sequence, Tom is wandering around the fish market in Naples, having left Marge on her own in a café to reply to the (fake) letter from Philippe that he has brought her. The music sounds as if it comes from a very old barrel organ, out of tune with notches missing; there are many rather disquieting shots of the fishes, including one with a monstrous, almost-human face and another severed, lying on the ground. Yet Tom seems merely interested, vaguely amused, in a touristic way, and the music labours on, neither embodying the cheerful feeling that barrel organs commonly do in films nor responding to the sinister overtones of the imagery.

The film ends as musically indifferent as throughout. In Mongibello Tom has finally seduced Marge (completing his incarnation of Philippe); the next day they go to the beach. As they leave the house, the main theme is played non-diegetically on a rather clunking piano, faintly comic, not registering the recent morbid development of the story, nor following the pace of Tom and Marge's movement. At the rocks from which they swim, there is wandering, affectless clarinet music. Marge goes off to meet Philippe's father and Tom runs up to the café and orders a drink, at which point the main theme comes in, cheerily, on accordion. There is no music behind Marge, Philippe's father and his associates inspecting Philippe's boat (with a view to selling it), but then, when Marge looks up at the line extending out from the back, the camera follows her eyes and runs down the cable, at the end of which is Philippe's body (caught up in the cable when Tom threw it overboard after killing him). As the camera moves down the cable, the main theme comes back in, now laboriously played on a rattly, echoey piano, so again slightly comic, but also louder now, underscoring the discovery of body, but in contrary mode to what conventional underscoring would do (that is, it is gleeful rather than horrified). The film cuts back to Tom lying back in the sun drinking, then to a shot of the bay, a fishing ship tranquilly sailing, then to inside the café and the police speaking to the proprietor, asking her to tell Tom he's wanted on the phone; all this has been accompanied by the rattly piano, but now as she calls out, the theme is taken up in a sweeter string arrangement, and then, as Tom walks towards the café, and the camera, and smiles, there is brief moment of clarinet and then fuller, louder strings, augmented at the last by some brass, as the camera tilts slightly to take in the bay and the island in it, the music serenely indifferent to Tom's fate, no more upset by his being caught than it has been by his deeds.

* * *

Running alongside creates a position vis-à-vis the events of the film, and everything else it is doing, that holds back from identification, immersion, absorption. Like the shifting use of motifs, unsettling fixed moorings in the text, or the copious use of reference and signalled imitation, thickening the texture while indicating what it is doing, or hovering on the cusp of diegetic and non-diegetic, neither within or without the film's world, running alongside is close to what the film appears to disclose, very close, and yet never quite at one with it.

Sometimes the scores work on the basis of a disjuncture between the music and everything else. *Plein soleil*'s brightness is almost insolent against Tom's behaviour, *Death on the Nile*'s blandness amoral.[86] There is a telling gap between Wild West music and Fernandel, the waltz and the battlefield carnage in *Waterloo*, the gentle lilt of 'Paese mio' and the tragedy of the Parondis, the wedding marches and the incipient violence of 'L'ora di punta', the cheerfulness of 'È primavera' and the eponymous film's claim to cynicism, the Venetianness of the music in *La mano dello straniero* and the sinister events, Ines in *La domenica della buona gente* and the genre of the film itself, and the gangster jazz at the station, the blithe romanticism of 'Sotto il sole di Roma' and class-divided and brutalist architecture in *Anni facili*, the maudlin or bawdy character of the songs in *La grande guerra* and the cynicism and fate of the characters.

Yet the most characteristic Rota tone of all, that catches both the attachment and the irony, the touching but held-back affection, occurs when the character of the music chimes with the film. Perhaps by virtue of pastiche: the waltz that ensnares Natasha, over-egging Arduino's fantasies, the exuberant confidence that goes sour in *Zazà*, the rumbustious goliardo that shows up Petruchio, the fun of the pastiches of pastiches in *I pirati di Capri*, teasing Neapolitan song in *Quel bandito sono io* and *Spara forte* … . Perhaps by combining elements together, as in the intertwined motifs in the quasi-realist, quasi-comic, quasi-sad, quasi-romantic *Campane a martello*, the twangy, overblown version of 'One Kiss Away from Here' in *This Angry Age*, the jazz on organ, harpsichord and barrel organ for the hip ghosts in *Fantasmi a Roma*. Above all by deploying the distinctive mixed quality so often observed in Rota's music: witty and melodic, sad but not tragic, romantic but not ardent, sentimental but not tearjerking, cheerfully rather than forcefully energetic, sentimental but with a sense of the absurd. There is the bland vulgarity of *Femmine di lusso*, offset plaintiveness surrounding signor Travet, the ironically creepy and the comically morbid in *Obsession*, the liveliness and melancholy of youth in *Sotto il sole di Roma*, the strange, perhaps sinister prostitute's music in *Le notti bianche*, the sweet sorrow of Linda leaving home in *Molti sogni per le strade*, élan, glow and disappointment all at once in *Un americano in vacanza*, the melancholy but graceful and charming 'valzer del commiato' in *Il gattopardo*, *Anni facili*'s two motifs, tarantella-like and emotional, that are variations on each other, the off-setting of upward against sinking phrases and both against an endearing rhythm in *Vita da cani*, the not quite romantic, not all-out sentimentality of the 'Sogni per due' signature tune in *Il maestro di Vigevano*, oom-pah-pah … oom-pah … oom.

4
Comedy

The credits for *Totò al Giro d'Italia* are watched in heaven by Nero and Dante (comic actors Catoni and Carlo Ninchi), who make comically disparaging comments as the names come up; when Nino Rota's comes up, however, they make a gesture and an 'aah' sound, indicating that at least this aspect of the film will be good. Perhaps they are responding to just how completely at home he is with comedy. It is a mode that forms a large part of Rota's oeuvre and also the one in which he adheres most closely to what is going on.

The comic runs right through Rota's work: his operas are either basically comic (*La notte di un nevrastico*, *Il cappello di paglia di Firenze*) or in large measure (*La visita meravigliosa*, *Napoli milionaria*), and there are many witty, even downright funny movements in the concert and chamber works. There is often humour in his music for films that are not comedies and the latter constitute the biggest generic category in his filmic output, both comedian comedies and the commedia all'italiana.

Rota wrote scores for films featuring most of the key comic performers in Italian cinema in the period: Walter Chiari (6 films), Vittorio De Sica (3), Aldo Fabrizi (4), Fernandel (3), Sandra Milo (1), Peppino De Filippo (5), Rascel (1), Tino Scotti (2), Alberto Sordi (12), Nino Taranto (3), Totò (4), Franca Valeri (1).[1] However, it is the five films with Macario[2] that produce his most inventive, detailed and engaged scores. In part this is because the silent-film, comic-book quality of Macario's performance style sits easily with a pointed musical style. There is, moreover, something unworldly and childlike about Macario (as was also commonly said of Rota); the comedy of his films is not rooted in the self-importance, self-deception, self-interest, wheeler-dealing, knavery and stupidity variously combined by Totò, Sordi and company, and while he gets into scrapes and sails close to the wind, he seems unfazed and unaware and above all untouched by the world around him. Played by Sordi, Felice in *L'eroe della strada*, who bends with every prevailing ideological wind only to be found out, would be a cynical – and incompetent – opportunist; played by Macario he is just an odd little fellow falling from one lark to another. This accords especially well with Rota's comic sensibility and inflects his work with the other, more worldly comedians.

Examples of commedia all'italiana in Rota's output include *Vivere in pace*, *Vita da cani*, *Campane a martello*, *Molti sogni per le strade*, *Lo sceicco bianco*, *Scampolo '53* (1953), *Anni facili*, *I vitelloni* and *Gli italiani sono matti* (1958). Commedia all'italiana married neo-realist observation with the comic, often involving strong elements of social comment or satire, ensemble playing (even when using star comedians) and often a disturbingly harsh undertow (see Giacovelli, 1990). It is characteristic of both Rota and such comedy that the comic tone of these films is not the only one; they may even involve tragedy (the death of Tigna in *Vivere in pace*) or bitterness (the defeat of a decent man in *Anni facili*), though it is sadness and sentiment that is Rota's most characteristic admixture. There is, however, a tone in many classic commedie all'italiana that is at odds with Rota's sensibility. It is not all that likely that he would have written most of a score like that for *I soliti ignoti*,[3] for a light modern jazz combo, or for *Sedotta e abbandonata*,[4] with its manically driven rhythms and sarcastic musical comments. However, while one can imagine him writing another kind of score for the former, with its cast of endearingly incompetent crooks (and his music was used after his death in the sequel *I soliti ignoti vent'anni dopo*[5]), it's much harder to imagine him producing the score for the latter, brilliant, pessimistic and almost intolerably cruel.

All Rota's comedy scores have a lot of fun with motifs that bespeak comedy, mischievous reference and play on the diegetic and non-diegetic. They also involve underscoring that emphasises, and overscoring that insists, that such-and-such is funny. Given the importance of reticence and disengagement in his approach, the latter might seem surprising. However, whereas standard underscoring and overscoring naturalise elicited responses, unobtrusively reinforcing the apparent rightness of an affective perception of characters and events or seeking to sweep you up in an emotional embrace of them, comic under- and overscoring signals the operation of the comedic, which is to say, taking up a distinctive positions in relation to what's on-screen, by seeing as funny things which are very seldom intrinsically funny. Moreover, much of the stuff of comedy is gags, business, funny faces and costumes, exaggerated bodies and movements – in short a whole range of elements that do not seek to present a seamless fictional world; Rota's music readily participates in this overt business of being funny. Comedy accords well with Rota's artistic temperament, of being in sympathy with but not wholly inside the effects it pursues (seeing as), ready to signal what it is doing even while not seeking to undermine its effects (let's laugh). At the same time, again in line with his never-quite-one-tone-or-the-other inclinations, his comedy scores are nearly always limned with sentimentality, not even invested single-mindedly in finding things funny.

I begin with an indication of the armoury of musical means deployed by Rota (and, of course, many other composers) that are of themselves comic: kinds of sound and rhythm, the role of parody and cliché. I then consider the way these are used in the films, sometimes augmenting comedy achieved by other means, sometimes enabling the perception of something as comic.

In many examples, a sense of the ambivalence of comedy comes through and I focus on this in the last part of the chapter.

* * *

Take the following example. A shot of the interior of a prison is accompanied, in this order, by 'The Song of the Volga Boatmen', with an instrumental 'bomp' at the end of each phrase,[6] with a fanfare-based melody over it; a cheerful, fast tune, played first on small orchestra, then on xylophone and what sounds like paper and comb; a spiralling, syncopated melody on clarinet, with perhaps a hint of sentimentality; the same tune in a more lumbering version on xylophone, reminiscent of the moment in *The Sorcerer's Apprentice* when the broom starts to get to work for the apprentice, with little pauses in the melody and occasional sigh-like phrases; until, on a cut to a shot of a man played by Aldo Fabrizi arriving at the prison, the 'Volga Boatmen' and fanfares return, in a perkier style.

This is the credits sequence of *Accadde al penitenziario* (1955). Nothing in the image says funny. Perhaps in 1955, the title might just about have suggested comedy,[7] and any film starring all four of Walter Chiari, Peppino De Filippo, Aldo Fabrizi and Alberto Sordi is unlikely to be anything but comic. Nonetheless the most explicit indication that this is to be a funny film is conveyed by the music, drawing upon many of the strategies of comedy music: referencing excessively familiar tunes (but not current popular songs), parodying them ('bomp'), providing jaunty, cheerful music, using instruments that tend to sound comic (xylophone, paper and comb) and slightly unexpected phrasing (little pauses, sighs). The music invites us to see a prison, a place of villainy, punishment, confinement and dreariness, as a site of comedy.

The music would probably sound funny without any images, not laugh-out-loud, perhaps, but smile-worthy. Or take the following succession: slurred strings, woodwind squeals, a squiggly phrase on clarinet and a short, loud slide on trombone. These accompany the opening moments of *Come scopersi l'America*, in which a man (Macario) wakes up and yawns (slurring), protestors run into a piazza (squeals) and Macario in perplexity draws a question mark over a poster map of Italy (the trombone raspberry). Rota makes copious use of the many sources of humour in music, even before we get to comic matching with other visual and aural elements, ranging from these rather primary funny sounds to kinds of comic reference.

Something may sound funny because it resembles other sounds that human beings tend to find amusing. The wind instruments, especially in the lower and higher registers, readily sound like the voluntary and involuntary non-verbal sounds emitted by the human body: belch, fart, hiccup, sneeze, wheeze as well as:

> BURP on trombone, in *Campane a martello*, to accompany Australia embarrassingly asking the marshal for a word;
> RASPBERRY in *The Best of Enemies* (1961), on trombone anticipating a (crashed and disbanded) plane blowing up, and, more derisively still, on

trombone, muted trumpet and clarinet, when the Alberto Sordi character, Blasi, foolishly lets slip to his English prisoner, Richardson (David Niven), his strategic plans for the fort at Eguadabada (the film is set in the war campaign in Abyssinia);

SQUEAK on piccolo, in *Come scopersi l'America*, as Cristoforo/Macario spits out water.

Even if they don't recall any specific such sound, winds may still sound comically naughty. When shy and proper young lover Walter goes to kiss sweet thing Grazia in the park in *Era lui ... sì! sì!* (1951), a rude trumpet sound stops him in his tracks (the rude non-diegetic sound of the trumpet as it were intervening in the naughty diegetic action). The fact that the odious Palocco (Sordi) in *Totò e i re di Roma* plays the euphonium already makes a comic comment about his self-important windiness, heightened by the contrast between his rather prissy, quite high-pitched voice and the low sound (albeit not actually heard in the film) of the euphonium, more comic still by virtue of the Italian word for euphonium, 'bombardino' (linked to bombing). Or the very putting of musical mimicry in place of a human sound not otherwise heard as funny may be comic, as in the slurred strings for Macario's yawning in *Come scopersi l'America*, noted above, this aural copycatting heightened by their playing an up-and-down phrase which Mickey Mouses Macario's up-and-down just-got-up arm-stretching movement. Yet other sounds recall the sounds of amusement themselves – laughter, chuckling, sniggering – such as the busy, high-register, pizzicato phrases on piccolo, oboe and strings that, in *Campane a martello*, mimic the giggling of the little girls when they come to take a look at Agostina and Australia on their arrival in the priest's house. This music is preceded by the actual sounds of the girls laughing and giggling, not at the two women – there is nothing funny about them – but from irrepressible high spirits. The music seems to arise out of the sounds they are making, carrying forward the infectiousness of laughter, smiling over the antics of little girls and setting up the ironic situation (that the girls are orphans of GIs, who have been looked after by Agostina's money, that she had sent to the priest merely for safe-keeping but which she got from sleeping with GIs).

Campane a martello: the little girls come to look at Agostina and Australia

Musically mimicked animal sounds too may be a source of simple merriment, baa, bleat, bray, chirrup, cluck, grunt, quack, whinny, as well as:

BARK on saxophone to accompany the entry of the seal in the opening sequence of *Era lui ... sì! sì!*, comic because, in what turns out to be a dream, an Eskimo wishes to swap the seal for the new bride whom Fernando is endlessly interrupted from making make love to on their wedding night;

HEE-HAW on violins as people unload black-market goods from a donkey in
Napoli milionaria;
MEOW in *Come persi la guerra*, Leo and Fritz making their escape from a
prison camp at night agree to have 'meow' as a sign, and violins mimic it shrilly
(perhaps there is even a further little gag here, in that violin strings are made
from cat gut); a little later an actual cat meowing gives a false signal with
consequent comic muddle;
MOO a trombone counterpoints the moos of the cow in *Vivere in pace* as
Tigna speaks affectionately to her; in *Marito e moglie*, a film rich in musical
onomatopoeia, trombone moos seem to mimic not only the cows but also
grumpy Rosalia herself (played by Tina Pica, peerless embodiment of comic
cantankerousness);
SQUAWK in *Marito e moglie* again, actual chicken squawks are set comically
against heavily treading music, as Rosalia takes first the hens' temperature then
her husband Matteo's (to see if he is hot enough yet to incubate the chicks).

In *Come persi la guerra*, Leo opens a wardrobe in the house in which he has
been billeted and discovers a German soldier, at which point there is non-
diegetic music of an oboe playing a cuckoo call, suggestive of a cuckoo
clock. When the German has told Leo that he is called Fritz (of course) and
is an anti-Nazi from Vienna in hiding, there is a brief fanfare (itself a little
joke acclaiming the revelation), which turns out to be actually made by a
clock that has a toy soldier in place of a cuckoo. Fritz is like a cuckoo (hiding
out in someone else's nest); his sudden beekaboo appearance is like a cuckoo
in a clock; when he reveals he is not a real Nazi and thus not really a soldier
any more, a real cuckoo-type clock heralds the fact with a pretend soldier.
Gag upon gag, all within seconds. (It's taken you much longer to read, and
me infinitely more to write, this account than the seconds the sequence itself
takes to unfold.) When Fritz appears later in the film, he is announced by the
cuckoo refrain on bassoon, counterpointed by Leo's (that is, Macario's[8])
motif, played, unusually, on horn (thus closer in register to Fritz's music,
perhaps suggesting they are both in the same – by this point, deserters'–
boat). There is cuckoo music every time Fritz pops up. Finally, at the end,
Fritz appears to shoot himself, but when news comes through that the war is
over, he comes back to life, heralded non-diegetically by the cuckoo clock
music.
    In all the above cases the music can signal humour by virtue of resem-
blance to sounds habitually (albeit not invariably) found funny, human and
animal. In other cases, kinds of wavering in the sound seem funny (perhaps
recalling the speech and movement of toddlers and drunks). Some
instruments are inherently wonky, the Jewish harp and the kazoo as well as
the following.

HAWAIIAN GUITAR This is by no means necessarily or usually comic, and
its primary association is with tourism and romance. However, it does have a
twang that takes it away from the strict regime of notes in Western music, a

departure always liable to suggest the comic (when it doesn't suggest the sinister). It accompanies the scene between Walter and Grazia in the park in *Era lui … sì! sì!* to comic effect, partly because Walter is the classic comic figure of the tongue-tied young man in love (one of Chiari's specialities), partly because a Hawaiian guitar in a park in Rome is incongruous (and even more so in 1951, when it was a still more exotic sound). In other words the music both partakes of the humour (Walter) and gives to it (the incongruous instrument). The humour of this is then milked for a later scene where we see Walter on the same park bench with a bunch of flowers in his hand proposing to Grazia, with the same Hawaiian guitar accompaniment, only for the camera to draw back to reveal he is rehearsing the speech to the friendly park policeman (at which point the music stops).

SWANEE WHISTLE In Fernando's dream of being in a harem in *Era lui … sì! sì!*, this is mixed in with cod Arab music (the gag being that Fernando is not the potentate in the dream, but Walter, the man who crops up as his rival in all his dreams and who in real life wants to marry his daughter). It is especially common in the Macario films, perhaps because it has a comic cartoon quality in keeping with the films and Macario's persona.

THEREMIN Commonly used in horror and outer space contexts, it is comically sinister in *L'ennemi public no 1* when used to help characterise the mobster hide-out whose denizens choose innocent, myopic Joe Calvet (Fernandel) as their boss, genuinely mistaking him for a hard man.

TRUMPET WITH MUTE PRODUCING WAH WAH SOUND This is heard when, in *The Best of Enemies*, the Brits' plane crashes and Richardson and Burke emerge shame-faced.

Even where an instrument is not intrinsically inclined to be wonky, its playing may make it so. The workings of the barrel organ that scrapes-prone Felice acquires at the end of *L'eroe della strada* have become laborious through age. Beppe's wild singing of the title tune at the beginning of *È primavera* sets him up as a comic (here, trickster) character. Drowsy strings and sluggishly played muted trumpet mimic Joe's state of mind when he is interrogated as a hoodlum (*L'ennemi public no 1*). In *Campane a martello*, at the end of the series of trumpet burps mentioned above, when Australia says she wants a word in private with the maresciallo and they go into his flat, the trumpet notes, already produced rather staccato and impurely, become sharp and almost strangled, registering how bad this looks to small-town morality.

The extreme registers of instruments may also seem funny.

HIGH Macario's theme is generally played on tin whistle (cf. Laurel and Hardy). In *Vivere in pace*, the kids look at a notice saying people who hide GIs will be severely punished and they have just found two whom they are going to hide, but when they look at each other there is a tootle on piccolo, high like kids' voices but also cheery, underlying their comic dismissal of problem. In *La grande speranza*, Fernandez, one of the Allied prisoners on the Italian submarine (in the Second World War), makes signs and gives a chirruping

whistle to one of the Italians dishing out coffee, which is his way of asking him
to give him a nip of booze; squeaky, busy woodwinds play in counterpoint to
his funny little whistle, to tell us this is endearingly funny, the humour
reinforced by rounding off with a particularly comic low bassoon phrase.
LOW The humorous potential of the low winds has already been noted above
(the bassoon to accompany Tigna's endearments to this cow in *Vivere in pace*;
trombone and horn to punctuate pompous masculinity in *Campane a martello*).
HIGH AND LOW TOGETHER *Vivere in pace*: the sequence of kids stealing
milk (direct from the cow), loaves and long johns hanging out to dry (all to
give the GIs they are hiding), accompanied by mock lugubrious bassoons and
low strings and then a quick piccolo and harp phrase. *Marito e moglie*: low
plodding winds plus squeaks as don Matteo pleads with Rosalia as she tucks
into a chicken, having refused to give him any because he refuses to hatch her
chicken's eggs.

Not only sounds, but irregular rhythms can also work comedically, suggestive of movements such as hobbling, hopping, limping, lumbering, sham-
bling, shuffling and skipping, bustling and careering, extreme dexterity, and
drunkenness. The melody in *Fortunella* that was to give Rota trouble when he
re-used it (romantically, uncomically) in *The Godfather* seems comical in the
earlier film because of its chirpy syncopation and sprightly little woodwind
comments at the break in the melody. In *The Best of Enemies*, burbling clarinet and bassoon in counterpoint accompany the Italian soldiers looking for
their mascot, Micheletto, a baby antelope, grown men scurrying around after
a little animal they've given a cute small boy's name to. The contrast of
extreme rhythms on the second day of the race is comic in *Totò al Giro
d'Italia*, fast and furious for the other contestants, lumbering and leisurely for
Totò (confident in the knowledge that the devil has fixed things for him to
win); later, when Totò is apparently going to kill himself because he thinks
he cannot not win the race, there is an alternation of the 'Funeral March'[9]
with standard comic music, which tends to make the former seem comic too.

Hiccups also have a comic rhythm as well as sound, and some percussive
instruments have the same quality: bones, spoons, xylophone. Plucked
strings make the rhythm seem funny at one point in *Era lui ... sì! sì!*, partly
because pizzicato is often comic and even more so when jazzy (jazz itself
often being perceived in the period as basically fun or frankly funny music,
especially in its 'Dixieland' mode) and even more so as here to accompany
Walter's three plump aunts whom he has employed as fashion models.

Rota also makes extensive comic use of fanfares. There is nothing
invariably funny about these, but they become so, party because they are a
feature of both the military and the theatre, especially *varietà*, partly because
they often have that 'duh-daah!' quality attendant on the completion of a
magic trick as well as on a performer's first appearance, partly because of
their pronounced syncopation, and often partly because they may seem
inappropriate, heralding something unworthy of being heralded. Perhaps
too they recall cock crows, evoking not only an animal sound but also the

absurdity of masculinity, always strutting and insecure (because strutting is an inherently unstable gait), crowing and strangled (because seeking to sound out beyond one's capabilities, something that the sometimes less-than-expert quality of fanfare trumpeters can catch). Some examples:

> *CAMPANE A MARTELLO* The maresciallo announces that he is not
> willing to take away the money left on don Andrea's dresser for the orphans
> and will leave that to others to do, and all the while, as he speaks, he is looking
> straight at the trio of old men, the town council, standing in the doorway of the
> town hall, in effect defying them to appropriate the money to put up a statue to
> Napoleon. When he finishes the townspeople look threateningly at the old
> men, who slink away into the doorway, accompanied by a rather sharp fanfare
> phrase, two trumpets tonally slightly at odds with one another, offset by a
> lower figure on horn. Here the fanfare announces the councillors' defeat and
> heralds their turning away rather than coming forward, that gag (an
> inappropriate fanfare) sharpened by the detail of the scoring.
> *TOTÒ AL GIRO D'ITALIA* A derisory little fanfare heralds Totò starting to
> learn to ride a bicycle (he has never ridden one in his life but he has just fallen
> foolishly in love with the winner of a beauty contest, who has tried to fend him
> off by saying she'll marry him if he wins the eponymous Tour of Italy, the
> most important bicycle race in a country in which bicycling is major sport).
> *TOTÒ E I RE DI ROMA* Ercole is anxiously expecting a visit from his boss;
> all the family await his entrance and Ercole even has a little band on hand,
> primed to play 'Entry of the Gladiators'. This is already doubly ridiculous:
> first, because, despite this tune's title, it is now primarily associated with the
> circus and not the grand entrance of powerful men; and, second, because in
> any case we are dealing neither with circus acts nor really powerful men, but
> self-important office workers. Then when the boss is announced and the music
> strikes up, it is only Giorgio, the suitor of one of Ercole's daughters, who
> comes in, and Giorgio is a nice young man but nothing more. The comedy
> comes from inappropriateness, but fanfares lend themselves to this because of
> their syncopated self-importance.

Music can also be comic by virtue of what it references. It can be parodic. The theme for signora De Ritis in *Un eroe di nostri tempi*, discussed below, is pastiche going on to parody, the very ambivalence contributing to the equivocal tone of its use. At the other extreme, the Neapolitan song that opens *Quel bandito sono io*, discussed in Chapter 3, is perhaps as mischievously parodic as Rota ever gets.

For *Giorno di nozze*, Rota wrote a couple of songs for the singer Chiaretta Gelli. He had already written for her with some success in *Il birichino di papà*, in which she was the main character. However, the cinematic treatment of her numbers in *Giorno di nozze* suggest there is gentle teasing going on in the music, with its perhaps over-abundant opportunities for Gelli's trademark light soprano trills, sustained high notes and coloratura tricks. She plays a secondary character, Marisa, best friend of the ingénue

Giorno di nozze: Marisa
(Chiaretta Gelli) sings away
while Giorgio (Roberto
Villa) and Muriella Mariella
(Anna Vivaldi [Anna
Proclemer]) would like to
be by themselves

lead Mariella and younger sister of Giorgio,
to whom Mariella is secretly engaged. In an
early scene, Marisa is seen as a pain, warbling
away at the piano in the room where Giorgio
and Mariella want to canoodle on the sofa.
At one point there is a loud, shrill phrase on
the words 'Tu sei mia speranza' ('You are my
hope') and a cut to Giorgio and Mariella,
looking rather fed up. The irritation is
underlined by the contrast between the way
Marisa/Gelli is dressed, with plaits and a
girly dress, and Mariella, with simply coiffed
hair and more grown-up clothes. The second
number occurs at the wedding party for
Mariella and Giorgio, where, after a certain
amount of fuss, Marisa starts to sing; however, the film keeps cutting away from her, to
various guests and the bride and groom talking, all ignoring the singing. In both cases,
the film showcases her only in order to
undercut her visually and emphasise her
exaggerated, at times piercing gentility.

One of the few sustained examples of,
albeit genial, parody in Rota's work is
L'ennemi public no 1, itself part burlesque,
part parody. The main source of its humour
is having Fernandel, a quintessentially
French comedian, play an American who is
taken for a dangerous gangster – this bur-
lesques the gangster set-up (rather than
mocking it); but aspects of the film also
parody it and other aspects of America,
including the music. These include the following. (1) A mixture of ersatz Gershwin
and big band, with occasional comic woodwind decoration of a kind common in Rota's
scores, for the pre-credits sequence, a faux
documentary introducing New York. (2) A
big-band tune carried on soaringly overripe
trumpet, suggesting especially the Harry
James big band. This greets the gag with
which the pre-credits sequence ends: 'Pour donner enfin à cette histoire toute
sa vérité on a choisi pour interpréter le rôle de l'américain –',[10] followed by
a cut to the credit announcing and showing Fernandel. Later, after Joe has
become Public Enemy no. 1, this tune is played on the radio, announced as
the big current hit 'Joe Killer Blues', in brassy James style. The parodic

quality is then heightened when a little later it accompanies Joe (believed by the tough guy gang to be their ruthless leader) walking past the men doing domestic jobs and watering plants, as he carries a basket of eggs as a gift to the local sheriff. (3) Trumpet and banjo cowboy music over Fernandel/Joe selling air-conditioning in a mock-up prairie in a department store, and old-fashioned (even for 1953) banjo music accompanying a Western on Joe's trip to the cinema. (4) Parodically sentimental music on harp and excessively sweet violin to accompany Peggy visiting Joe in prison (when she worked with him in the store she was not romantically interested in him, but now that he is Public Enemy no. 1 she is). When he escapes out of prison – accidentally – he walks in Central Park, passing a Salvation Army band playing in the over-enthusiastic manner Rota often accords to amateur bands; their raucous tone gives way to a non-diegetic version of the sentimental tune, absurdly sweet, almost paradisiacal, as Joe walks away towards birds on the path, in sunlight. These elements are combined in the final sequence, first Joe escaping the gang on the high ledge of their building, with Gershwiny piano and then Theremin versions of the 'Joe Killer Blues' motif, and then in the closing shot, following him saying that a film like this can only end in the Far West, with the cowboy music over him on horseback, riding a trail.

A rather different technique, that nonetheless works in a similar way to parody, is the use of very obvious cliché. In *The Best of Enemies*, 'Rule Britannia' plays non-diegetically as Richardson inspects the latrine that he has made the captured Italians build in the middle of the desert. It is just a single cubicle made of straw, but it has a Union Jack on the door. The music mocks the absurdity of building it (and the ridiculously neurotic toilet habits it implies) and the pomposity of inspecting it, in the process suggesting that this is all typically British silliness.

This comic use of cliché is especially developed in the films with Macario.

L'EROE DELLA STRADA Felice/Macario gets a job painting slogans on walls. As he starts, over an energetic underlying figure used throughout the film, the Italian communist anthem 'Avanti popolo' plays over him daubing a hammer and sickle, which, however, gives way to 'Deutschland über alles' when two men walk past and turn and upbraid Felice in German, at which point he hastily changes the symbol to an outline representation of Hitler's face. Then two old ladies pass in a carriage and the music becomes operetta-ish, and now he substitutes a royalist image. Dull solemn music on trumpet accompanies the arrival of Christian Democrats and Felice changes the image again to look ecclesiastical. Later, Felice has been appointed a vigilante and appears, twirling his baton, with a brief burst on tin whistle of the Laurel and Hardy theme (referenced elsewhere in this and other Macario films – he has much of the innocence of this duo). On his first day he is sent to break up a crowd of strikers and sets off to the accompaniment of the Rota–Macario theme tune. However, when a large crowd of strikers start to chase him, the

L'eroe della strada: Felice (Macario) transforms a hammer and sickle ('Avanti popolo') into Hitler's face ('Deutschland über alles') into royalty (operetta) into a cleric (church music)

music is the last, 'chase' section of the 'William Tell' overture, until he realises that they are striking on his behalf (because he stood up to the boss, albeit inadvertently, and because he wanted to fit into with the prevalent workerist attitude), at which point the music becomes the theme tune for the weekly communist broadcast 'La radio dei lavoratori'.[11]

COME PERSI LA GUERRA Leo/Macario is shown successively in Spain, wearing a vaguely Spanish hat (the Toreador song from *Carmen*), then somewhere very cold ('The Song of the Volga Boatmen'), encountering Americans ('Over There', 'Anchors Aweigh'), Germans (cod Wagner) and the French ('La Marseillaise') and playing judo ('Chinese' music).

COME SCOPERSI L'AMERICA In the opening montage of postwar life, the 'Stars and Stripes' plays over a headline about the ERP[12] and 'Santa Lucia' over a poster announcing 'Visitate l'Italia' ('Visit Italy'); the Wagner Wedding March (on very mournful bassoon) accompanies Gaetano obliged to marry a rich old woman (in a sense he is the bride), and then, after the marriage is postponed, in comically dotted arrangement; 'La Cumparsita',[13] the tune most people think of when they think of tango, when Cristoforo (Macario) and Gaetano arrive in Latin America (the country is not more precisely specified), with the latter gesturing towards the city, saying 'il paese del'ordine' (the country of order), and a cut to someone breaking into a shop; 'Where Is My Brother?', a cod Negro spiritual arranged in correct choral fashion with a Paul Robeson soundalike solo, for a missionary meeting; Offenbach's 'Barcarolle' then 'Santa Lucia' for Cristoforo and Gaetano rowing to get back to Italy, clichés of Italy and also a gondolier – not a rowers' – song (even if the first is an invention of Offenbach and the second is really an Neapolitan song adopted by Venetian gondoliers for tourists).

Come scopersi l'America has a particularly complex sequence musically, using many of the devices discussed above. When Cristoforo/Macario by accident looks like Hitler, his motif is played on bones when he first catches sight of himself in mirror, followed by an upward rush on violins for his double-take when he realises the horror of whom he resembles; when some German Nazi sympathisers crowd round him, he struggles to get away, to the accompaniment of the 'Ride of the Valkyries', given an oom-pah, oom-pah bass figure, with occasional hysterical bugle calls; and the sequence ends with a trombone raspberry.

* * *

So far in this chapter I have been detailing some of the musical means Rota uses to be comical. I now turn to the way these relate to what is on-screen (visually and sometimes aurally). Music sets an overall tone, but it also interacts more precisely with what's on-screen, sometimes straightforwardly reinforcing it, at others producing humour from kinds of mismatch with it.

Music sets the tone, virtually always from the word go. Characteristically, the music for the credits sequences of *L'ennemi public no 1* and *Accadde al penitenziario*, described above, set up the fact of funniness. *Quel bandito sono io* begins in darkness with first a dramatic phrase (eight staccato, uneven notes involving big leaps) on full orchestra and then a fast-pounding figure, reminiscent of silent movies,[14] with a fast, chirpy melody over it. If the first element could be taken straight, the second, already suggesting comedy by virtue of anachronism, is pushed further in that direction by a xylophone pointing the rhythm of the melody and by hiccup-like phrases on woodwind at breaks in it. A tone of fast hysterical comic energy – in short, farce – is established at once and maintained throughout the film.

Whatever comic tone is established in a credits sequence remains in place for the rest of the film, but the scores are nonetheless usually also quite precisely inflected by the antics and business on-screen. An early comedy like *Giorno di nozze* has cheerful music on small orchestra, at a very low level of volume, playing pretty well continuously throughout, with scant regard for the specifics of the comic action, but this is unusual in the comedy scores as a whole, and even this film has moments where the music becomes more precisely allied to what is going on. Most of the comedies are a succession of such moments within the ongoing overall comic tone of the music.

The most obvious index of this is the high degree of Mickey Mousing. The obviousness of the coordination is what makes it funny. This perhaps relates to Henri Bergson's observation that what we often find funny is the perception of the mechanical within the human: the man slipping on a banana skin reveals the motor basis of walking; he also thereby has his human dignity undermined, which is especially entertaining if the person involved has much invested in their dignity (and may explain why men are more often at the centre of comedy than women). Some examples (to add to those scattered above and below):

> *ANNI FACILI* Fastish, bouncing music accompanies Luigi pursuing Larina, who can unblock the process of getting a licence for the drug Virilon; at a certain point, he seems to have lost him, we see Larina getting into big car and the music comes slowly to a halt – until suddenly Luigi appears from round the corner and runs up to car, when the music comes racing back in, this time on fanfare-like trumpets.
>
> *QUEL BANDITO SONO IO* When the remorselessly avaricious Rosana snatches the wad of notes left on the mantelpiece by Leo for his departing girlfriend Stellina, there is a comic stinger: a sudden peal on mandolin.
>
> *COME PERSI LA GUERRA* Both the Germans and the Americans (to the latter of whom Leo/Macario and his mate Checcho have been drafted) are seeking to establish themselves in a mine; in one shot, the Germans go down corridors on either side of the screen while Leo comes up one in the centre. This farcical gag is emphasised by having booming Wagnerian music that goes down (both melodically and in terms of sound level) and the main comic theme on flute coming up, a contrast in musical registers (stentorian orchestra/silly flute). The comic theme is then given a swing (= American) treatment. In a shot with Leo and Checcho on one side of the screen and a German on the other, unable to see each other in the darkness, this swing version is counterpointed with the heavy German music, the music getting faster and faster as they make the phone connection (supposedly to the Americans outside) and then stopping suddenly when, the connection made, Checcho finds himself speaking to the German, with just some suspenseful strings behind; the sudden stop of the music comically underlines the farcical turn of events, the comedy increased by having strings which are both appropriate (enemies confront one another) and inappropriate (it's farcical). The pause is brief, but then the intertwined music recurs, getting ever faster in the comic confusion in the darkness, until there is another sudden pause plus suspenseful strings, when Leo and Checcho start speaking on a phone each has got hold of and find they are speaking to each other.

Later a very drunk Leo is about to be shot by a German; the latter tells him to stand still by a wall, turns round and goose-steps away, and Leo drunkenly follows him. On each step down there is a drum beat, the already comic effect (given an hysterical edge by Leo's plight and perhaps a satirical one by sound mimicking goose-stepping) is reinforced by each step and beat accompanied also by a note on a tuba. When the German realises what Leo is doing, Leo runs around him back to the wall to the sound of a quick clarinet flourish, in its contrast to the beat and tuba itself comic.

Reprieved, Leo is sent out to fight for the Nazis. Bassoon notes underline his steps, while a phrase from the main comic theme played on clarinet mimics his hand gesture up to his helmet, which has camouflage branches in it. The clarinet phrase would be comic anyway but the lightness of touch is still more comic when Leo picks a berry out of the camouflage branches and pops it in his mouth.

Even when not so precisely allied to movement, music may underscore the humour, reinforce it, bring it out. Sometimes it underscores the basic comicality of a character: the brilliant little flourish that greets Barbarotti/Sordi's every appearance in *Le miserie del signor Travet*, the pompous winds for the marshal and town councillors in *Campane a martello* or the plodding music for Donna Rosalia amid her cows in *Marito e moglie*. Other times it points a gag: the over-egged paradisiacal versions of 'Un ora sola ti vorrei' in *Via Padova 46* , the changes of music as Felice changes his wall painting in *L'eroe della strada*. In *È primavera*, when randy Beppe realises that 'la donna' that he is going to meet is the Madonna, a cello plays a tipsy version of the theme, with descending plink-plank-plunks on piano, to tease his disappointment. Early on in *Un americano in vacanza*, Dick waits for Maria outside the palazzo where he has dropped her off; his sweet eagerness is rendered comic by a trumpet, with an opening and closing mute, playing a slowed-down version of the galop theme used previously for the journey to Rome; when we see Maria sneaking out the back of the palazzo to catch a tram, clarinet twiddles reinforce the comedy of love.

These cases would be funny without music. In other instances, music may also bring out humour that is not so marked in the action.

LA BELLA DI ROMA (1955) Nannina is speaking with Gracco about Oreste having pulled out from helping her set up her own trattoria, to the accompaniment of serious music; however, as it dawns on her that she might be able to draw Gracco into her plans, the comic motifs of the film, one lumbering on double bass and trombone, the second syncopated and spirited on high clarinet, come in intertwined; her manner does not change, but the music indicates the humour of her manoeuvring. Later in the same film, Gracco finds himself in a trap. His son has been missing but is now found; however, his wife Ines made a vow that, if the son was found, she would not have sex for six months, while Gracco himself made a vow to be faithful only to her (and thus not pursue Nannina any more). When he realises that he has made a vow to be faithful to someone who has made a vow not to have sex, the second comic motif comes in, funnier still by being played lugubriously on low clarinet.
ERA LUI … SÌ! SÌ! In the opening sequence, there is a shot of Fernando's bride in bed from his point of view; she clearly has her breasts exposed, albeit below camera, and on the cut to his point of view there is a harp glissando moving downwards, mimicking and also laughing over his thrill at looking her over; then there is a sudden knock on the door and the music stops at once, bringing the moment of reverie to an abrupt halt, the amusement now at him in, albeit husbandly, flagrante delicto.

The comedy may be achieved by means of a cut, and the gag reinforced by music, notably fanfares.

> *LA GRANDE GUERRA* The shirker Milanese Giovanni pays the shirker Roman Oreste, whom he mistakes for an orderly, to get him put on to orderly duties; 'Sei a cavallo,' says Oreste, taking the money (meaning 'I've fixed it for you to be rejected as medically unfit'); there is an immediate cut, along with very spirited fanfares, to Giovanni clambering over a fence, with heavy back pack, undergoing very heavy obstacle training. The joke continues, with several fanfares played in counterpoint and underlying march rhythm, all suggesting bright liveliness, in contrast to the heavy-duty training on-screen.
> *THE BEST OF ENEMIES* Braggadocio Blasi goes to a local village to request local recruits: a quick bright fanfare cues Arab music of the kind usually reserved for snake charmers and belly dancers and a cut to the success of his appeal: four men who are tall, very dark, with spears and shields, in short not many, not slinky charmers, not even Arabs.

Quel bandito sono io is a notably sustained instance of comic underscoring. As already noted, the credits music sets a tone of farcical energy, which gives way to the parodic Neapolitan song. Together these respond to the film's rather extraordinary character: the intricate farcical machinery of its plotting and the caricatural playing, to say nothing of the fact that in this

La grande guerra: Giovanni (Vittorio Gassman) and Oreste (Alberto Sordi)

Quel bandito sono io:
Dorothy's father (Gordon
Harker) and mother
(Margaret Rutherford),
Dorothy herself (Jean Kent)
and the lawyer Catoni (Max
Adrian) get into their
monkish disguise

film set in Naples, all the main actors are British, whether or not they are playing Brits.[15] There are two farcical climaxes, the comedy of each whipped up by the music.

As the Pellegrinis are getting ready to escape to Sorrento, spirited phrases on strings, suggestive of a mazurka, come in on the soundtrack, adding a nervous energy to what is already a situation of high anxiety. Everyone repairs to their rooms to get into their disguises (as monks), leaving the entrance hall empty and the door open. The same melody is now played on trombone, greatly slowed down, recalling the music for the heavies used elsewhere in the film, two of whom are waiting outside the block hoping to capture Antonio. The music is already comic by association and by virtue of the trombone; it also adds to the hysteria, on the one hand by such an extreme change of pace and on the other by suggesting that the heavies are about to enter the flat. In the event, the heavies turn out to be Mr and Mrs Wilson, the British consul and his wife, who have been invited for a visit. The musical gag, preparing us for menacing presences instead of these flutteringly ineffectual ones, nonetheless also sustains the hysterical effect of the slowing of pace against the frenzied need of the Pellegrinis to get out of the flat as soon as possible. Then, as the Wilsons look about them perplexed that no one comes to greet them, the music, using the same motif, becomes refined, reminiscent of classical ballet music, mainly on high violin and flute, at once teasing the Wilsons' respectability and maintaining the sense of holding up the Pellegrinis' desperate escape. The latter effect is heightened by every so often interpolating trombone phrases (a reminder of the heavies in waiting) and squealing strings (mainly, in comic stinger mode, when members of the family suddenly appear in their monk's garb). As the farce is ratcheted up, so the music gathers pace until finally all the family, dressed as monks, are running around the bewildered Wilsons and then making their escape, the melody only now fully expressed and as a bouncy mazurka. The comedy is as much in the speed of everything as its craziness, something emphasised by having music more suggestive of dance than either suspense or slapstick. The family run out of the block and past the heavies, who of course only see a row of monks carrying large crucifixes, albeit running and albeit the last (Ciocio) very small; the dancing music continues as they shrug their shoulders at the sight, not realising it is their quarry getting away.

The second farcical climax in the film has lookalikes Antonio and Leo both in the Pellegrini household, as well as the brutish Faccia d'angelo and the police, and Dorothy now thinking Antonio has been leading a double life as Leo, and running about and water pistols and much else. For this mayhem the score folds the two motifs established for Antonio and family and for the heavies into the pounding silent-movies music of the credits, in other words bringing everything together in a brilliantly coordinated, rather than cacophonous, counterpoint, analogous to what the farce itself is doing. At the end of the film, when Antonio kisses Dorothy – but with a bit more fire than earlier, in other words, a bit more Leo-like – Antonio's motif predominates, but with little embellishments from the heavies' music, the latter spicing the sweetness of the former, just as Antonio has now been spiced with some of Leo's macho glamour.

Music then may reinforce the funniness on-screen, but it may also be a contrast to what is going on that itself produces humour. It may be comic music with straight action. In *Come persi la guerra*, Leo walks over a bridge holding in his hand a bomb with the fuse lit. One of the film's comic themes

Quel bandito sono io: Antonio (Robert Beatty) kisses Dorothy, but is he 'her favourite husband'?

runs alongside, interspersed with mounting phrases that in certain circumstances might be used to up the suspense but here add to the comicness, partly because it is hard to take the situation seriously (because it is Macario, the bomb itself is anachronistic and the whole thing has a cartoon quality), partly because the music is reminiscent of the kind of suspense music used for children's adventures. At the funeral of Filippini, one of Ercole's co-workers, in *Totò e i re di Roma*, a band plays mournfully a theme already established as comic, partly by virtue of its jerky rhythm, partly by its association with comic business, the comic quality upped here by the less-than-perfect playing of the band. The seriousness of the situation seems funny because of the generic context and the music, and also because the mourners, all Ercole's co-workers, are shown to be thinking more of their own promotion as a result of Filippini's death than their sorrow at his passing, so much so that they begin discussing the matter as they walk along behind the coffin, to the point that their chatter drowns out the music.

Or it may be straight music with comic action. Gentle, reflective guitar music accompanies the scene in *La legge è legge* in which Donadieu, the owner of the trattoria in which Ferdinand (Fernandel) was born, explains the circumstances; as he recalls his being born in the kitchen, he picks up a plucked chicken and holds it as a baby, saying 'How lovely you were then – it was before you had your teeth' (Fernandel has famously large teeth), then plunges it into boiling water, at which Ferdinand winces – but the guitar carries on in its own sweet way. Similarly, in *Quel bandito sono io*, sweet music accompanies Antonio returning home with a bunch of flowers not knowing that his family mistakenly think he's having an affair. In *Totò e i re di Roma*, when Palocco is first announced, a tune virtually the same as (though subtly not) the fanfare music for the entry of the toreadors in *Carmen* is heard, appropriate because Palocco is Ercole's nemesis but absurd because of Sordi's prissy performance and the fact that, after all, he is only a clerk not a toreador; when, after Palocco has reversed the decision of the examination board (who out of pity were going to pass Ercole) Ercole attacks him, this same tune comes in, still comic even though this time covering a physical combat.

In yet other cases there are elements of the serious and the comic in both the music and the action. In *Mio figlio professore* excessively dramatic music accompanies the killing of a beloved hen (which gets away anyway). In *Totò al Giro d'Italia*, when Totò says he'd sell his soul to the devil if it'd win him the Giro d'Italia, there is dramatic music (a churning figure on cellos and double bass and over it 'razor-like slashes on strings'[16]), preparing the entry of the devil; only because Totò is indelibly comic, and because the idea of the devil often is in comedy, does this music then itself seem funny, in effect a parody of sinister music. Or neither element is comic but the juxtaposition is: hunting horns over the children looking for the piglet in *Vivere in pace*, youthful jazz over the antics of middle-aged men in *Un eroe dei nostri tempi*.

All the above preserve the notion of the diegetic and non-diegetic (even if the very use of such pointed music may denaturalise the former). Elsewhere, fun is had from playing about with the distinction. Music is sometimes brought to a halt by something on-screen: the busy music accompanying Mariano and Amalia scurrying to get out of the house in *Giorno di nozze* is cut short, as they are, by the sound of the doorbell; when the car judders to a stop in *Molti sogni per le strade*, so does the cheerily syncopated music; when Gracco drives up to Nannina's trattoria in *La bella di Roma*, he is accompanied by the non-diegetic motif established for him, which he then switches off on his (perforce diegetic) car radio. In the last example, the gag turns on Gracco's/Sordi's conviction of his own control of the situation and our knowledge that he hasn't a hope with Nannina.

The joke may be about the functioning of the music in the film.

> *L'EROE DELLA STRADA* Felice – who has all along bent with the prevailing ideology, with non-diegetic musical commentary to match – gets a barrel organ; when he starts to turn the handle, it plays 'Lili Marlene' and fascist-related tunes,[17] and in horror he runs away (and the films ends). Earlier he has been able to improvise if he got things wrong – changing slogans, voicing approved opinions – and the non-diegetic music merely highlighted this; now, in the world of the film itself, the barrel organ is implacable.
> *QUEL BANDITO SONO IO* At the end of the sequence of the Pellegrinis escaping to Sorrento, as the heavies watch the monks scurry past, the mazurka motif fades away to be replaced by the comic-sinister trombone motif associated with them elsewhere in the film. A little later, at the party in Sorrento, Catoni decides to liven things up and cries out 'Samba!'; the music at once changes to a very effervescent samba version of the heavies motif. Further on, when Dorothy sees Leo and Rosana at the night club, the same motif is played on blowsy saxophone, with a lazy piano accompaniment over an easy beat. As with the escape-to-mazurka, the humour resides in turning things into a dance, here the heavies music into samba and slow jazz.

Petruchio and Grumio diddle dum along to music they should not be able to hear in *The Taming of the Shrew*. Macario dances along to it on at least two occasions.

> *L'EROE DELLA STRADA* Felice is looking after Giulietta's baby in the shack in the shanty town where she lives; a Hollywood movie star, Paulette Jones, arrives in the town to distribute gifts and display her and America's caringness, to the non-diegetic sound of, first, the 'Stars and Stripes', then, at the moment Miss Jones enters the shack, a sudden switch to swing music – and there is Felice apparently dancing, rocking and waggling a finger at the baby in his arms, in time to this swing; when Miss Jones steps forward, she puts her foot through one of the fragile steps, bringing the music to a jolting halt.
> *COME PERSI LA GUERRA* The English Captain Thompson, on whom Leo is billeted, insists on practising judo with him. The non-diegetic musical accompaniment is cod Chinese chords with the Macario theme played over them very fast on high wind and xylophone. At one point the Captain holds his arms out and Leo takes them and dances with him to the non-diegetic music.

What all the above examples indicate is the score's high degree of involvement in the comedy. Music that evokes various species of high spirits, good fun and cheerfulness runs alongside the film's action, but what are striking are the detail, range and precision of comic sounds, pastiche and parody, the meticulousness of the synchronising of music to image, even to cut, the care over matching comic with comic, comic with straight, straight with comic, the moments of self-reflexivity. All of this is rare in the rest of Rota; he is usually close but not adherent, interested but not involved, appropriate but not synchronised, sometimes auto-plagiarist but hardly ever self-referential. But comedy is different. It invites a stance of seeing as comic, so that all the elements of a film, and thus also of the music, are involved in the production of that stance rather than, as tends to be the case in other modes, drawing us into the action or the characters. Rota's involvement in producing the comic tone is not at odds with his practice of keeping out of the way.

Comedy involves seeing things as funny because by and large nothing is intrinsically funny, not farting, falling over, dropping your trousers, wearing clothes that don't fit or belong to the opposite sex, not gurning, puns, misunderstandings, deceptions. Seeing things as funny can, in comedy and in life, entail distance and result in satire, mockery and sadism. There are famous moments in classic comedy – Malvolio imprisoned in *Twelfth Night*, Harpagon believing he has lost of his hoard of money in *L'Avare*, feckless, rascally recruits Oreste and Giovanni dead in the mud at the end of *La grande guerra*, Edmund, Baldrick and their comrades gunned down in the very last episode of *Blackadder* – when the enterprise of finding things funny that aren't is pushed over the edge and they aren't funny any more. This is almost never the case with Rota (*La grande guerra* is thus very exceptional), but nor are his scores straightforwardly comic.

The sentimental is seldom far away in Rota's comedy scores. Very often an alternate motif to the comic is announced in the credits. An energising fanfare-based tune opens *Vivere in pace* but then gives way to a full string orchestra, cantabile melody whose emotional tones include romantic, sentimental, sad and noble, but decidedly not comic or light. It is the other way round for *Come persi la guerra*: the film opens with a maestoso romantic theme only subsequently giving way to the Macario theme, first on trumpet, then on piccolo. In *Era lui … sì! sì!* the romantic motif is sandwiched between two comic motifs, one slightly infernal on swirling strings over a fast oom-pah tuba, the other more cheery and fanfare-based, with xylophone pointing, both played before and again after the romantic motif. In the case of *Quel bandito sono io*, unusually, when the romantic element comes in following the hiccuping mock thriller music, it is in the form of the parodic Neapolitan song.

The sentimental element may offset the comic, perhaps in effect heightening it by way of contrast. It may though be part of the comic. The vicissitudes of young love are a venerable basis of comedy and the music may simply play to this, in *Un americano in vacanza*, for instance, and the Walter Chiari vehicles. In *La bella di Roma*, the introduction of the sentimental motif at one point is part of the joke: Nannina is stringing both Gracco and Oreste along; when they pursue her to a boxing match, she reassures them that she is simply a fan of the sport, and then runs off to the match, at which point the sentimental motif comes in, reminding us that she really wants to see her beloved Mario (who is in the match); the tune expresses her feeling but it's also a joke at the expense of the two men foolish enough to believe the gorgeous Nannina could possibly be sexually interested in them.

Often though, the sentimental plays on the ambiguity of comedy itself, the sense that we are seeing as funny something that is not so, that is, in the present context, often sad. The music may effect a segue to the sad. In *Come persi la guerra*, Leo, now a prisoner-of-war, is called out of his hut and the main comic theme of the film is played, albeit in a sad string arrangement. He is led to speak to a young woman, Gemma, who is his madrina di guerra (the girls who 'adopted' solders as pen-pal sweethearts). The music gives way to a romantic theme. The earlier string arrangement of the comic music paved the way for the introduction of the romance theme, although there is a further complexity, perhaps comic, perhaps even more sadly sentimental: Gemma is in fact the madrina of another soldier of the same name as Leo, and the conversation between them, notwithstanding the romantic music, keeps them on either side of a barbed wire fence – there is no romance for Leo. At the end of the sequence, the Macario theme is played a little sadly once on bassoon, once on piccolo, echoing the comic-sentimental mood established.

Sentimental music is seldom associated with Totò, yet in *Totò e i re di Roma*, when Ercole (Totò) is shown writing a grovelling apology to his boss for the rude things his parrot has said about him (itself, of course, a comic situation), it is accompanied by a very pretty little tune over a gently throbbing violin figure, which is then repeated on oboe and piano: certainly not tragic or tearjerking, but allowing the moment to drift into the orbit of the tender and poignant. It is touched on again (on high cello) a few minutes later when, to get his revenge on Ercole for his parrot's words, his boss, who has discovered Ercole does not have an elementary school certificate, makes him take an exam. This is potentially a moment of considerable humiliation – Ercole is middle-aged and established in his job – and the music might reinforce this were the situation not so patently preposterous. At the end of the oral examination, itself a typically brilliant series of plays on words as Ercole/Totò tries to run rings round his interlocutors, the examiners tell him that they cannot pass him as he has not been able to answer questions that a child would know (such as any Italian words beginning with H or the names of the kings of Rome); he replies by saying that that's the problem, he is not a child, pointing out the pressures on a married man, a civil servant with little money, and that he would know if they asked him how much things cost rather than the pointless questions they have posed, and the consequences of his failure for his job and what his children will think of him. The musical motif is as before, the light darkens barely perceptibly behind him, the camera moves in slowly to a mid-close-up and the whole of this monologue is one long take.[18]

How are we to respond to this? On the one hand, it is Totò, the film is a comedy, the reply could be another variation on Totò's speciality, trying to argue his way out of situations, and the rhetoric, of words but also of lighting, could be seen as parodying a lachrymose appeal to the situation of the common man.[19] On the other hand, the use of the long take and close-up tends to connote interiority and seriousness and Totò's performance is certainly not marked by his characteristic comic grimaces and inflections; moreover, it does move the examination board and there is never any indication to the audience that Ercole/Totò thinks he has got away with something. Critics at the time did think the film had serious moments (though on the whole they didn't think the film carried them off) and this was surely one of them;[20] they may have taken their cue from the fact that the film is based on two short stories by Chekhov and that the central character belongs with a number of treatments of the humiliations of the (male) office worker, including *Le miserie del signor Travet* and *Il delitto di Giovanni Episcopo* (1947), in both of which, though predominantly sad, even tragic in tone, the eponymous role was played by an actor primarily associated with comic roles (Carlo Campanini and Aldo Fabrizi respectively). The latter may take us to the heart of this post-examination sequence, for it is poised on just that moment in some comedy when what we have been laughing at all along (here not just Ercole but Totò's persona more generally) has been taken to a logical conclusion where we are no longer sure whether it can be found funny (Malvolio and company). The music plays its role in this ambiguity. The motif itself remains essentially the same from its first use, any change in instrumentation merely providing variation, not a change in tone, and no change in tempo or dynamics, but that first use was in the context of the clearly still comic (apologising for a parrot). Perhaps the fact that it does not deploy any of the conventions of the funny in music eases the tone of the film towards one of unalloyed seriousness in the treatment of the monologue. On the other hand, the fact that nonetheless the motif's first association is with the comic, that it has not changed since then and that, characteristically of Rota, it does not make a direct, tearjerking appeal, allows the film to remain suspended at that moment when the comic risks descending right down into the unfunniness that underpins it, but just holds back from emotional and socially critical high seriousness. This is not just a technical matter of ensuring that the comic tone can be recovered but also an engagement with the ambivalence at the heart of comedy, an engagement possible in part by virtue of the subtle disengagement of Rota's pretty, gently throbbing music. The motif is used again when Ercole returns home and as before the moment is poised on the precipice of grief. Yet now the film draws decisively back. Ercole tells his wife Armida and their daughters that he is going to die, and as he says it, the motif comes in again, very quietly but also for the first time in a different arrangement, low alternated with high winds, funny music. He has clutched at his heart in pain and is in despair at his circumstances, yet the music suggests we be amused. It is a reversal of the earlier use of the motif: previously it hinted at the sadness within the comic, here it nudges the comic out of the mournful. The shift back to the comic macabre is then fully effected when, after the music comes to a halt, Ercole suddenly thinks of the expense of a funeral and says that, to save money, he'll make his own way to the cemetery – 'And please, no donations to charity, just flowers'; cut to him walking at the head of (his own) funeral procession, with the same music as for Filippini's funeral earlier in the film (discussed above), played here even more inaccurately and squeakily, with enthusiastically banged drums. The motif does occur again, attenuated, when Ercole, now in paradise, is calling out the winning lottery numbers to Armida in her sleep and again when she and the daughters remember him sentimentally, having won the lottery. The camera tracks in on Armida saying that now they are all happy and there is an immediate cut to Ercole carried off by the police in paradise for having cheated the lottery. The motif is a remembrance of the earlier glimpses of sadness but in the contexts of the directly comic (Ercole/Totò still trying to buck the system after death) and the happy (winning the lottery), and any possibility that sentimentality might set in is at once wiped away by the sudden, and comic, cut from Armida saying they are all happy to Ercole being carted off by the paradise police.

The moment of Ercole's monologue to the examining board is one of tonal ambivalence, not just comic and serious mixed together but the maintenance of the classic dilemma of whether to laugh or to cry. In 'L'ora di punta', Arturo chases Dorotea through the house with a gun to Theremin accompaniment; is this nightmare or farce? or perhaps farce is anyway always the nightmarish seen as funny and here not securely kept in check? Characteristically, Rota's score is poised on the brink.

Once past the bright and breezy opening sequence (Beppe singing along on his delivery round), there is an ambiguity of tone throughout *È primavera*, notably in the intertwining of the cheeriness of the title tune with the old-fashioned, minuet-like motif associated with his first wife, Maria Antonia, in Catania, and with the more modern sounding one for his second wife, Lucia, in Milan, both motifs sweet and pushed in the arrangements towards poignancy. The eponymous theme tune stays with Beppe, beguiling in his carelessness; but the music for the women also suggests the price others pay for his lack of care, and the intertwining of their motifs with his suggests the inextricability of male devil may-care with female having-to-put-up-with-it. At the end of the film, as the first marriage to Maria Antonia is declared the only legal one and Lucia is paired off with Beppe's military chum (and Maria Antonia's previous fiancé) Cavallucio, 'È primavera' is played continuously alongside on what sounds like a piano roll. The old-fashioned quality and its rolling along perhaps suggest that these problems are from time immemorial, perhaps that life after all must go on; yet the decision to do it this way is striking. Perhaps the piano roll sound softens the rather uneasy resolution to the film (Beppe is out of hot water and without remorse, Lucia is conveniently paired off), but perhaps in its distinctiveness it registers the very fact of having to soften. It becomes full orchestra for the end cast list, over a shot of a new boy delivering bread and singing the title song: a happy end or a nasty taste?

There is a tiny scene in *La bella di Roma*, just one shot of less than half a minute, that is on the face of it merely a banal moment of transition, but which is transformed into one shot through with melancholy, desire, comedy and bitterness. Nannina has just got away from the importunate Gracco and got into a taxi to go to visit Mario in prison; Oreste is on his way to his wife's grave with a bunch of flowers in his hand; seeing Nannina get into the taxi, he joins her; they have a rather desultory conversation, in which he initially implies he was on his way to see her before admitting he is really on his way to the cemetery. This is of itself only very slightly comic: Oreste pursues Nannina into the taxi she got into to evade the pursuing Gracco; when Oreste says he is going to the cemetery, she says that every-one has their obligations. Nor is the scene of itself particularly sad: it's a nui-sance but not a tragedy for Nannina that Mario is in prison, and Oreste, though all too aware of Nannina's charms, is a loyal but not deeply grieving widower. What gives the scene its particular tone is the music. It uses one of the motifs of the film that is usually played in a quick, high-spirited, synco-pated fashion, usually on high winds; here though it is played on solo violin with slightly hiccupy phrasing. In other words a cheery tune played on a tearjerking instrument in a faintly comical way. In this way it responds to several currents: old men's desires and a young woman's ability to manipu-late them, a beautiful and capable young woman dependent on a rather use-less hunk and a couple of old lechers, a loyal widower mooning over young flesh, a smart woman eager to see her man but needing to keep the lecher on board and so on. It does not come down on the side of the comical or the serious, nor does it say that one is the reality hiding beneath the other – it maintains a perception of the two fused ineluctably together.

For the character played by Franca Valeri in *Un eroe dei nostri tempi*, sig-nora De Ritis, Rota uses one of his salon pastiches. It sounds like the kind of music played in the lobbies and tea rooms of grand hotels in earlier times, the violin given a particularly sweet timbre, each phrase of the melody ending on two little, equal, separated notes ('dink dink'), echoing in miniature the similar phrase in the *Blue Danube* waltz. Valeri was the peerless imperson-ator of slightly fake gentility, whose most famous revue sketch creation was 'la signorina snob';[21] De Ritis claims, falsely, to be the widow of a diplomat, thus a cut above the office worker she in fact is. The motif perfectly captures her fragile aspiration to refinement, teasing it but in its charm only gently so. However, the motif becomes darker, on low strings, when the character Alberto (Sordi) learns that De Ritis has the job of sacking people in the office where both of them work; it returns in its original, genteel form when Alberto accompanies her to her husband's grave, hoping to ingratiate him-self with her by his sympathy, the tune thus playing off her habitual gentil-ity and his specially assumed one. When it appears later, still in its genteel version, when she visits Alberto in hospital, it perhaps evokes the sadness and the (cruel) comicality of her imagining that he might genuinely be fond of her. Finally, at the end of the film, it becomes nearly genuinely pathetic as she overhears Alberto telling people of the rumour that she murdered her husband and then as she tells a policeman that her husband was just a Major Domo in an embassy, not a diplomat. The sense of the underlying sadness, of De Ritis and of Valeri's persona, nearly comes to the fore, yet not quite.

If Rota's comedy scores are unusual, for him, in their adherence to the action, they are characteristic in their lack of commitment even to the enterprise of unalloyed laughter. The major exceptions are the Macario vehicles, which pick up on that sense of the performer's unworldliness, as if untouched by whatever is thrown at him, allowing the films and their music to inhabit an almost abstract realm of comicality. Elsewhere though ambivalence is always to hand and this has to do with the character of Rota's music. The typical stance of his work, indicating but not eliciting emotion, forever on the brink, within and without, allows the comedies – not always, but typically – to play on the ambivalence of the very enterprise of comedy, that is, by and large, seeing as funny things that are not intrinsically so. This might be a matter of keeping the tragic and terrible at bay, but that would be to hierarchise a tragic sense of life over a comic one. All Rota's music tends to suggest that no such hierarchisation is possible. Things here are not 'really' awful so let's make them seem laughable, not basically sad but let's keep smiling, not grim but when you stop to think of it risible – they are ineluctably both. With Ercole before the examination board, Beppe and his women, Nannina and her men, signor De Ritis and her pretences, you literally don't know whether to laugh or cry.

5
Fellini

Nino Rota's work with Fellini is one of the most celebrated of all composer–director collaborations, invariably listed along with Eisenstein and Prokofiev, Hitchcock and Herrmann, Leone and Morricone, Spielberg and Williams. It also risks eclipsing the rest of his prodigious output: when he died in 1979, one newspaper announced it with the headline, 'È morto Rota, il musicista di Fellini' ('Rota, Fellini's composer, dies').[1] The association is nonetheless inescapable, for it constitutes the most sustained realisation of Rota's aesthetic.

A concert of his music for Fellini at the Barbican, London, was entitled 'Perfect Partners'.[2] Yet on the face of it they were not an obvious combination. Rota came from a well-to-do family in the Northern capital Milan and then lived in Rome from the age of fourteen; Fellini's father was a comfortably-off commercial representative in the provincial seaside town of Rimini. Rota came from an artistically very well-connected background with a high cultural education; Fellini's cultural formation was the circus, cartoons and revue (the last two of which were his first forms of employment). Rota was discretely or asexually homosexual; Fellini was very publicly married (to Giulietta Masina), a notorious womaniser and, if the films are anything to go by, pruriently fascinated by homosexuality.[3] Above all, Rota was steeped in and lived for music, whereas Fellini had little formally developed interest in it.

Yet from *Lo sceicco bianco*, Fellini's first film as sole director,[4] until Rota's death, the latter wrote the score for all the former's films (fifteen features and two shorts), with the exception of 'Agenzia matrimoniale', Fellini's contribution to the 1953 compilation film *L'amore in città*. In 1947 they had already both worked for Lattuada (Fellini as scriptwriter) on *Il delitto di Giovanni Episcopo* and *Senza pietà* but not, it seems, met. When in 1952 Fellini came to make *Lo sceicco bianco*, he only had the vaguest idea of Rota as a composer, but when he went to visit him, Rota had written a melody for the film, one that 'andava già benissimo' ('already went very well') with it. Theirs was, said Fellini later, 'un convergere di due temperamenti' ('a convergence of two temperaments').[5]

Despite his protestations of ignorance and even dislike of music,[6] Fellini is the most musical of directors. M. Thomas Van Order (2009: 21–5) argues that Fellini was comprehensively involved in choosing and determining the music for his films, even to the extent that one could consider him to some extent its composer.[7] Rota himself noted that Fellini would have musical 'insights that only a musician ... could have had and yet which he achieved purely by instinct'.[8] Even without Rota, the use in 'Agenzia matrimoniale' of a burble of Latin-American rhythms to convey the bustle of interactions in a working-class block of flats, or in *E la nave va* (1983) of a range of classics to evoke the fragile world of a decaying artistic aristocracy, is consummate.

However, it is not his actual, untutored musical knowledge that makes Fellini a musical director so much as the musicality of the film style itself. Film and music are both arts of movement: movement that unfolds over time, yielding pace and rhythm; movement that takes place in space, in where it is produced, in the way sounds take up space (loud and soft, the different timbres of instruments), in the perception of melody going up and down. It is this that informs Fellini's use of the tempi and gestures of camera movements, the rhythms of editing, facial and bodily movement and the interactions between them and actual music itself.

He could perhaps have achieved this with other composers. What unites him and Rota is their relationship to their material. They come at this from different social, cultural, musical directions, but both occupy a position that is neither wholly within nor wholly without that which they present. Rota, in his upbringing and his day job, came from high culture, yet was working in a popular medium and drawing upon popular musical traditions. Fellini was shaped by popular cultural traditions – the provinces, popular Catholicism, circus, vaudeville, the movies – of which, as a high-prestige, Rome-based film director, he was no longer actually a part. Both inhabited a position within-and-without the worlds in which they worked and also the worlds that their films disclose and construct.

Consider the second sequence in *Amarcord*, in the barber's shop. The barber and his customers chat about this and that and a bright little tune is heard, coming from nowhere. A customer asks the barber what he is going to play at the bonfire later that day. 'I've composed a new tune,' he says, 'listen to this', and picking up a flute proceeds to play the bright little non-diegetic tune we have just heard.[9] His playing is set up by the non-diegetic soundtrack: from the beginning of the sequence, a flute, muted trumpet, piano and light percussion combo play the tune a couple of times; then they play a second, related tune, before giving way – as Gradisca, the hairdresser in the backroom, welcomes her little sister Fiorella – to strings that play the 'Amarcord' theme already played in the credits, though at breaks in the melody playing a little riff echoing the previous tune; then there is a return to the combo, but now just vamping the earlier underlying rhythm until the barber comes in with the tune he says he has composed. The break with the tune (the little bit of the 'Amarcord' theme) and the vamp pitch the barber's playing at an undecidable point between diegetic and non-diegetic. It is as if the non-diegetic music wants to showcase the barber a little (the break with the first playing of his tune) and is ready to wait for him (the vamp), while the barber is listening to the moment in the vamping rhythm when it is right for him to come in. As he plays and the combo continues its rhythmic support, Gradisca dances backwards into the shop, the men applauding, until she laughs, draws the curtains on herself, crying 'Via! Via!' ('Off with you!') and the film at once cuts to the next scene. Gradisca dances to the barber's tune but also the non-diegetic combo's rhythm; when she says 'Via!' it is as if she is bringing the sequence to an end, which is indeed what happens.

Perhaps no sequence in Fellini, Rota or the cinema achieves such poise as this (which lasts just under a minute), so charmingly, so seemingly casually, so little concerned to labour a point about disclosing and constructing a world, about the ontology of fiction. Yet such procedures are typical of Fellini and Rota and a fortiori Fellini–Rota.

One aspect of this is the way established pre-existing tunes and Rota-composed ones are put on a par and regardless of diegetic belonging. The films' scores slip between tunes so that music indicated as occurring in the film's world because it's taken from the real world is undifferentiated from music composed especially to construct that film world. In the night club and at the party in *Il*

Amarcord: the barber (Cesare Martignon) plays the tune he has 'just composed', Gradisca (Magali Noël) dances to it until telling them all to shoo

bidone, tunes from the credits sequence and non-diegetic score crop up diegetically alongside current hits such as 'La pansé',[10] 'Coimbra',[11] 'Te voglio bene tanto tanto'[12] and 'Souvenir d'Italie',[13] the latter also, on mandolin, in the restaurant where Augusto takes his daughter Patrizia out for lunch. In *La dolce vita*, the previously non-diegetically established Rota tune 'Notturno' is played on guitar at Steiner's party by a woman who then sings the blues 'I'm goin' away'; in the final party the film's two main motifs take their place besides 'Jingle Bells' and 'Why Wait' (the B-side of the contemporary hit 'Patricia'), all in uniform, blandly jolly versions.

For *La dolce vita* Rota also wrote two pastiches of popular music. One is an irritatingly catchy 'Canzonetta' (little song), first heard from a transistor radio on the terrace where some sunbathing girls wave at Marcello and Paparazzo, then on Maddalena's car radio, on a radio at a photo shoot and at the Cha Cha night club. The other is a waltz, 'Parlami di me' ('Talk to me about me'),[14] played twice at the Cha Cha club; the first time it is mixed in with the dance-band version of 'Entry of the Gladiators'[15] for the dance girls' act; the second time, it is the basis of the clown's trumpet solo (the one that amuses but also saddens Fanny, the dancer who has joined Marcello, his father and Paparazzo at their table). This tune was originally intended to be 'Charmaine' (Miceli, 1982: 185) and it is played by Polidor, one of the biggest comic stars of Italian silent cinema. One nostalgic reference piles upon another, but first folded into a blandly cheerful version of the rumbustious 'Gladiators' and then sandwiched between 'Yes Sir That's My Baby!'[16] and 'Stormy Weather'[17] in what is regarded by Marcello and Paparazzo as a has-been night club that they have only visited at the request of Marcello's father, who has heard about it back home, that is, in the provinces.[18] The sequence mixes pastiche and impacted reference with dated songs, but all on a par in terms of cheery arrangement.

In addition to promiscuously running together pre-existing and specially composed music, the movement of diegetic elements into the non-diegetic music and vice versa is often nudged towards greater complexity. This is so in sequences set in cinemas, where the music on-screen relates to what is happening in the cinema. Van Order (2009: 47–8, 75–7) discusses the detailed way that Fausto's flirting with his glamorous neighbour in *I vitelloni* and Augusto's visit to the cinema with Patrizia in *Il bidone*, cheerfulness at being with her undercut by his being recognised by a victim of his scams, are both underscored by music coming from the film being shown. The effect is heightened by the tendency of both Rota and Fellini usually not to underscore in any precise way: they choose to deploy underscoring at the very moment it becomes most implausible, the mere coincidence of music playing in the film's world with events taking place in it. Further, in *Il bidone* the music in question is that of the opening credits of *Lo sceicco bianco*. The latter is in part, like *Il bidone*, about a con man, although Fernando is an altogether more transparent and ridiculous conner than Augusto; likewise the bright and sentimental motifs of *Lo sceicco bianco* play against *Il bidone*'s altogether bleaker tone.

The cinema sequence in *Roma* (1972) begins during the screening of an epic film; quiet, ancient-sounding music plays behind the vamping of a femme fatale; then the music gets excited, rises, accelerates, crescendos, while in the cinema some people in the front row leave and there is an frenzied rush to take up the vacated seats. Here the music from the screen under-

Amarcord: vamping in the cinema

scores what is actually going on in the cinema, activity that has, however, nothing to with the emotions on-screen. All is still again in the cinema as the music becomes more tragic and the film ends. Next up is a documentary about the glories of the fascist regime; when this turns to the splendours of Florence, a languidly romantic melody on piano comes in and the camera in the cinema moves in on a woman flirting with the man to her left; as they turn to look at each other, there is a brief, erotically suggestive phrase on brass and then the melody is picked up again on guitar. This shift to a slightly sexier, jazzier musical tone augments but also moves away from the music's diegetic source (the not particularly sexy splendours of Florence), and this continues as the film cuts to the woman now seen having sex in a car, with, it is soon revealed, a line of young men waiting outside for their turn with her. The music is now in full up-tempo 1930s dance-

Amarcord: vamping like in the movie

band style and the original diegetic source in the cinema is left far behind – except that visually the film now itself looks like an old movie, first naughty slapstick (what we see of the love-making is the woman's high-heeled feet peddling up in the air) and then cutting to her dressed pretty well as the femme fatale had been in the epic film. Previously diegetic music had uncannily shadowed goings-on in the cinema; now non-cinematic, non-diegetic music accompanies movie-like activity away from the cinema.

Especially common in Fellini–Rota is movement from non-diegetic to diegetic music, perhaps because it contributes to the sense of both telling a story, constructing a world, while at the same time becoming – kind of, almost – part of that world. In the opening sequence of *Il bidone*, Roberto, one of the con men, dances and sings along with the burbling little tune that is carrying on behind; towards the end, another of the con men gets out of the car and stretches, whistling one of the film's otherwise always non-diegetic sentimental themes. In *La dolce vita*, a quiet version of the opening credits music accompanies Marcello, Maddalena and the prostitute Ninni in the car back to her block of flats, but when she says to be quiet, they'll wake the neighbours, they turn off the radio and thereby the credits' theme, as if this non-diegetic element at some point morphed into a diegetic one. In *Giulietta degli spiriti* (1965), José, Giulietta's husband's attractive business visitor, sings to her what is everywhere else non-diegetically her theme, perhaps in effect being one of her spirits. 'Notturno' in *La dolce vita* occurs first wholly non-diegetically behind the conversation between Marcello and Maddalena sitting in the car in Piazza del Popolo and then, as already noted, diegetically at Steiner's party. At the end of the party in Bassano di Sutri, it is heard as the partygoers return in the early morning from the haunted castle; they stop as they see the principessa madre and the chaplain going into Mass, and the other members of the family fall in to accompany them; throughout the sequence, there is the sound of the church bell, to which 'Notturno' keeps time; when everyone stops, the music too stops, though the bell continues to toll; when they walk into Mass the music resumes: there is perfect accord between the sounds of the non-diegetic and diegetic realms.

As many of the examples discussed indicate, it is often near impossible to say whether, or at what point, something is diegetic or not. This is a recurrent perception of writers on Fellini–Rota. Van Order traces the slipperiness and uncertainty regarding diegetic and non-diegetic music, the refusal of a hard-and-fast distinction, in all of Fellini's films up to *8½*; Gorbman (1978: 89) notes the way that in *La notti di Cabiria* music 'works to erase distinctions between diegetic, narrational and the spectator's framework'; Miceli (1982: 286) discusses the way that in *8½* 'music is not limited to exhausting the possibilities of the three "levels"[19] but mixes them up, sometimes with calculated ambiguity, sometimes obviously, until they are synthesised in the finale in a form that obliterates all such classification'.[20]

The result, however, is not, mainly, confusion. This is partly because both Fellini and Rota have such a light touch. It is also because their films hold in play a sense of the ontology of perception; that is, that one perceives a world and one knows oneself to be in that world and yet once cannot perceive oneself in that world in the same way that one perceives everything else. This sense is heightened when what is involved is a world that behaves like a real world, existing beyond the frame and the running time, and yet which has been put there by film-makers. The films remain poised on that perception, not falling into solipsism (there is only what an 'I' perceives) nor empiricism (the world is just there, separate from all perception of it), not concealing their involvement in the construction of worlds but nor wishing to prevent the willing suspension of disbelief in them.

When in *Lo sceicco bianco* Wanda sees the photo-romance troupe arriving to catch the bus to their location shoot, they are accompanied by a single drum beat, played by a young man leaping along dressed as an Arab, seen in the distance behind her. Wanda looks about open-mouthed as they assemble; when, finally, she looks up and sees two of the stars, Felga and Oscar, coming down the stairs with the other actors, the drum roll is augmented by a little march on a small orchestra which has no diegetic source. Editing establishes that the shots of the actors are from Wanda's point of view, but a closer shot of Felga and Oscar shows him whispering something to her and her laughing raucously; this closer shot also allows us to see that he is smoking and holding book matches in his hand, not really a glamorous Bedouin. The shots are point-of-view shots and yet they also allow us to see what they disclose in a way that is at odds with Wanda's enchanted perception. Similarly, the music indicates her excited feeling at seeing the troupe, while also being a pompously silly little march, already used in the credits. If it expresses how she feels, it also indicates the absurdity of what is so delighting her. Yet there is fun and energy in this music and the editing pattern, such that the film catches something of the way she sees the troupe even while it sees through them.

In what follows, I consider the significance of such within-and-without procedures in relation to three dimensions of Rota's and Fellini's converged temperaments: movement, memory, magic.

MOVEMENT
In the circus sequences of *I clowns*, where a band can be glimpsed in the background, the music is roughly in tune with the different acts but, bar the

odd drum or rattle to Mickey-Mouse slapstick, oblivious to the detail of what's going on. This is most probably how circus bands worked in this basically non-narrative form, in contrast to the relatively attentive-to-the-events procedures of melodrama, one of the main precursors of film music. In 1923, aged twelve and fresh from the prodigious success of *L'infanzia di San Giovanni Battista*, Rota and his brother Luigi went to see the Fratellini brothers, a clown act subsequently celebrated in *I clowns*, and visited them backstage, where, both holding musical instruments, they were photo-graphed with them (De Santi, 1992: 20). Perhaps it was a decisive moment. The burbling little marches and the blithe carrying on regardless through-out Rota's work suggest that the circus was important in Rota's formation as it is well known to have been in Fellini's.[21]

In Fellini, circus is a paradigm of life – and cinema – itself,[22] and at the heart of this is the perception of circus as an amalgam of arts of movement, of acrobats and animals and clowns, its music that of non-stop, banging away, on-with-the-show enthusiasm. Its shape is the circle, something that promises perpetual motion, a promise at once affirmed and denied in the walk-round finale, since it takes the form of circular motion that also signals coming to an end.

Peter Harcourt (1974) bases his account of Fellini's films on the per-ception of the centrality of the sense of movement to them. Movement – movement for its own sake, not goal-directed – is the essence of life that ratiocination, social organisation and religious ceremony, inter alia, seek to stymie. There is, though, movement and movement. Movement may be restless and neurotic, listless and enervated, just as it may be flowing and exhilarating.

There is the headlong confusion of movement in the party sequence in *Il bidone*, people moving in all sorts of different directions, crossing the field of view of the camera, blocking each other off, and music that struggles against pandemonium and changes abruptly, an urgent mambo rhythm replacing a romantic ballad and so on. There is the disturbingly, menacingly driven quality of *La dolce vita*'s credits music and the crazed drive of the galop and can-can in *8½*, the first associated with Carla (and also briefly with the French actress), the second with various other nuisances, the constant pressure on Guido to make his mind up, literally to get a move on, both tunes combined in the inferno of the press conference.

There is also music whose lack of drive and brio conveys feelings of listlessness and enervation. In *La dolce vita*, especially at the parties, the music rolls on bright and relaxed, yet nonetheless also remorseless, deadly, on and on. The score of *Satyricon* is based on continuous sounds, the soft cacophony of a pullulating, directionless world. *Giulietta degli spiriti* uses Giulietta's theme not only to keep her at the centre of the film, but also to catch the sense of her drifting, apparently peaceably, actually anxiously, through the pastel, luminescent *mise en scène*, at once a pretty, pleasant envi-ronment for Giulietta's position (with which in itself she does not seem dis-contented) as housewife to a well-off businessman and also a contrast with the anxieties (disturbing memories and visions, discovery of her husband's infidelity) and spirit voices that assail her. Only at the end of the film does this music disappear, replaced by a calm solo flute as, having made friends with the spirits, she walks calmly towards the sea.

Yet there is also energising movement. Sergio Miceli (1982: 265ff.) discusses the way an eruption of music may jerk a character out of stasis: the sudden appearance of the bersaglieri fanfare as Ivan has come to a standstill in his search for Wanda in *Lo sceicco bianco*, giving him new resolve; the arrival from nowhere of the clown musicians in *La strada*, whose burbling music leads Gelsomina into town and to il Matto; the arrival at the Caracalla night club in *La dolce vita* of Frankie, who gets the band to displace the staid, bland 'Arrivederci Roma'[23] with 'Caracalla's',[24] releasing Sylvia to lead everyone in a conga. The music that the orchestra finally manages to play in *Prova d'orchestra* is a galop, but whereas Carla's galop in *8½* has an insistent, foregrounded, restless rhythm, here it is cheerfully energetic.

There is also circular, healing movement: the young people turning around each other and Cabiria at the end of *Le notti di Cabiria*, with their tune segueing effortlessly into hers, diegetic into non-diegetic; the roundup of tunes at the end of *8½* that do not so much end as fade away. And easefully flowing movement. The bliss of Cabiria's theme in *Cabiria* is the way it joins up melodically with itself: it consists of two sections, one (A) based on a series of upwardly yearning phrases, the other (B) on a more even keel with a more relaxed rhythm; they generally give way to one another but the melodic resolution of B is actually achieved by returning to the opening upward phrase of A. Throughout *Amarcord*, one tune flows into another, Rota's and not Rota's, the rhythms evened out, the sense that there'll always be another melody and that they'll all come round again.

In this context, an alteration or contrast of movement can be highly significant.

ALTERATION The theme that accompanies the scams in *Il bidone*, at first suggesting 'comic theater and … narrative suspense', becomes each time slower, heavier, so that by the last time 'the narrative suspense has dissipated' and the bleak spiritual and ethical implications of the actions are to the fore (Van Order, 2009: 84). Van Order notes the way that each episode of *La dolce vita* 'begins with a lively adventure that eventually concludes with *immobility* and death (symbolic or real)' (2009: 107, my emphasis), qualities conveyed in the pace and energy of the music as well as camera and on-screen movement. Sections of *I clowns* work in the opposite direction, accelerating rather than decelerating. The music in the opening sequence, in which a little boy becomes aware of the circus setting up next door and apparently goes to it, builds up from snatches of people humming and bells jingling, through various pieces of circus music, that get gradually louder and faster, with bits of music with castanets (for a knife-throwing act), lumbering Orientalism (the lions) and the 'Ride of the Valkyries' (the wrestler Miss Matilda), climaxing with Fučík and the *8½* passerella. The combination of getting faster and louder, plus the rapid shifts in musical register and an overlay of other sounds, notably of slapstick, create a tempo of enthralling confusion. There is a similar increase, of speed, loudness and confusion, at the clown funeral, starting with a very heavy tread and portentous chords, but then accelerating with the use of the film's own clowns motif as the pantomime horse pulling the hearse breaks into a dance and the funeral procession picks up speed, eventually careering round the ring (here using *Lo sceicco bianco*'s circus-like march), until things get manically out of control and 'Stars and Stripes Forever' heralds the arrival of the clown-manned fire brigade.[25]

CONTRAST I clowns ends on two clowns in a deserted circus ring playing the slow 'Ebb Tide',[26] on solo trumpets in a deserted circus ring to up the maudlin quality, perhaps suggesting elegy for the circus much more than the mayhem of the immediately preceding funeral has. The galop and can-can are both absent from the final walk-round of *8½*. In so far as this is a glimpse of ideal movement, of reconciliation and happiness, such driven music must be absent, even though the 'Ninna nanna'[27] and 'Ricordo d'infanzia' are both folded into the passerella. Earlier, Guido's mistress Carla arrives at the hotel café, much to his embarrassment, to the sound of the galop; when, on Guido's 'Basta!', it stops, it is replaced by 'Ninna nanna' and the passerella on piano, preparing the way for the harem sequence; this is also a vision of reconciliation and happiness, but one that turns out to be a false dawn; nonetheless, banishing the driven music of the galop and replacing it with the dreamy flow of the lullaby and the cheerful motion of the passerella is part of the process of finding the right movement.

* * *

Il Casanova di Federico Fellini (1976) is an especially developed treatment of movement, this time in terms of repetition. Simone Perugini (2009) links this to Casanova's obsessive character. There is, to begin with, a motif derived from two piano pieces by Rota based on the musical values designated by the letters of Bach's name;[28] their titles suggest the spirit in which they are composed, bright and pealing (Valzer Carillon) and stumbling fun (Circus Waltz (sic)), and waltz suggests lilt and brio. However, in their transformation into the *Casanova* motif they take on a very different character, bringing out from what Rota considered 'leggeri, piacevole, scherzosi' ('light, agreeable, playful') something that Fellini found 'diabolico'.[29] Bach is often thought to be a mathematical composer and the fact that the tunes are based on the letters of his name already suggests a cerebral starting point; the waltz, as well as being a by-word for intoxicating sensuality, is also one for endless repetition. It is this mechanical, joyless, remorseless quality that is emphasised in the film, more staccato, using instruments with a harsh, metallic sound, including electric piano, harpsichord, celeste and chimes, sometimes altogether (Perugini, 2009: 38). The motif is first heard emanating from a music box Casanova carries about with him and plays every time he has sex. It has a mechanical bird on top, which, in an obviously phallic way, pumps up and down and flaps its wings as the music plays. On it first appearance, it still has a music-box sound, though louder and with more attack. Each time it recurs, it becomes musically more infernal: for the sex competition in the palace of the Prince Brando (where Casanova demonstrates he can come more times in an hour than can the coachman Righetto), for instance, there is a greatly augmented orchestra, a pounding underlying beat and crude brass squeals,[30] or, for the group sex in Dresden, it is accompanied by a side drum, likening proceedings to a military exercise,[31] before segueing into the atonally uncomfortable finale of a version of *Orpheus and Eurydice* performed by members of the troupe with whom he is having sex.

But repetition does not have to be horrible. Another motif, 'Pin Penin', its eponymous refrain itself a repetition, is like a nursery song. It is first heard sung (off-screen) by a woman in the sewing workshop Casanova visits for sexual trysts. It accompanies his fascination in this setting with Anna Maria, the quiet, anaemic girl who keeps fainting. It is then briefly interpolated into music during Casanova's escape from prison and the evening at the Count du Bois' but only again properly in London, sung by the giantess Angelina. In the case of Anna Maria, Casanova has sex with her during one

Il Casanova di Federico Fellini: the giantess Angelina (Sandra Elaine Allen)

of her fainting spells, whereas he just spies on Angelina bathing. Yet while in the first case his pleasure is undercut by his furtive glances (lest someone discover his taking advantage of the girl), in the second, despite the fact that he cannot have access to Angelina, he smiles beatifically on at her: 'Pin Penin' here 'becomes, for Casanova, a lullaby sung by the Great Mother that finally allows him to sleep',[32] releasing him from his obsessions.

There is also a motif, established in the credits, using very short repeated phrases, overlaid with backwards and forwards and up and down melodic-rhythmic figures;[33] Perugini (2009: 29–33) links the inherent tonal precariousness and open-endedness of this to the fragility and insatiability of Casanova's obsessiveness. It becomes associated especially with the mechanical doll that Casanova first sees, and is enchanted by, at the Wittenberg court. Already there the music creates a contrast to the inferno of the crazed, cacophonous organ music at the court,[34] a cross between *Carmina Burana* and heavy metal at their most barbarian. In the final sequence – apparently a dream that Casanova says he had the night before of dancing with the doll on the frozen Grand Canal in Venice – the music provides a moment of happiness in the context of Casanova's humiliating decline, ill, mocked, sexually spent, at the castle of Waldstein in Bohemia. The music that was wandering and mysterious in the opening is now dance music, whose lilt, along with the turning movement of Casanova and the doll and the eventual fade, suggests movement going on blissfully forever.

MEMORY

The wealth of reference in Fellini–Rota signals the past. This may be thought of as something that once existed and can now be indicated, the activity of history, or else as something that one once experienced, the knowledge of which one carries within one and can evoke, the activity of memory. In both cases, Fellini complicates the case, in ways which at bottom have become commonplaces of thought about history and memory: the past is not just there to be known, memory is not reliable, nor the self that remembers stable, both are inflected by the needs of the moment in which they are produced.[35] Fellini does not labour the point, nor does he wind up in radical scepticism (the past is just an invention of the present, memory only a personal fabrication). Rather histories and memories are shot through with shards of matter from the past, and not least music; and if film cannot actually be the past or a memory, it can explore historiography and remembering.

In the reprising of musical material, both within films and across their joint oeuvre, Fellini–Rota's work itself constitutes a form of memorialising, and I turn to this next. There is also a very particular way in which Rota's music was often a memory of the music that Fellini had in mind during the making of a film. Moreover, many of the films are also an attempt to convey history and memory, even while acknowledging the limitations on the possibility of doing this.

Repeating material in the form of motifs is a standard procedure of film music and there is no lack of these in Rota-Fellini.[36] More unusual are

sequences which round up motifs. In the sequence in *Le notti di Cabiria* following the visit to the sanctuary, when no one has been saved, an accordionist plays all the themes of the films, one after another. The harem
sequence in *8½* brings together the passerella (the 'circus' theme), 'Ricordo
d'infanzia' ('Memories of Childhood') and 'Ninna nanna' (both associated
with childhood) and 'Fiesta'[37] (the tune the adolescent boys pay la Saraghina
to dance to) in a fantasy of harmony among the women of Guido's past and
present; the flow back and forth between them (very loosely aligned with
which women appear on-screen at any point) is interrupted by the women's
rebellion, with Guido restoring order by means of a whip and to the accompaniment of the 'Ride of the Valkyries'; thereafter, 'Ninna nanna', the most
infantile motif, plays behind, along with, in a very softened version, the can-
can theme that elsewhere conveys intolerable movements and demands; at
the end of the fantasy, Guido is at peace, back in nursery mode, the demands
of the world lulled. However, here the passerella does not return. In final
sequence of the film, on the other hand, where Guido imagines (?), sees (?),
makes a film of (?) everyone from his life dancing together round a circus
ring, the passerella dominates, with all the resonance of circus in Fellini's
work. The music in the sequence is triggered by Luisa, Guido's wife, saying
she will try to understand and accept him, and on her words a little group of
clown musicians come in. They play 'Ricordo d'infanzia', and the fact that
Luisa triggers this suggests a desired fusion of childhood and marriage; but
the fact that the motif is played in a circus-like way also folds it into the
vision of life as a circus. Also included is 'Ninna nanna' but not the disrup-
tive sexuality of 'Fiesta', leave alone the threatening drive of the galop and
can-can. The lack of the passerella at the end of the harem round-up is of a
piece with this as a regressive, egotistical fantasy. The final sequence grasps

for a more collective, inclusive vision of reconciliation and harmony, as embodied by the paradigm of life and movement itself, the circus.[38]

There is also repetition of musical material across the Rota–Fellini oeuvre. The music for *I clowns* is a compendium of the circus/clown music that Rota wrote for Fellini (the fast main theme of *Lo sceicco bianco*, the little band that leads Gelsomina into the town in *La strada*, the *8½* passerella, the circus flashback in *Giulietta degli spiriti*) and even that to come (the music for the mermaid act and Anita Ekberg is the accordionist's theme in *Amarcord*),[39] not forgetting Wagner's 'Valkyries' (*8½*) for Miss Matilda and Fučík's 'Gladiators' (*passim*). *Roma* is especially rich in non-Rota preexisting material (including 'Ciccio formaggio'[40] in Trastevere, 'Stardust',[41] 'Rosamunda',[42] 'Tu che mi hai preso il cuor'[43] and 'The Donkey Serenade'[44] at the varietà show, 'La società de li magnaccioni'[45] at the present-day street party), but also draws on Fellini and Rota's own Roman past, using *La dolce vita*'s credits music (already reprised by a group of African-American tourists in Rome in 'Le tentazioni del Dottor Antonio') during the ecclesiastical fashion show and the 'Via Veneto' theme for the hellish vision of arriving by motorway in today's Rome (it too already re-used, in a nightmarish vision of Roman arrival, in 'Toby Dammit').

During preparation and shooting, Fellini would often have in mind, and even literally have playing on set, music that he wanted to use in the film in hand. But then:

> When it comes to the moment of making the actual music, of recording the soundtrack, I'm confronted with this problem, of having to let go of the music I've chosen. This is when the truly angelic quality of Nino's nature comes in, for instead of finding him against me, he'll immediately say, 'Oh, but the music you've chosen fits perfectly, there's nothing for it, I'll let go of these [his motifs], I couldn't possibly do anything better'. Of course such an accommodating manner disarms me. While he's saying this, he begins to doodle with his fingers on the piano, bringing out motifs as if distractedly, as if he isn't really putting his mind to it.[46]

These distracted motifs were very often a version, an echo, of Fellini's own choices and were the ones that ended up in the film.

Fellini's musical default was Fučík's 'Entry of the Gladiators'. Not only was it very widely used in circuses, but it is also quintessential circus music in its form, starting with a fanfare and then tumbling over itself, with much booming and banging, ending on an expectant note, as if always disposed to start up again. Its first direct use in Fellini is sardonic, far from the spirit of circus, at the Cha Cha club in *La dolce vita*, where a clown cracks a whip at showgirls in tiger leotards, and the tune soon turns into a quickstep and departs from Fučík's melody. Only in *I clowns* does it come into its own as a signature tune for what that film recognises is a dying, perhaps dead, entertainment form. However, from the start of his collaborations with Rota, 'Gladiators' was in Fellini's mind. When they met to decide on the music for

8 1/2: the clown musicians
in the final sequence

Lo sceicco bianco, Rota brought some music he had prepared, but Fellini said he'd wanted to use the Fučík.

> While Nino said he would let [his music] go, because he too thought that
> [Fučík] would work well, he put his hands to the piano and began playing
> another little march, which ended up seducing, moving, exalting and
> enchanting me more than the old traumatising march of the gladiators for
> which, regularly, Nino's little marches were substituted, much more adorable
> and to the point.[47]

The main theme of *Lo sceicco bianco* is like an echo or memory of Fučík, with all that it connotes, without actually being it. It enables a particular perception of people and events as circus-like without creating any cognitive dissonance from the fact that they are not circus. It's an entire program. The music emphasizes the circus-like aspects of some characters and some situations that strictly speaking do not belong to the circus and cruelly underlines the grotesque nature of the characters and their actions (quoted in Colón, 1981: 30).[48] Rota was substituted for Fučík for the music for the clowns that lead Gelsomina into the town in *La strada* (De Santi, 1978: 101), much more delicate and spirited. Fellini again wanted Fučík for *8½* and again ceded, to Rota's *passerella*. The finale was originally cut, by Leo Catozzo, to Fučík, and he was considerably upset by the rhythmic discrepancy produced when Rota's little march was substituted.[49] Yet Rota's characteristic lack of complete obedience to the on-screen action (and, according to Rota, Fellini's perfect indifference to such synchronicity[50]), as well as the fact that the music is like but is not the Fučík itself, maintain the sense of a vision of life being like, rather than being, a circus.

For other films, Fellini also had other tunes in mind.

I VITELLONI The old music-hall song, known in Italian as 'Titina',[51]
especially famous in Charlie Chaplin's nonsense version of it in *Modern Times*
(1936), is whistled by Guido, the boy at the station, and then played at the
carnival. The main lads' theme was first used by Rota for *Roma città libera* in a
ballad form, sometimes sung to the words 'Vola nella notte', and it appears like
this in *I vitelloni*, with Leopoldo putting it on his gramophone at night and the
voiceover telling us it is his favourite song. However, it is also used in quicker
and more syncopated versions inflected by the formal character of 'Titina'.
LA STRADA The theme on set was Corelli's Violin Sonata Opus 5 Number
12 (1700), known as 'La Follia'.[52] One can readily imagine the appeal of the
title of this work, and its mixture of grave and sprightly variations, in relation
to both Gelsomina and il Matto, and the music's spiky rhythms have some
affinity with Giulietta Masina's darting movements and expressions. However,
although given his erudition Rota must have been aware of the music's history,
there is no discernible connection between the Corelli work and Rota's score. It
seems that during the editing Rota handed Fellini a music manuscript marked
'tranquillo' and this became the theme, replacing Corelli (Baxter, 1993: 112). It

very closely resembles the fourth movement, larghetto, from Dvořák's
Serenade for Strings, 1875, although it is hard to see any point in there being
deliberate reference: perhaps this is a case where there is just similarity.
LA DOLCE VITA (1) The on-set music was the 'Morität' from Kurt Weill
and Bertolt Brecht's *Der Dreigroschenoper*,[53] better known as 'Mackie
Messer'/'Mack the Knife'. In this instance, the rights could not be obtained and
Rota produced a variation on it so close as to call forth accusations of
plagiarism.[54] The tune itself is whistled by one of the guests at the aristocrats'
party (Van Order, 2009: 113), perhaps very briefly asserting its difference from
Rota's 'La dolce vita' motif. Rota's version uses the opening phrase of Weill's
tune with one alteration: Weill's ends on the same note repeated twice, Rota's
omits the repetition and instead lengthens the note; perhaps because of its
association with Brecht's words, the repeated note seems insistent, where
Rota's single long note is more drawling. The Weill version contains some
melodic development, whereas Rota's 'dolce vita' keeps repeating the same
basic phrase with just the odd shift of key; the Brecht–Weill version is making
a point, each strophe coming to a cynical/socially critical conclusion, whereas
the Rota is simply, perhaps inanely, repetition. In *Der Dreigroschenoper*, and in
perhaps its most famous recording, by Lotte Lenya, 'Mackie Messer' is sung in
a rasping voice to a grinding, dissonant hurdy-gurdy accompaniment; for 'La
dolce vita', the rhythm is slackened, the accompaniment lounge-bar piano or
combo, with brushed percussion. The change to the melody and the
arrangement draw the sting from the Brecht–Weill, just as *La dolce vita*
presents a world from which energy and critique are draining away. Much of
what Rota does to 'Mackie Messer' had already been done. It had become a hit
again in the 1950s in just such a jazzed but depoliticised way. In Italy, it was
especially a hit for the glamorously gowned, soft-voice singer Jula de Palma, in
a lounge-bar arrangement. Perhaps 'La dolce vita' references what had already
happened to 'Mackie Messer' and all that it represents. (Compare also the film's
sapping of the energy of Fučík and Prado discussed elsewhere in this chapter.)
LA DOLCE VITA (2) The 'titoli di testa' (opening credits music), used
motifically throughout the film, derives from 'Pini presso una catacomba', the
second of Ottorino Respighi's symphonic poems *Pini di Roma*.[55] Van Order
(2009: 100ff.) discusses the derivation in detail, concluding (102):

> Rota has transformed the layered structure of Respighi's piece, where
> spirits inhabit the darkness of the underworld and slowly release their
> chanting voices from within that space before returning to stillness and
> silence, into a pattern of quick, contrasting themes that seem to imply the
> momentary victory of a vital impulse but then conclude with the hopeless
> resignation of the coda.

Once again, music suggesting energy, here with specifically Roman
connections, is used to suggest the loss of energy central to the film's vision.
SATYRICON During the filming, the signature music was a classic of early
modernism, one that opened the way to dodecaphonism, Anton von Webern's

Five Pieces for Orchestra, 1911–13, and also three much more recent, electronically based pieces, *Trois visages de Liège* (Henri Pousseur, 1961), *Ensembles for Synthesiser* (Milton Babbitt, 1964) and *Electronics and Percussions – Five Realisations* (Max Neuhaus, 1968). These provided a reference point for the score, composed by Rota with the assistance of the electronic music composers Ilhan Mimaroğlu, Tod Dockstader and Andrew Rudin. *AMARCORD* (1) The 1930s song 'September in the Rain',[56] played on set, provided the basis for the main theme. The title in itself seems to have no relevance to *Amarcord*, but the song is about remembering, and one phrase from the Italian lyrics (that are overall are sadder than the English) is suggestive of the film's fleeting tenderness:

> fu tanto triste e breve il nostro amore,
> come un fiore
> che sfiorì.[57]

Even without the associations of the words, the tune's long descending line readily expresses nostalgia. For the sequence of Gradisca and the Prince, Fellini wanted to use 'Fascination'.[58] This had already been used in *I clowns*, swelling up sumptuously on the entrance of a German couple into a provincial bar asking for champagne, she ultra-blonde and draped in white fur, much to the stupefaction of the men playing pool there; as so often in Fellini, 'Fascination' here allows one to see and to see through the couple's glamour. In the event, Rota wrote an arrangement of the main *Amarcord* theme for massed close-textured strings, evoking the ersatz opulence of 'Fascination' while also maintaining the consistency of the theme's dreamy repetitiveness. This version was then also used in the credits and in the scene of Titta's approach to Gradisca in the cinema.

AMARCORD (2) The theme first used for the fogarazza night (burning the witch of winter) seems to me very close indeed to 'Titina', though I have no evidence that this was conscious. It is especially appropriate here. *Modern Times*, with Chaplin's famous version, was released in the diegetic period of the film, and, as already noted, it is used in *I vitelloni*, a film set in the same kind of small seaside town as *Amarcord*, dealing with the same kind of people. The echo of 'Titina' in 'La fogarazza' is thus a – vague – memory of both a tune from the period and also of a previous Rota–Fellini construction of the place.

PROVA D'ORCHESTRA The music that the orchestra finally plays is very similar to Rota's own *Concerto for Strings*, composed in 1964–5 but revised in 1977. Rota was also, most unusually, present at the rehearsals and shooting, giving advice on how orchestra rehearsals were conducted and helping the actors take up the correct positions for the instruments assigned to them (Comuzio, 1979: 78).

Music like but not actually being pre-existing pieces acts like traces of the past, traces that may have their origin in very personal associations and responses, but which, precisely because they are based on widely known and available works, are also historical. The Fellini–Rota films (or parts of films) set in the past convey this sense of the apprehension of the past through traces or left-overs, an apprehension that is not total or transparent but also not an utter misapprehension. They recognise the ways in which memory is inextricable from the historical legacy and lightly insist on something at once obvious and ignored, that films can actually be neither the historical past (already gone) nor memories (which are what sentient beings have, not artworks).

The choice in *Il Casanova di Federico Fellini* of Rota's two waltzes places the film at the cusp of such considerations. Though in their precision and regularity they recall Bach (1685–1750), they were composed in a form, the waltz, and, originally, for an instrument, the piano, that were only coming to prominence in the late eighteenth century. On the other hand, Casanova (1725–1798) would certainly have been in a position to be familiar with form, instrument and Bach (though – and this adds to the delicacy of the reference – Bach did not hold the place in the musical canon in the later eighteenth century that he holds today). Rota's pieces had been commissioned in 1975 by the contemporary music theoretician Mario Bortolotti and Rota had included them in concerts of modern works composed in honour of Bach in Brescia and Bergamo. All this allusive complexity – a twentieth-century homage to a composer from before the period of the film, and not securely remembered in it, in a form unavailable to him but fashionable in the period of the film – at once signals the film's attention to period detail and its refusal of period recreation. This is then heightened by the use, and mixing up, of period and modern instruments and modes (Perugini, 2009: 38–9).

Satyricon is even more rigorous in its engagement with the past. There is a tune that recurs, a brief series of notes, heard first played by a man on a loosely strung instrument in the Insula Felicles, as Encolpio and Gitone walk past, subsequently at Trimalchio's feast on flute and light percussion, then sung by Gitone to a small lyre and by the servant girl who sleeps with Encolpio and Ascilto, accompanying herself with tiny cymbals, and finally over the freeze frame on Encolpio at the end of the film. The tune is based on the ancient Greek scale, recognisably melodic but nonetheless outside the normal Western harmonic range. It functions as a song people sang at the time, familiar to everyone in the film but not to us.

On the other hand, the template of Webern and even more Pousseur, Babbitt and Neuhaus provides the sense of an unfamiliar modernity, of music that was conceptualised as opening up a future, Webern and dodeca-phonism in turning their back on Western harmonics and the others in making music out of the instruments of the future, electronics, synthesisers. This is both defamiliarising and also suggestive of the otherness of a world that by definition we cannot know but may think we can glimpse, the future. *Satyricon* overwhelmingly references the past, in being an adaptation of a Roman text, in its visual iconography, in the recurring song, yet its refusal of any sense of direct access to the past is achieved also by casting its aural frameworks partly in terms of the future, so that the film has no secure temporal position.

The soundscape is far from wholly futuristic, although there is a rigorous exclusion of
cinematic ancient-world music (*Ben Hur*,
Rota's *La Regina di Saba*, the peplum[59]), that
signifies the exotic past while remaining
within familiar Western modes. We see
instruments on-screen that look ancient, even
if we cannot identify them or work out their
connection to the sounds we are hearing.
Traditional Western instruments are used
(including modern ones like xylophone and
electric organ), sometimes played straight,
sometimes treated to manipulations in the
recording (the sizzling sound in the fight
between Trimalchio and Eumolpio, for
instance, was achieved by hanging a micro-

Ancient, sometimes
unfathomable musical
instruments in *Satyricon*

phone directly over piano strings); the first tune heard at Trimalchio's feast is
Neapolitan but played on archaic instruments, including a zitar. Non-Western
instruments are also used, sometimes in recordings: African and Asian instruments on and off throughout, Indonesian gamelan for the sequence on Lica's
ship, the Cameroonian 'Dance of the Monkeys' for Encolpio's encounter with
the Minotaur in the labyrinth. The layering of these non-Western sounds
over worked Western and futuristic ones is a further refusal of precise time-
space coordinates and yet also reaffirms temporality and spatiality. Layering
suggests a palimpsest, which is how anything from the past comes down to us,
bits of the actual past (remains or images of musical instruments, for instance)
overlaid with what has come between (Western instrumentation and the
invention of harmony) and what surrounds us now (a knowledge of global
music, developments in creating a future music).

The music is fragmentary and yet what most characterises the soundtrack is continuousness. Ermanno Comuzio (1986b: 155) characterises the
result as composed of 'indistinct sonorities, indefinite threads, disquieting
underlinings, achieved above all by subterranean vibrations, light touches,
obsessive vocalisations, combinations of metallic sounds and so on'.[60] The
music comes and goes, but when it is there it is founded principally on long-
held notes or chords or apparently meandering sequences of notes, which
instil no expectation of development or resolution, and on percussive or
chanted repetition, which yet do not set up rhythmic regularities. The music
merges with ambient sounds also characterised by continuousness: wind, air
currents, mechanical throbbing, rumbling. These form part of a dense overlay of sounds: barking, dripping and running water, unidentified bird calls,
crickets, wordless cries, wailing, and human languages that, since they are
mostly unfamiliar and never translated, function as much in terms of sound
as utterance. In other words, though it comes and goes, the soundscape of
the film emphasises flow. Moreover, because the music refuses expectation,
development and resolution, it is hard for it to work narratively in the way

even Rota's scores generally do, in some kind of rough coordination along-side the action. The ongoing music accompanies the characters but does not underscore the events or suggest their feelings; it is diegetic and rigorously so, just the environment in which the characters find themselves, an in fact rare instance of music in film being indifferent to the fates of particular characters or what is unfolding alongside it.

This music is wholly in tune with the overall project of the film. Unfamiliar yet recognisable as music, melodically and rhythmically ungraspable, layered, coming and going, all this is of a piece with some of the other distinctive procedures of the film: visionary, hallucinatory land- and city-scapes, a *mise en scène* mixing the apparently new with ruins, lack of space-time coordinates (what time of day it is, how long a sequence lasts, inexplicable spatial transitions),[61] unidentifiable food, artworks that look like Klee and Mondrian, depthless composition across the widescreen (often invoking – and in the opening and closing shots actually being – a wall), lateral tracking and panning that emphasises horizontality, people looking out towards us, sometimes turning to do so, but by definition unable to see us, characters making gestures baffling to us but clearly understood by those around them and bursting into laughter at nothing that we could be supposed to find comic, narratives gaps,[62] interpolated stories, opening in media res, ending in mid-sentence. None of this – music, sound or image – draws us in or even very close. It gives us access to the things of history but not the feeling of being able in imagination to enter the past.

The opening melody in the credits for *Roma* resembles (but is not) the song in *Satyricon*; both seem to use ancient modes, and doing so in the case of the former, a film about twentieth-century Rome, again suggests the palimpsest, ancient Rome showing fitfully through the contemporary. The tune is used repeatedly.

It is sung by a woman over a shot of a damaged statue of Julius Caesar. A rather manic character seems to suggest that it has been damaged by fascists but it might just be wear and tear; either way it bears witness to the processes that diminish left-overs over the course of time. This brief moment is not in Rome itself, but is part of a sequence about reference to the Roman in a provincial town, another aspect of the processes of accretion and destruction that produce the palimpsest. The fact that a woman is wordlessly singing it suggests perhaps folk memory of an ancient tune (its formal qualities disqualify it from being considered a part of contemporary or even modern popular song tradition) – women are often the bearers of this aural memory, often, in Fellini, with nostalgic-erotic overtones (cf. *8½*, *Amarcord*).

It is the music for the opening section (that we see) of the film set in ancient Rome seen in a cinema in the provincial town. The visual imagery comes from silent cinema but there is speech, thus yet more layering (of periods of film history). The climax and end of this film deploy two romantic themes from *Lo sceicco bianco*, another film about Rome and of fantasies of going to Rome.

It is again sung by a woman outside an upmarket brothel, as inside young Fellini talks with the pretty prostitute he has just had sex with (there is a picture on the wall, itself suggesting a copy of a tapestry, depicting two women in ancient Rome, layer upon layer of imagery: the film shows a picture which copies a tapestry which imagines a distant past (behind which there is one more distant, since it is a truism that prostitution is the oldest profession).

It is played on a slightly twangy guitar for the arrival of the Cardinal at the palace of the Princess Domitilla for the ecclesiastical fashion show, Christianity imposed upon paganism, adapting itself to modernity.

Like *Roma*, *Amarcord* is a mixture of history and memory, but it evokes more centrally the texture of remembrance. Though the title is often taken to mean 'I remember',[63] the film is not straightforwardly a set of someone's memories. Both using musical analogies, Natalia Ginzburg spoke of the film as 'a choral memory sung out loud in a synthesis of reminiscences, fantasies, dreams and actual experiences'[64] and, to catch its collective quality, Franco Sciannameo calls it a 'cinematic folk opera'. The music is not what anyone in particular remembers but rather the music of the period available for the construction of memories. They are the tunes of the time, popular and political songs, 'La facetta nera'[65] and the 'Inno a Roma'[66] at the fascist parade and the communist 'Internationale'[67] in protest against it,[68] 'Siboney'[69] (the first tune we hear played by the accordionist), 'Abat-jour'[70] and 'Salome'[71] for the visit of the Emir, 'Vorrei ballare con te',[72] briefly sung by Titta's uncle and so on, cited, pastiched (Rota's various themes and arrangements) or echoed ('September in the Rain' and 'Fascination'). While some tunes ('Stormy Weather', 'La Cucaracha',[73] 'The Internationale') were still widely known and played at the time of the film's making and release, others ('Quel motivetto che mi piace tanto',[74] 'Siboney', 'Inno a Roma') were less so, refrains that might be vaguely familiar but hard to name.

Music is often heard in snatches and somewhere off-screen. Tunes are woven together in a way that shows little regard for diegetic and non-diegetic belonging, for exactness of origin (Rota and non-Rota) or temporal precision (when exactly they were composed). This contributes to the uncertain temporality of the film, structured as an archetypal year in the life of a town but also including at least one absolute and unrepeatable event (the death of Titta's mother) and one fairly confined historical reference point (the launching of the ocean liner, the *Rex*). The fuzziness, and yet occasional exactitude, about dating relates more broadly to the quality of the music. The main theme ('September in the Rain' + 'Fascination') mixes together a dance-band rhythm with excessive, glossy strings (with sometimes the former, sometimes the latter more to the fore), two registers of

1930s popular music but not two that generally occurred simultaneously; it provides a basic musical framework of remembrance as something imprecise, wistful, unfocused. In short, the patchwork of tunes in their dreamy, distracted frame is like the rest of the film, made up of fragments and moments, often fleetingly seen and heard, not rooted in any particular consciousness but in what is available to be constructed into remembrance.

Take the sequence of the evening struscio (evening promenade). The main theme is played here by dance band and accordion 'with a bouncy Fox-Trot flair' (Sciannameo, 1975: 61), linking it with two of the sources of music in the film's world[75] without actually showing it to emanate from either of these. It gives way seamlessly to 'Quel motivetto che mi piace tanto', then 'Stormy Weather' (already heard sung by a woman somewhere in the Biondi household), then back to 'Quel motivetto' followed by a snatch of the main theme before turning to 'La Cucaracha' for the arrival of 'Madame's new girls', but then back to the main theme, then 'Stormy Weather' again, then the main theme (now just on accordion). There is no particular reason to segue from one tune to the other, no alignment with the various little incidents on-screen, with the exception of the introduction of 'La Cucaracha' (which even has, unlike the drift between tunes in the rest of the sequence, the minutest pause before it); even here the main theme returns before the girls have completed their open carriage ride through the town; when 'Stormy Weather' reappears, as the girls arrive at the brothel, it is played on slurred trumpet rather more steamily than before. The final statement of the main theme plays over the camera, hitherto in continuous movement, coming to a halt at a shop window full of religious imagery, an evident contrast with 'Madame's girls' – but the theme itself carries neither sexual or religious connotations except in so far as it is part of an aural–visual flow that encompasses both.

A film of reminiscence cannot straightforwardly be someone's actual memories, partly because memory is constructed out of cultural rather than purely personal artefacts and partly because a film is not a person. *8½* presents both these perceptions. Music comes and goes continually in both the frame story (Guido trying to make a film) and the various inserts (dreams, memories, day-dreams, ideas), diegetic and non-diegetic mixed up, constructing a sense of a musical unconscious, vaguely registered tunes actually playing in the frame cropping up in the inserts, tunes from the inserts made present in the frame and so on. 'Ricordo d'infanzia', played in the encounter with Guido's parents in a cemetery (dream?), the children's bedtime sequence (memory?), from time to time in the harem (fantasy?) and in the final sequence (?), is first heard sung by a woman working in the hotel where Guido has Carla stay and later on piano in the lobby of Guido's hotel. The passerella is heard first as part of the illusionist's act, then doodled on piano at the hotel by Mezzabotta, then on the radio in the production manager's office, then by the dance band on Luisa's first evening in Chiancino; it is only with the harem sequence that it is no longer part of the space-time of the frame, and it reoccurs in the latter in the viewing theatre, before its apotheosis in the final sequence. Similarly the 'Ninna nanna' that Carla is imagined singing in the café before the cut to the harem sequence (where Gloria and Carla are seen playing it on harp), is in fact first heard playing idly on piano at the spa when Guido meets Mezzabotta and Gloria.

'Ninna nanna' is also mixed in with the can-can at the press conference. Here the infernal arrangement (staccato strings, blaring horns, tremendous speed) cannot possibly be being produced by the five-piece band at the conference – yet when we do actually see them, when Guido runs off behind them, the music is temporarily adjusted to just those musical forces without there being any break in the flow in the music. The role of music in producing the world of the film is acknowledged. 'Fiesta' is first heard non-diegetically (conceivably in Guido's mind) on slow clarinet as Guido catches sight of a large peasant woman during his interview with the Cardinal, leading to the sequence in which la Saraghina dances to 'Fiesta'. The simplest way of understanding this is that the sight of the woman triggers the memory of la Saraghina, but as always with this film, any formulation about what is going on is likely to oversimplify. In this case, at the end of the sequence the film cuts to Guido and Daumier, the latter saying that such an episode is of no interest. This may alert one to the elements of obvious cinematic construction in the sequence: the extreme close-up of the mother (revealing that her tears are fake), the speeded-up motion of the priests chasing the boys away from la Saraghina, the music, with no evident or even imaginable diegetic source, in an implausibly acrid arrangement.[76] Though the Saraghina sequence, like much of *Roma* and *Amarcord*, and all Fellini's, all anyone's

8 1/2: la Saraghina (Edra Gale) entertains the boys

work, may draw on memory it can never be memory. Fellini and Rota give us that recognition while still evoking the texture of reminiscing.

MAGIC

The term 'magic' is ambiguous. It can refer to a realm of actually occurring phenomena, fabulous but real, explicable only by recourse to notions of the supernatural or numinous. In the case of Fellini and Rota this means both esoterism and Catholicism. Magic can also mean tricks, fabulous illusions wholly explicable in everyday, material, though generally secret, terms. There is awareness of this too in Fellini and Rota but, rather than stress illusoriness, they cherish the capacity for wonderment.

Fellini and Rota took magic very seriously. Both consulted and made decisions on the advice of clairvoyants. Fellini took guidance on the auspices for his films from various necromancers, including the Turinese magus Gustavo Adolfo Rol, who claimed that on his advice Fellini cancelled a film long in preparation, *Il viaggio di G. Mastorna*.[77] His discovery of the ideas of Jung provided a further gloss to this. Rota and Vinci Verginelli amassed one of the biggest collections of hermetic literature in the world, now in the Accademia dei Lincei in Rome (Scianammeo, 2005: 13), and esoteric ideas inform the libretti Vinci wrote for Nino, notably the *Mysterium*, 1962, *Aladino*, 1963–5, and *Il Natale degli Innocenti*, 1968–70.[78]

The spirits of *Giulietta degli spiriti* are real, although contact with them is not accompanied by music but by wind (often a sign of spirituality in Fellini) and silence; there is a lot of music in the film, but it is either the somewhat remorselessly repeated bright little motif associated with Giulietta's life or raucous intrusions of various kinds, giving special force to the silence of the spirits.[79] Hermetic ideas are more directly addressed in *Il Casanova di Federico Fellini*. The mysterious – repetitive, strange – motif in the film, linked to the mechanical doll, has an incantatory quality. It is heard behind the credits over the elusive movement of the surface of the water, a prelude to the opening ceremony of the Carnival in Venice, an attempt to raise a huge ship's figurehead from the water accompanied by fanfare versions of the motif. It recurs again to accompany the Marquise d'Urfé 'surrounded by wizards, clairvoyants and psychics' who persuades Casanova to perform an esoteric rite of immortalisation, which for him is nothing but paid sex. The first occasion is a failed incantation and the second a fantasy of a batty aristocrat, yet the motif becomes associated with the doll, culminating in Casanova's enchanted dancing on the ice at the end of the film. There is here a trajectory from magic embraced by all but Casanova (the crowd at the Carnival are wildly enthusiastic, the Marquise tremulously credulous) to his readiness to give in to enchantment, to the magic of magic.

The idea of there being something mysterious about music itself is suggested in *Prova d'orchestra*. Musical instruments are just bits of wood, metal and other matter, yet the players all speak of their instruments in anthropomorphic, 'animistic' (Blanchard, 1984: 194) and often spiritual, 'shamanistic' (Vinay, 2002: 53) terms. The oboist for instance claims the instrument as one of 'spiri-

tual elevation [which] develops certain powers in those who play it, an interior vision that enables one to see the colour of sound. I play and I see a golden atmosphere, luminous, the colour of the sun! Like a vast mirror that blinds me with beatitude.'[80] The flautist at first claims merely that 'the flute alone is truly a human voice' but then eggs this up with it being 'an instrument of solar and also lunar witchcraft', the organist adding that 'Apollo [the sun god] played the flute'. For the harpist, 'the harp has a celestial voice … [It belongs] in the kingdom of evanescence'. Moreover, despite their personal rivalries and shared (and mutual) contempt for the conductor, and the shattering of their rehearsal space, at the end they are able to conjure a harmonically and rhythmically perfect and unified sound (emphasised, as Michel Chion (2003: 370) notes, by the contrast of the separating close-ups of the players in rehearsal and the unifying long panning shots of the whole orchestra playing together).

Fellini and Rota were also both Catholics. There is criticism of the church in Fellini and teasing of priests and nuns, but there is also a respect for simple Christian piety and a fascination with angels as figures of salvation. Rota shares this fascination (most obviously in the figure of the angel in *La visita meravigliosa*), and he produced a considerable quantity of sacred works throughout his life. Some of these are touched by his characteristic impish humour, but in a spirit of joy, laughter as a gift from God. This informs his two most overtly religious films, *Peppino e Violetta* (1951) and *The Reluctant Saint* (1962). The former deals with a little boy's persistence in getting permission to take his sick donkey (the source of his livelihood) into the crypt of the church of St Francis in Assisi; the ingredients, a comically resourceful little boy, a donkey, a saint with a reputation for simplicity, make the film overdetermined as praise of folly. Likewise, the subject of *The Reluctant Saint*, St Giuseppe of Copertina, is portrayed as a simpleton

Prova d'orchestra: the magic of music in spite of everything touched by grace. The music in both films is straightforward, lively and good humoured, as required, as well as reverent.

Rota joins in the teasing of the religious in the ecclesiastical fashion show in *Roma*, literally pulling out many comic and sinister stops. He also supplies a gentle motif for both 'the man with the sack' and the lay brother Don Giovanni in *Le notti di Cabiria*, figures who suggest to Cabiria the possibility of a simple piety only indirectly related to the church. More commonly, in Fellini–Rota, the sacred is found in the popular.

This may mean actually fusing the sacred and the popular musically. Claudia Gorbman (1978: 89–92) shows how this is effected in *Le notti di Cabiria*. After the sequence in the sanctuary Cabiria and her friends are picnicking, Cabiria laments that no one is changed. A procession of choirboys passes singing an 'Ora pro nobis'. It produces a moment of stasis, often, as the antithesis of movement, negative in Fellini. Here though it seems to offer a glimpse of something other than the scrum of the sanctuary and the subsequent random partying movement, Cabiria gazing on in something like wonderment. Gorbman points out that the notes of the melody for the 'Ora pro nobis' form the basis of the Neapolitan song that brings Cabiria back to life after the shock of Oscar's theft and abandonment of her, this time the holiness of melody caught up in the healing movement of the music and the young people's gambolling.

In *La strada*, when Gelsomina is jerked out of her stasis by the little band of circus musicians, she follows them into a town, to the religious procession accompanied by a large band playing with a heavy tread and on to a tightrope act high above the street, performed to what sounds like a tinkling music box. In all three cases the melody is in fact the same, suggesting a connection between clowns, procession and acrobat. The connection is reinforced visually in the transition from the church service in which the procession culminates to the tightrope act: the last shot of the ceremony is a tilt upwards disclosing the pomp of the building; the next shot is a tilt up towards the tightrope act. Moreover, the acrobat, il Matto, has wings, making him look like an angel. The equation suggested, above all by the consistency of the melody across the sequence, is that there is something sacred about the circus just as there is something of a show about the procession.

The main theme of the film is also touched with the mystical. It is a tune that Gelsomina already knows before she meets il Matto: she sings a snatch of it and tells Zampanò they heard it from a window one night in the rain and how beautiful it is. However it is il Matto who teaches her to play it. She is enchanted when she hears him playing it in the early morning on a miniature violin; it occurs non-diegetically during his talk inspiring a sense of self-worth in her; thereafter she plays it on the trumpet (as Van Order (2009: 59) notes, with considerable, almost magical accomplishment[81]). Someone, like her not quite normal (vagabond, angel?, queer?), has to give her the gift of listening to and playing her own music. The music soars, notably on the run-up to the high opening note each time the melody is repeated, suggestive of spiritual reaching and salvation.

La strada: il Matto (Richard Basehart) plays the theme on miniature violin that Gelsomina (Giulietta Masina) learns to play on trumpet

Much depends on the ability to hear the music of salvation, to respond wholeheartedly to magic, and this can be in any kind of music. The tune that 'saves' Cabiria is a Neapolitan song, one that she knew casually before (she sings a snatch of it in the opening sequence). Yet we have already seen her capacity to respond. In the stuck-up Kit Kat club to which film star Alberto takes her, the band plays a mambo (in fact the prostitutes' motif in the film); people dance stiffly and the band leader occasionally delivers phrases like 'O che mambo!' flatly and stone-facedly. Cabiria though goes straight for the spirit of the music, improvising movements that are more vaudeville than mambo. It is naff, yet there is an energy and glee to it that the other clients clearly envy.

Something similar occurs in the scene in *Lo sceicco bianco* when Wanda first meets 'The White Sheikh', Fernando. They are in the beachside bar

Le notti di Cabiria: Cabiria
(Giulietta Masina) mambos

near where the photo-romance shoot is taking place; as if out of the blue, a car drives up with the radio playing and stops, but the driver leaves the radio on and the door open. It plays a romantic tune and seems to seal the magic of the moment for Wanda, as Fernando asks her to dance and the customers, in a series of shots, look on in delight. The music, there arbitrarily, nonetheless catches the mood that both Wanda and Fernando want, she because he is her dream man, he because he is happy to play that role. It is conventional popular music, part of the film's account of the constructedness of romance and the gullibility of the audience for it, but also, in the suddenness of its appearance and the delight on the other customers' faces, magical.

There is even something of this in the use of Perez Prado's 'Patricia' in *La dolce vita*. It is first heard on the juke box in the seaside trattoria where Marcello is trying to write his book. He asks the young waitress, Paola, to turn it off, which she does, but she goes on la-la-ing it. Finally, he gives up trying to write and as soon as she realises this, she asks him if it is OK to put 'Patricia' back on, and the scene ends with it blaring away again. Marcello tells Paola that she reminds him of an angel in an Umbrian church and the sense of this is present in her reappearance at the end of the film, signalling across an inlet of water against the roar of the surf, trying but unable to make contact with him, he now irremediably lost to the dolce vita. Yet this angel figure loves 'Patricia', responds to its raucous fun and vigour.

'Patricia' figures again later, first in a toned-down version at the Cha Cha club (alongside an equally weakened 'Entry of the Gladiators'), then in the Prado version, for Nadia's striptease. Perhaps the latter suggests the degradation of Prado's music in this tawdry striptease performed by the newly divorced Nadia, played by has-been starlet Nadia Gray. Yet Nadia/Nadia Gray performs it with apparent good humour and aplomb and no sense of embarrassment, and this version of 'Patricia' contrasts with the treatment later in the party of its original B-side, 'Why Wait', which has all of Prado's thrilling angularity and brassiness ironed out. Perhaps even at the nadir of

La dolce vita: Nadia's (Nadia Gray) striptease

La dolce vita's enervation, some can still respond to music's offering of magic.

In *8½*, there is a night club mind-reading act. Guido takes the master of ceremonies, Maurice, aside and asks him what the trick is; 'There is some trick in it', says Maurice, 'but sometimes also something real.' Guido asks if he can try it and Maurice's assistant, Maya, the mind reader, correctly guesses that Guido is thinking the apparent nonsense phrase 'Asa Nisi Masa'. This introduces a sequence of children being put to bed, which explains the phrase as a childhood incantation that, as one of the boys says, will bring to life 'the woman in the picture' who will give the children treasure. The likelihood of Maya guessing correctly what is in Guido's mind is so remote as to be impossible, suggesting that she really does read it. Moreover, it is magic heralding magic: what she reads is itself a magic incantation; the phrase is made up by a standard childhood game of adding syllables to words, in this case 'Anima', that is, spirit, mind, soul. The music accompanying Maurice is the passerella, the first time it is heard in the film, which is the signature tune of the final sequence. The latter is perhaps a vision, Guido embracing all those he has known, perhaps the apotheosis of his 'anima'; but it is also, of course, only a vision, indeed only a film, a conjured moment. The magic of the sequence – if it works for you – is Guido's/Fellini's/Rota's/our capacity to respond to the magic of film and music, even as we know there is something of the trick about it, to be open to the something real within it.

> [Nino always] arrived at the end, when the stress of shooting, editing and dubbing was at its height, but he arrived, stress vanished and everything became a party, the film entered a light, serene, fantastical phase, in an atmosphere from which it gained as it were a new life.
>
>   Federico Fellini[82]

Notes

CHAPTER 1

1. Mario Soldati (1986: 54) claims that the music was developed from the main theme of his own film *Daniele Cortis* (1947). Soldati is not making any criticism nor any claim to prior rights on his, Soldati's, part. However, I am not convinced about this even though Soldati's description of the similar feeling of the two motifs is felicitous in suggesting that they evoke a 'nostalgia for a life never lived'.
2. Rota also re-used it as part of the grotesque music for the court of Wittenberg in *Il Casanova di Federico Fellini* (1976).
3. *Sleuth* was the substitute when *The Godfather* was disqualified.
4. Namely that it had only been shown for the first time in Los Angeles in 1972 (Wiley and Bona, 1986: 779)
5. '… si prenda un'idea già sfruttata e la si trasformi, la si rielabori'. Rota in an interview with Francesco Canessa, in Lombardi, 2000: 174.
6. Review in *La Notte* (Milan) 15 March 1958, reproduced in Fava, 2003: 119.
7. Martino does not sing 'Speak Softly Love' in this or the subsequent films (and nor does anyone else) and the song he does sing, 'I Have But One Heart', is not by Rota. There is, however, a further thread of imitation. Martino was, like his character Johnny Fontane, a successful crooner, but the latter has always been supposed to be based on Frank Sinatra, himself in turn a model, as singer, for Martino. Vito's help for Johnny occasions one of the most famous scenes (the horse's head) and phrases ('to make someone an offer he can't refuse') in the film. Sinatra seems never to have recorded or performed 'Speak Softly Love'.
8. The others were Ennio Flaiano and Tullio Pinelli, among the most important scriptwriters in Italian film, and also, uncredited, Eduardo De Filippo himself.
9. He had made *Dementia 13* (1963) under a pseudonym for Roger Corman, a crypto-new wave comedy *You're A Big Boy Now* (1966) and a flop musical *Finian's Rainbow* (1968). If the first two promised a certain energy and contemporaneity, *Finian's Rainbow*, though full of lovely things, did not suggest he should be trusted with a mega-budget production like *The Godfather*.
10. There is also diegetically a use of melodies from *La traviata* (Verdi) and *La sonnambula* (Bellini), as well as a popular patriotic song 'La bella Gigogin'.
11. This itself re-uses a cadence from the second movement of Rota's Second Symphony 1939.
12. It was first performed in concert in 1972, with the sub-title *Per il Gattopardo* (Miceli, 1982: 300).
13. See Tomasi, 1963.
14. On Verdi and the Risorgimento, see Parker, 2000, and Rostagno, 2000.
15. Cf. Dyer, 2006: 32–4.
16. The Choir of the Society of Trentine Alpinists (i.e., in the region of Trento, principal city of the North East Italian Alps).
17. See Ernesta Rota's diary entry for 24 August 1948 in Lombardi, 2000: 43.

18. Nino Rota in correspondence reproduced in Ibid.: 61.
19. Anonymous, 'Nothing Like It in Italy: Nino Rota and Our Film Music', *The Cinema*, 6 October 1948, reproduced in Ibid.: 44–7.
20. Ibid.: 47.
21. As it happens, in 1958 Rota was called in in a case made against Domenico Modugno that his massive hit 'Nel blu dipinto di blu' (better known as 'Volare') was a plagiarism; Rota showed through detailed analysis that this was not so (De Santi, 1992: 99).
22. Probably in origin an Irish jig, it seems to have been first arranged in an English context by Henry Purcell in 1689. It is familiar now for its use from 1955 until recently as the signature tune of the BBC World Service.

CHAPTER 2

1. 'Quando sono al pianoforte, quando cerco una musica, può essere che tendenzialmente io sia felice; ma come uomo, come si fa a essere felici in mezzo all'infelicità degli altri? … Il sentimento che anima la mia musica è teso a far sì che coloro che la ascoltano possano avere almeno un momento di serenità.' Quoted in De Santi, 1992: 8.
2. Counting the two episodes each in *Cento anni d'amore* and *Boccaccio '70* as separate films and the television serials each as one, and also including films for which he arranged the music but not those which used his music posthumously.
3. See appendix for complete filmography, but Borin, 1999, for the most detailed version of this. See De Santi, 1983, for catalogue of other musical works.
4. 'Nino è un amico angelico fatto da musica, assistito dell'angelo della musica che gli sta sempre accanto, attorno con dalle grandi alone.' In Pier Marco De Santi (ed.), *Omaggio a Nino Rota*, Pisa: Comune di Pistoia, 1981: 22 (taken from a roundtable discussion in Martinafranca of Rota's work shortly after his death). Quoted here from extract in Fabris, 1987: 55.
5. There is no biography of Rota, but the most detailed account can be found in De Santi, 1983. Unless otherwise indicated, factual details in this chapter are taken from this.
6. See Miceli, 1982: 297, and Sciannanemo, 2005: 4.
7. 'Una chicca dei salotti milanesi.' Suso Cecchi D'Amico, quoted in Pellicciotti, 1998.
8. Witnessed by Fedele D'Amico and recounted in Fabris, 1987: 105.
9. Rota's recollection in an interview, quoted in De Santi, 1992: 54.
10. 'Mi ricordo che una volta arrivò in casa mia una telefonata con la quale Luigi Zampa chiedeva a Nino se avesse fatto la muscia di un suo film. Nino se ne era completamente dimenticato. Anzi, in quel momento era impegnato a scrivere musica per un'altra colonna sonora. Ma non ebbe il coraggio didire a Zampa che non l'aveva fatta e Zampa lo invitò ad andare a Cinecittà all'una e mezza per fargli ascoltare la musica. Era mezzogiorno. Nino fece colazione e partì per Cinecittà. Si mise al pianoforte e, stabiliti i tempi di durata della musica sequenza per sequenza, suonò tutta la musica di quel film. … Mi ricordo una sera in cui Visconti pregò Nino di eseguire "E lucean le stelle" secondo gli stili dei grandi musicisti, da Bach a Debussy.' In Fabris, 1987: 105–6; see also Cecchi D'Amico, 1996: 172.
11. Aria from *Tosca* (Puccini, 1900).
12. A musical form in which one melody is repeated by different voices or instruments coming in successively before those already performing have completed the melody.
13. '… di improvvisare la composizione a sei voci, secondo il brano original. Senza scomporsi, egli sedette al piano e suonò tranquillamente tutte e sei le voci!'
14. Gianandrea Gavazzeni, the conductor of its first performance (Parma, 1942), apparently declared himself perplexed but admiring of this 'perfect nineteenth century opera' (Cecchi D'Amico, 1996: 171).
15. Produced by Franco Zeffirelli at the Old Vic in London 1960, the music re-used for his film version.

16. Visconti's production of Goldoni's play, Venice and Paris, 1958.

17. Film and opera.

18. 'La mia musica appare facile, e non sono pochi coloro che dicono che sembra sempre si "saperla tutta"; ma poi, alla fine, nessuno ricorda più nulla perché le note gli sono scomporse davanti.' Quoted in Malorgio, 2001: 100.

19. See 'Re-uses' for a listing.

20. '… sono assolutamente convinto che il plagio in musica non esiste. È materiale musicale a disposizione: se uno lo prende e lo fa suo, resta la gratitudine che il nuovo autore deve avere per il vecchio, ma che cosa più bello fra noi nella musica?' Nino Rota in an uncredited interview, quoted (103) from sleeve notes by Lorenzo Arruga to record *Omaggio a Nino Rota* n.d., reprinted in Fabris, 1987: 103–4.

21. Ibid.: 78.

22. Igor Stravinsky, already an old friend, had dedicated a manuscript copy of this to Rota at a performance of it in Turin. The music for the typhoon in *This Angry Age* draws on Stravinsky's *Le Sacre du printemps/The Rite of Spring*, 1913 (perhaps influenced by Disney's revisioning of this in relation to primeval forces of nature in *Fantasia*, 1940); on the soundtrack LP this section is entitled 'Hommage à Igor'.

23. Quoted (without source) in Catucci, 1996: 14.

24. This also references French neo-classicism more generally; see Giannelli, 1987: 71.

25. '… con la chiarezza costruttiva e la trasparenza del tessuto polifonico del fondatore del neoclassicismo italiano'.

26. Rota's music was also used for ballets made after his death: *Amarcord* (choreography: Luciano Cannito; Naples 1995) and *Filumena Marturano* (Beppe Menegatti; Cagliari 2000), and a performance piece, *La strada* (Neil Armfield and Kate Champion; London 2000).

27. Choreography Mario Pistoni; Milan 1967.

28. 'In essa, il compositore rivela pienamente una tecnica e una conoscenza dello strumento e della tastiera (suonava egli stesso il pianoforte con estrema facilità), paragonabili per la stupenda intuizione delle diverse sonorità e per l'equilibrio del linguaggio, a quella di Chopin e di Ravel.' Quoted in De Santi, 1983: 55.

29. 'In realtà questo musicista è sempre "doppio", impastato di allegria e tristezza, ironia e patetismo, grande musica e piccolo mestiere; è disponibile e refrattorio, modesto e conoscio di sé, realista e nutrito di belle illusioni. È un finto semplice.' Comuzio, 1986a: 34.

30. See my accounts of the waltzes for *The Godfather* and *Vita da cani*.

31. From Enrico Cavallotti, 'Inattualità di Nino Rota', *Il tempo* 2 August 1978: 18, reprinted in Fabris, 1987: 65–7.

32. '… io non temo di essere melodico e orrechiabile … che la musica sia subito percepibile; abbia cioè i canoni dell'immediatezza'. From an interview in 1978 with Guido Vergani, quoted here from extract published in Fabris, 1987: 77.

33. '… arguta, ironica, subito pronta a stemperare la propria consapevolezza nella più disarmante e spiccata vena melodica'.

34. www.mfiles.co.uk/composers/Nino-Rota.htm

35. Quoted in De Santi, 1992: 50–1.

36. 'Adamo non ha un passato, noi non possiamo tornare Adami, saremo dei primitivi con un passato.' Bontempelli, Massimo 'Rapporti con l'avanguardia. Postilla' in *L'avventura novecentistica*, Florence: Vallecchi, 1935, 105; quoted in Finotti, 2001: 3.

37. '… capovolgeva sistemi e metodi togliendo alla musica la possibilità di essere essa stessa un racconto, negli schemi e nelle forme tradizionali (primo tempo di sonata, adagio, scherzo, rondo, ecc.)'.

38. 'Un connubio difficile', *Rassegno musicale* 16, 2 February 1943; quoted in Calabretto, 2000: 92.

39. Co-productions were common in postwar Italian production, but I have considered 'abroad' here only those films originated and produced in countries outside Italy.
40. *War and Peace* had an American director and mainly American lead stars, but it was an Italian production, shot in Italy with an Italian crew.
41. See Lombardi, 2000: 33.
42. Ibid.: 119.
43. See De Santi, 1992: 13.
44. Arrangements co-written with the play's director and author, Eduardo De Filippo.
45. But see Calabretto, 2001, for an analysis of the ways in which Rota did manipulate Bruckner for the *Senso* soundtrack.
46. Beethoven's Sonata in A for Violin and Piano, Op. 47, 1803.
47. Information on Italian box-office success derived from Spinazzola, 1985.
48. On Morricone, see Cumbow, 1975, Frith, 1988, Morricone and Miceli, 2001.
49. Three co-directed with Steno.
50. 'Your passion for music isn't even a passion – it's a vice!' Luigi was Nino's brother, two years younger than him, who died at the age of thirty-seven in 1950. The quotation is a remembrance of Nino in an interview with Leonardo Pinzauti ('A colloquio con Nino Rota', *Nuova Rivista Musicale Italiana* 1 (1971)); quoted here from De Santi, 1992: 38.
51. 'I am a musician and only a musician'; on an audiotape interview played in the television documentary *Zwischen Kino und Konzert. Der Komponist Nino Rota* (Munich: Media Res, 1993, Vassili Silovic).
52. She also arranged for her adoption in America when her English mother abandoned her, and saw that she, along with two other unspecified persons, inherited after Nino's death (Cecchi D'Amico 1996: 173–4). There has been some speculation as to who the mother really was.
53. 'Silobarapni muemso maerepa: Icniv atoronin' (= 'Apeream os meum in parabolis: Vinci Nino Rota'). For further discussion of *Aladino* see De Santi, 1983: 140–4.
54. On the issue more generally of homosexual/gay/queer music see inter alia Brett et al., 1994, and Fuller and Whitesell, 2002.
55. 'Forse questa musica sarà "amabile", ma il film, in ogni caso, non lo sarà affatto.' In an interview with Ornella Volta, *Positif* 181, March 1977, reprinted in Comuzio and Vecchi, 1986: 80–1.
56. 'He is a young man, with a very handsome face, long hair, dressed in a golden tunic, his knees and feet bare.' (From the opera libretto, published with recording on Discantica 02/03 DDD (1995), 32.)
57. 'What have you done, Reverend? To let a half naked, indecently dressed man into your house …' (Ibid.: 33).
58. There was a BBC television adaptation in 1952, starring the young and perhaps even then evidently gay Kenneth Williams as the angel. Rota was visiting London in this period.
59. 'I see … I see … an infinite land, without space, without time, it's him, it's his country. Other worlds, other heavens, all is light.' (Opera libretto, op. cit.: 36.)
60. On the trumpet and masculinity, see Gabbard, 2008.
61. Quoted in De Santi, 1983: 145.
62. Including his writing music for children, such as *Tre liriche infantili per canto e pianoforte* (1935) and *Pezzi pianistici per bambini* (1971) and the operas *Il principe porcaro* (1926), *Lo scoiattolo in gamba* (1959) and *Aladino e la lampada magica* (1968).
63. Cf. Finotti, 2001: 11ff.
64. In an interview in the video *Nino Rota* (Rome: Istituto Luce, 2000, Mario Monicelli).
65. '… cercava di uscire da porte che non c'erano, e poteva realmente uscire anche da una finestra come una farfalla' (Fellini, 1986: 47).

66. In *Ciao Federico!* (US/Italy, 1971, Gideon Bachman).
67. '... lo spirito del film, più che la materialità della successione delle immagini'. Quoted in Saponaro, 1987: 32.
68. 'Affascinava tutti proprio per la sua estrema disponibilità e nello stesso tempo per la sua totale assenza. In qualunque ambiente e in qualunque occasione lo si incontrasse, quali che fossero o potessero essere i motivi per i quali lo si incontrava, dava sempre l'impressione che fosse capitato lì per caso, ma nello stesso tempo dava la sicurezza che si poteva contare su di lui, che poteva accompagnarti per un tratto ...' (Fellini, 1986: 47).

CHAPTER 3

1. On the notion of motif, see, inter alia, Gorbman, 1987: 26–9; Kalinak, 1992: 103–10; Larsen, 2004; London, 2000.
2. Strictly speaking the song, written by Giovanni D'Anzi and Michele Galdieri in 1941, is called 'Mattinata fiorentina' ('Morning in Florence'), but 'È primavera' ('Spring is Here') are the opening and frequently repeated words of the song. When it is sung in the film, it is often only these words that are sung, followed by la-la or whistling a snatch of the rest of the tune.
3. '... un film cinico, volutamente cinico, distaccato dalla sorte dei personaggi, alle cui spalle veramente Castellani mostra di divertirsi'.
4. '... una sfoglia leggera e soffice che si scioglie in bocca'. Luigi Chiarini in *Cinema* 33 (1950), quoted in Trasatti, 1984: 53.
5. The painting is in the Brera Gallery, Milan (though there are other versions elsewhere). It is referenced in *Senso*, in the kiss that Franz gives Livia when she agrees to give him the money to pay a doctor to say he is too sick to fight, money that she gets from the Risorgimento funds her cousin had given her for safe-keeping; in other words, here love is a betrayal of the Risorgimento, one of the many ways the film critiques the standard view of the latter.
6. See Reference section, page 69, for a discussion of this.
7. For further discussion of the Marxist schema of *Rocco*, see inter alia Nowell-Smith, 2003: 123–37, and Canova, 2000.
8. He and Nadia were lovers but broke up; now he is jealous that she and Rocco have got together and rapes her in front of Rocco.
9. '... lui mi fermava e diceva, "Questo è quello che ci vuole". E allora io elaboravo quel principio di tema: perché, con Luchino non è che ci volessero dei piccoli brandelli musicali. Ci volevano dei brani in pieno sviluppo. Quindi, non è che quella prima intuizione fosse sufficiente; ma da quella partivo.' Quoted in De Santi, 1983: 93.
10. I am always wary of making this claim, but was assured by music students attending my MA course in Music and Film at King's College London in autumn 2008 that it was so. Certainly the music sounds as if it makes that transition from sad to bright, negative to affirmative, pessimistic to optimistic, so often achieved by the shift from minor to major.
11. The family come from Lucania (Basilicata) and the words of the song are by Gian Giagni, who was born in Potenza (also Basilicata). On the other hand, De Santi (1983: 94) and Chiarelli (1997: 118) say that 'Paese mio' is based on a Pugliese lullaby and Rota had already used it for a religious procession in Puglia in the Mascagni biopic, *Melodie immortali*.
12. See Aristarco and Carancini, 1960: 57–61
13. In *The Godfather*, Sonny is lured to his death by rushing out of the house without bodyguards on receiving a phone call from his sister Connie, whose husband, Carlo, has beaten her up; Carlo, inclined to be rough anyway, has been put up to this by a rival gang, knowing that Connie will turn to Sonny and that he will act precipitately and fatally.

14. Michael visits Cuba with his brother Fredo to do a deal to control hotels and casinos there; they are thwarted by the Revolution. In Cuba, Michael realises that Fredo has betrayed him and the family to a rival gang. The Kefauver committee, 1950–1, was set up by the US senate to investigate organised crime. Michael is called before it.

15. On the established musical conventions in film for indication of place see, for instance, Gorbman, 1987: 83, and Brownrigg, 2003: 30; also Brownrigg, 2003, more generally and Scheurer, 2007, for generic music cues in film.

16. For a fuller account of Rota's use of citation see Mangini, 2001.

17. 1906, Charles A. Zimmerman.

18. 'How It Rained', 1917, the signature piece of the Neapolitan café chantant star Armando Gill (1877–1945).

19. 1932, Marf and Vittorio Mascheroni.

20. 1940, Mario Panzeri, Nino Rastelli and Gorni Kramer.

21. '… serpeggia nella descrizione dell'ambiente rurale ma assume anche valore di definizione sociologica'. See also Comuzio, 1979: 67 and 1986a: 35–6.

22. Wilfred Josephs is credited as music consultant. According to Miceli (1982: 300), the musical elements are all to be found on the LP *Military Fanfares, Marches and Choruses from the Time of Napoleon*.

23. 'Des pas sur la neige', *Préludes* Book 1, Number 6.

24. This connection is indicated by De Santi (1983: 64). The opera was first performed in 1955, the year before the film appeared.

25. Beginning with *Cronaca di un amore* (1950); he also composed for *Hiroshima mon amour* (1959).

26. The piano part perhaps evokes the style of Rinaldi (1840–1895), who was known in Germany as 'the Italian Chopin'. This already gives the music an anachronistic flavour, in itself nothing unusual for Rota, especially in his concert music; perhaps though there is a further resonance relevant to the film. Rota pays homage to his grandfather, but the latter died before Rota was born: as I am suggesting more generally of the film, this music suggests both connection and disconnection.

27. His term in an interview quoted in De Santi, 1992: 64.

28. The film is a version of a seven-times-filmed novel, itself adapted as a highly successful stage melodrama. The most familiar film version now is probably D. W. Griffith's version, *Orphans of the Storm* (1922); the property was familiar enough in 1947 for Totò to make a spoof, *I due orfanelli* (i.e., the two male orphans).

29. I take the term 'stylized imitation' from Samuel A. Floyd's discussion of William Grant Still's *Afro-American Symphony* (1995: 109). Dunham and Still were both key players in the project of using African-American cultural elements as a basis for extended works such as symphonies and ballets. On the relation of this to pastiche, see Dyer, 2007a: 150–6.

30. Dunham did anthropological fieldwork in Haiti in the 1930s, paying particular attention to its dance traditions.

31. Mendelssohn's is from his 1842 incidental music to *A Midsummer Night's Dream*; Wagner's is from *Lohengrin*, 1850, and is better known in English as 'Here Comes the Bride'.

32. *Pavane* (Fauré) 1887, *Pavane pour une infante défunte* (Ravel) 1899.

33. Symphony No. 1, 1917.

34. These are identified in Mangini, 2001: 143.

35. Ibid.

36. Ibid.: 155.

37. 1934, Ernesto Tagliaferri and Nicola Valente.

38. 1898, Giovanni Capurro and Eduardo Di Capua.

39. *Il medico e lo stregone* (1957) has a parodic, sung, tarantella-style tune over the credits, which is then used as part of the film's making fun of backwardness and wiliness in a mountain village outside Naples.

40. On Eduardo (as he is always referred to), see, for instance, Bentley, 1954, Di Franco, 1975, Puppa, 1990: 144–52.
41. Nine if you count *Un ladro in paradiso*, based on Eduardo's 'cantata' (a playlet with songs) *De Pretore Vincenzo*, although he was not directly involved in the film.
42. *Miseria e nobiltà* is the title of a play by Scarpetta, twice filmed, and produced in a 'free adaptation' by Eduardo on stage and television.
43. 'Eyes that speak' (without talking), 1904, Rodolfo Falvo and Alfredo Falcone-Fieni.
44. 'Quanto è bravo! La canzone Napolitana – la rifà!'
45. 1880, Luigi Denza and Peppino Turco; composed on the occasion of the opening of the Vesuvius funicular and presented at the Piedigrotta Music Festival, one of the most important vehicles for the establishment of Neapolitan song.
46. 1950, Tito Manlio and Salve D'Esposito.
47. 1900, Vincenzo Russo and Eduardo Di Capua.
48. 'Domani a Eduardo il Premio Feltrinelli', *Il messagero* 17 December 1972; quoted in Di Franco, 1975: 74. ('La napoletanità di Eduardo scrittore è proiettata verso la sua italianità, anche se la scelta fra i due termini non è mai definitiva. Così la napoletanità si trasforma in una teatralità universale.')
49. '… il dialetto si stempera, si filtra, si mimetizza e si adatta alle strutture portanti del discorso alto dove però travasa carica communicativa ed immediatezza espressiva, restando … quale cadenza, ombra lessicale, patina sonora'.
50. Quarenghi, 1995: 28.
51. Ibid.: 25. The film 'suscita polemiche accesissime a Napoli, dove viene accusato di dare della città partenopea una immagine deformata e venata di razzismo, che, non a caso, piacerebbe agli spettatori del Nord perché li confermerebbe nelle loro idee preconcette nei confronti della gente del Sud'.
52. A form of boisterous Italian Renaissance students' song.
53. One might also see here a vestige of the play's play-within-a-play structure, acknowledging that the whole thing is play acting.
54. On the distinction, see Gorbman, 1987: 3, 14–26, and for a critique of it see, inter alia, Kassabian, 2001, and Holbrook, 2003. Chion uses the terms 'pit music' and 'screen music' as 'terms that designate the place where each (supposedly) comes from' (1994: 80), which relates to his wider discussion of music, sound and space in film. Miceli (1982: 223–30) uses the terms 'internal' and 'external' and also 'mediated' for instances 'which at once incorporate the characteristics of the other two and negate them' (227); although I have stuck here with diegetic and non-diegetic as these are more or less standard in English-language film music analysis, Miceli's account is attractive for incorporating the mediated as a given rather than an aberration.
55. Cf. Stilwell, 2007.
56. c.1927, Paolo Citarella, possibly based on a song by Rossini, itself possibly based on an anonymous Neapolitan tarantella. (Cf. http://www.bobshannon.com/stories/lazymaryback.html)
57. Gorbman draws here on Chion, 1985: 125.
58. The bersaglieri are an elite infantry brigade, whose fanfare is one of the most familiar of all Italian military refrains.
59. In fact composed by Henry Mancini, whom Paramount had wanted to do the whole score.
60. See also the discussion of motifs in *Zazà*, pp. 46–7.
61. Many of the points in this paragraph derive from the discussion of the sequence with my 2008–9 MA Music and Film group at King's College London.
62. On instrumentation in *Romeo and Juliet*, see Rothwell, 1977.
63. See Gorbman, 1987: 76.
64. 1938, Paolo Marchetti and Umberto Bertini; in the credits it is named as 'Magdalena'.

65. It is also the waltz discussed in Chapter 1.
66. Michel Chion, 2003: 411–2, discusses the potential 'acousmatic' quality of off-screen music, that is, the uncertainty about where it is coming from that may be consequent on one's not seeing its source. This facilitates the plausibility of the sense of pervasiveness explored here.
67. '… nei film di fare una musica … che sia a sé stante come musica, che si affianchi al film, non che si sottometta, che vi si adegui solo materialement'. From an unpublished interview with Guido Vergani, quoted in De Santi, 1992: 46.
68. For analyses of his work, see Gorbman, 1987: 70–99, and Kalinak, 1992: 113–34.
69. In Lombardi, 2000: passim.
70. Another of Gorbman's rules for underscoring (1987: 76–7).
71. FS [Filippo Sacchi] in *Corriere della Sera* 15 November 1933, quoted in Savio, 1975: 364.
72. Most readings of the disquiet see her as a figure of sexuality, bringing out perhaps the ambiguity in Mario's befriending of Natalia, or emphasising the difference between sex and love (cf. Pravadelli, 2000b: 164; Bacon, 1998: 201). While this is undoubtedly right, there is (not least by virtue of her being played by one of the divas of 1940s Italian cinema, Clara Calamai) something at once melancholy and hostile in the prostitute's demeanour that adds a feeling that is more than symbolic and more than just about sex.
73. She uses money from the movement entrusted to her by her cousin Roberto, a Risorgimento leader, to pay for Franz (of the occupying Austrian army) to get a doctor to say, falsely, that he is too sick to fight.
74. But for the reticence with which it is actually played, this is an example in Rota's work of what Kalinak (1992: 170) indicates was known in Hollywood as the 'theme score'.
75. Quoted in Buhler et al., 2000: 15.
76. '… il netto distacco del musicista dalla vicenda filmica, dalla storia'.
77. '… esprima sopratutto lo spirito del film più che la materialità della successione delle immagini'. In an interview with Giorgio Saponaro for the Pugliese edition of *Il Tempo*, 5 November 1967: 4, reprinted in Fabris, 1987: 31–2.
78. 'Se le dicessi in quanto tempo ho scritto la musica per … lei non ci crederebbe. … Ma lo sa in quanto tempo Mozart ha fatto *Le nozze di Figaro*?' Quoted in Miceli, 1982: 316 (he suppresses the name of the film). The answer to Rota's question is, according to the opera's librettist Lorenzo Da Ponte, six weeks, though this is widely disputed.
79. 'Rota lavorava, infatti, principalmente su appunti; il film in genere lo vedeva in moviola, dopo aver composto gran parte delle musiche, e solo per risolvere problem tecnici (durate, stacchi, orchestrazioni). Il film, tutto intero, nella sua versione definitiva, non la vedeva quasi mai, neanche dopo la sua uscita' (Lombardi, 2000: xvii).
80. See note 1.
81. Ernesta Rota noted in her diary (25 December 1945) that 'Nino wrote the score [for *Un americano in vacanza*] in three hours without a break, music which ought to have been rubbish, but which Nino made delightful and elegant: he's not capable of producing rubbish' (in Lombardi, 2000: 28). Perhaps it is these circumstances, with none of the distraction of working with the drawn-out film itself, that give the score its strong structure of repetition.
82. That is, Southern Italian but without narrower regional specificity.
83. Cf. Comuzio, 1979: 68.
84. His films include *Murder My Sweet* (1944, UK: *Farewell My Lovely*), *Crossfire* (1947), *Warlock* (1959), *A Walk on the Wild Side* (1962), *Bluebeard* (1972).
85. On neo-realism and such women stars, see Farassino, 1989.
86. Rota speaks of way that the suspense in *Plein soleil* and *Death on the Nile* is all in the images and dialogue, not in music (in De Santi, 1992: 112).

CHAPTER 4

1. Chiari: *Era lui … Sí! Sí!*, *Noi due soli*, *Accade al penitenziario*, *Gli uomini, che mascalzoni!*, *La via del successo … con le donne*, *Femmine di lusso*; De Sica: *Lo sbaglio di essere vivo*, 'Pendolin', *Il medico e lo stregone*; Fabrizi: *Vivere in pace*, *Vita da cani*, *Accade al penitenziaro*, *La via del successo … con le donne*; Fernandel: *Le boulanger de Valorgue*, *L'ennemi public no 1*, *La legge è legge*; Milo: *Fantasmi a Roma*; Peppino: *Ragazze da marito*, *Via Padova 46*, *Accade al penitenziario*, *La via del successo … con le donne*, 'Le tentazioni del Dottor Antonio'; Rascel: *Napoleone*; Scotti: *È arrivato il cavaliere*, *Vita da cani*; Sordi: *Totò e i re di Roma*, *Lo sceicco bianco*, *Via Padova 46*, *I vitelloni*, *Accade al penitenziaro*, *La bella di Roma*, *Un eroe dei nostri tempi*, *Fortunella*, *Il medico e lo stregone*, *La grande guerra*, *The Best of Enemies*, *Il maestro di Vigevano*; Taranto: *Un ladro in paradiso*, *Anni facili*, *Italia piccola*; Totò: *Totò al Giro d'Italia*, *Napoli milionaria*, *Totò e i re di Roma*, *La legge è legge*); Valeri: *Un eroe dei nostri tempi*.
2. *Come persi la guerra*, *L'eroe della strada*, *Come scopersi l'America*, *Il monello della strada* (1950), *Italia piccola* (1956).
3. 1958, Mario Monicelli; music Piero Umiliani.
4. 1963, Pietro Germi; music Carlo Rustichelli.
5. 1985, Amanzio Todine, selected, arranged and augmented by Bruno Moretti.
6. If it were being sung in English, this would go 'Yo-oh heave ho! BOMP!; Yo-oh heave ho! BOMP!' etc.
7. It was a follow-up to the previous year's highly successful comedy, *Accade al commissariato*.
8. Rota uses the same motif for Macario in the three Borghesio–Macario films he scored.
9. Chopin's *Marche funèbre*, 1837, although, like 'Here Comes the Bride', so familiar as to seem traditional and anonymous.
10. 'Finally to make this story truly authentic we have chosen for the role of the American – .'
11. The Workers' Radio. I am grateful to Giorgio Marini for identifying this connection.
12. That is, the European Recovery Plan, aka the Marshall Plan, the largely American-financed plan for postwar European recovery.
13. 'The Little Parade' by Gerard Matos Rodriguez, Uruguay 1917.
14. It is very reminiscent of the *Devil's Gallop* by Charles Williams, used as the theme tune for the popular British radio thriller series *Dick Barton Special Agent*, running from 1946–51. Given that Rota spent some time in the UK in this period and that *Quel bandito* is a British co-production, the similarity may not be coincidental.
15. In fact the main actor, Robert Beatty, who plays the dual roles of Antonio and Leo, was Canadian, but most of his career as an actor was in Britain. Tamara Lees was of mixed English and Russian parentage; uniquely among the main cast, her career was in Italian cinema.
16. 'rasoiate negli archi' (Comuzio, 1986b: 121).
17. 'Lily Marlene' (Hans Leip and Norbert Schulze, 1938) is unusual in being a song adopted by both Allied and Axis forces. Perhaps the point here is that it is so strongly associated with first the Nazis then the equivocally welcomed Allies, whereas Felice's experience throughout the film has been of the perils of any kind of alignment.
18. There are, in fact, shots of the examination board listening to the monologue cut into it at various points, but the quality of the sound recording and the cutting from and back to him in mid-flow indicates a single take.
19. The words themselves have their comic potential, as when he says: 'To study and learn the things you have asked me, you need people with no problems, children, lunatics, the rich.'
20. Cf. Caldiron, 1980: 125.
21. She is seen doing this routine towards the end of *Luci del varietà* and she reprised it often on radio and occasionally later on television.

CHAPTER 5

1. *Il giorno* 11 April 1979; article (by Lorenzo Arruga) reprinted in Comuzio and Vecchi, 1986: 81–3.
2. 24 April 2004, produced by Hal Willner.
3. Male queers generally form part of the gallery of grotesques in his films: the camp chorus boy in *Luci del varietà* (1950), the has-been actor in *I vitelloni*, the drag queens and camp hangers-on in *La dolce vita*, the paedophilic teacher in *Amarcord*, the Count Du Bois and his 'mantis' opera in *Il Casanova di Federico Fellini*, the exquisite young man in *E la nave va* (1983). However, the treatment of the relations between Encolpio, Ascilto and Gitone in *Satyricon* and of the sweet comedian in *E la nave va* are much more complex and tender. There is no such balancing film to set against the ugly, joyless, man-hating lesbians of *La città delle donne* (1980).
4. *Luci del varietà* (1950) was co-directed with Alberto Lattuada.
5. Interview on television programme *Voi ed io*, part 9; quoted in De Santi, 1983: 74.
6. 'I don't know anything about music' ('Fellini parla del suo mestiere di regista', *Bianco e Nero* XIX: 5 (1958); quoted here from Miceli, 1982: 263); 'The fact is that music depresses me, fills me with remorse; it's like an admonishing voice that upsets you because it reminds you of a dimension of harmony, peace, completeness from which you are excluded, exiled' (Fellini, 1986: 50).
7. Van Order draws on and synthesises from Alpert, 1986, Borin, 1999, Boyer, 1978, Cardullo, 2006, Kezich, 2006, Lombardi, 2000, Miceli, 1982, and Rizzardi, 2001, including interview material with both Rota and Fellini contained in these.
8. 'intuizioni che soltanto un musicista … avrebbe potuto raggiungere, ma che Fellini ottiene puramente col suo istinto'. Quoted in Miceli, 1982: 263.
9. Cf. the barber composer in *Marito e moglie*.
10. 1955, Renato Carosone and Gigi Pisano.
11. 1952, José Galhardo and Raúl Ferrão; Amalia Rodrigues' version was a big hit in Italy.
12. 1954, Renato Rascel.
13. 1955, Lelio Luttazi, Giulio Scarmicci and Renzo Tarabusio, a hit for Jula de Palma and the basis of an eponymous film (1957, Antonio Pietrangeli).
14. So called from the lyrics composed for it by Antonio Amurri but in the end never used (Morelli, 2001b: 383).
15. 'Vjezd gladiátorů', 1897, Julius Fučík.
16. 1925, Gus Kahn and Walter Donaldson.
17. 1932, Harold Arlen and Ted Koehler; it was a hit in Italy in the 1930s in various American versions, including Ethel Waters, Ted Lewis and Guy Lombardo.
18. The father is played by Annibale Ninchi, a silent film star as well as the eponymous *Scipione l'Africano* (Scipio the African) (1937), the biggest and most explicitly fascist spectacular of the 1930s, adding a further layer of reference.
19. Miceli refers here to his distinction between internal, external and mediated levels; see p. 189, n. 54.
20. '… la musica non si limita ad utilizzare a fondo le possibilità offerte dai tre "livelli" ma li mescola, ora con ambiguità prestabilita, ora in maniera palese, finché li sintetizza nel finale in un intervento che ha il potere di annullare ogni classificazione' (Miceli, 1982: 286).
21. Cf. De Santi, 1978.
22. See Stoddart, 2002.
23. 1955, Renato Rascel, Pietro Garinei and Sandro Giovannini.
24. An amalgam of the bersaglieri fanfare and the opening phrase of the motif 'La dolce vita'.
25. Sousa's 1896 march is only played in circuses to signal fire or other disasters. See en.wikipedia.org/wiki/Circus_music (accessed 24 June 2009).
26. 1953, Carl Sigman and Robert Maxwell.

27. This is a standard Italian term for nursery rhyme, though in this instance the tune is Rota's.
28. That is, B♭-A-C-B♯.
29. Rota in an interview included in De Santi, 1978: 114.
30. See Perugini, 2009: 66–8, for a more detailed analysis.
31. Ibid.: 68–70.
32. 'diventa, per Casanova, una cullante ninna-nanna cantata dalla Grande Madre e sulla quale può, finalmente, addormentarsi' (Ibid.: 65–6).
33. 'two series of simple intervals of a fifth, repeated obsessively, over which alternate two thematic elements: one with a melody harmonised in thirds over a rocking barcarolle rhythm, the second an ascending and descending step movement based on a single chromatic relation' (Ibid.: 30–1).
34. See ibid.: 73ff.
35. See Burke, 1989, 1996, for a discussion of Fellini's work in relation to modernist and postmodernist thought.
36. See Miceli, 1982, and Van Order, 2009, for discussion of motifs in the films up to *8½*; Gorbman, 1978, on those in *Le notti di Cabiria*; Sciannameo, 2005, on *Amarcord* and Perugini on *Il Casanova di Federico Fellini*.
37. 1931, Walter Samuels and Leonard Whitcup.
38. On this sequence, cf. Dyer, 2010.
39. The Fratellini brothers (their act recreated for the film) play Schubert's Moment musical no. 3 at the piano, as do the singing teachers, the Rubetti brothers, on glasses in the kitchen of the ship in *E la nave va*, although this, of course, was made after Rota's death.
40. Neapolitan song, 1940, Gigi Pisano and Giuseppe Cioffi, made famous at the Teatro Bellini by Nino Taranto.
41. 1927, Hoagy Carmichael.
42. Italian title of 'Modřanská Polka' ('The Beer Barrel Polka'), 1927, Jaromí Vejvoda, known in English as 'Roll Out the Barrel'.
43. Italian version of 'Dein ist mein ganzes Herz' (English 'You Are My Heart's Delight'), by Franz Lehár (from *Das Land des Lächelns*, 1929), sung in the variety show by the soubrette 'Loredana Fiorini'.
44. 1937, Rudolf Friml , Herbert Stothart, Robert Wright, George Forrest.
45. One of the most famous Roman stornelli (traditional popular songs).
46. 'Quando arriva il momento di fare la musica vera, di incidere la colonna sonora, mi trovo davanti a questo problema: dover rinunciare alle musiche che ho scelto. E qui interviene l'aspetto proprio angelico, voglio dire, della natura di Nino, per cui invece di trovarmelo contro, Nino dice subito, "Oh, ma le musiche che hai scelto van benissimo, non c'è altro da fare, io lascerei queste, non riuscirei a far niente di meglio". Naturalmente questo atteggiamento così arrendevole mi smonta. Mentre dice così, comincia a giocherellare con le dita sul pianoforte, tirando fuori dei motivetto come distratti, come se veramente non stesse applicandosi.' Quoted from a class with students at the Centro Sperimentale di Cinematografia in Comuzio, 1986a: 27.
47. 'Mentre Nino diceva di lasciarla, perché anche a lui sembrava che andasse bene, mette le sue manine sul pianoforte e comincia a suonare un'altra marcetta: che, alla fine, mi seduce, mi commuove, mi esalta, mi incanta molto di più della vecchia marcetta traumatizzante dei gladiatori che, regolarmente, viene sostituita con le marcetta di Nino, molto più affascinanti e pertinenti.' Ibid.: 31.
48. Quoted from Van Order 2009: 245 (his translation). Colón is referring specifically to *Lo sceicco bianco*. I demur at 'cruel'.
49. This led to Fellini breaking with Catozzo, one of his closest collaborators (De Santi, 1978: 104–5, 1992: 92).
50. Quoted in De Santi, 1978: 104–5.
51. 'Je cherche après Titine', 1917, Léo Danideiff.

52. Based on a traditional Portuguese dance of this name, which formed the basis for innumerable works from the sixteenth to the eighteenth centuries and even beyond (e.g., Liszt: *Rhapsodie espagnole*, 1897; Rachmaninov: *Variations on a Theme of Corelli*, 1931).
53. *The Threepenny Opera* (1928).
54. See correspondence in Lombardi, 2000: 53–5. On the validity of the accusation as well as the use of the motif in the film, see, in addition to Van Order, Morelli, 2001b: 393–422. *Der Dreigroschenoper* was itself based on John Gay's *The Beggar's Opera* (1728), which used entirely pre-existing tunes.
55. 1924, 'Pines near a Catacomb', *The Pines of Rome*.
56. Harry Warren (music). Italian words by Alfredo Brecchi, a hit for Barbara Monis in 1940. Despite the new lyrics, the English title was retained.
57. 'Our love was so sad and brief/Like a flower/That fades.'
58. 1932, F. D. Marchetti.
59. 'The effect was as far as possible from the pomp of the peplums, since Fellini demanded that the music have no conventional emotional associations of any sort' (Baxter, 1993: 252).
60. 'sonorità indistinte, filamenti indefiniti, inquietanti sottolineature, ottenute sopratutto da vibrazioni sotterranee, tocchi leggeri, vocalizzi ossessivi, fasci di suoni metallici, ecc'.
61. Cf. Curchod, 1984: 32. My understanding of the film, and many of the observations in this paragraph, derive especially from this article.
62. In this respect as in many others the film is in fact faithful to Petronius' text as it survives (Ibid.: 30–1).
63. For discussion of the title, see Gaudenzi, 2002, Gianetti, 1976, and Tassone, 1978.
64. 'memoria corale cantata a voce spiegata in una sintesi di reminiscenze, di fantasie, di sogni e di esperienze attuali'. Quoted, without source, in Verdone, 1994: 91.
65. A fascist anthem; 1935, Mario Ruccione and Renato Micali.
66. 1919, Giacomo Puccini and Fausto Salvatore, and appropriated by the fascists. See Sciannameo, 2005: 64.
67. 1888 (music), Pierre de Geyter; Italian words 1901, E. Bergeret.
68. See Sciannameo, 2005: 64–5, for a fuller account of this sequence.
69. 1929, Ernesto Lecuona.
70. 1920, Mario Robianco and Ennio Neri, a hit for the Italian singer Anna Fouguez (Sciannameo, 2005: 68).
71. 1919, Robert Stolz (Italian lyrics by Riccardo Rossi); its use here emphasises the element of Orientalist fantasy in the presentation of this sequence. The Italian sheet music describes it as a canzone orientale and foxtrot; it had been a hit in the period for major café chantant stars such as Anna Fouguez and Gino Franzi. Thus it was already old music by the putative time of film, the mid-1930s, but plausible as already-dated music played in a provincial Grand Hotel. It also contributes to the palimpsest quality of the film: not only a 1919 song being played in the 1930s, it had also become a hit again in the 1960s, notably as sung by Milva, a version more readily available to the memories of contemporary viewers of the film. (The song and tune is better known in English as 'Romeo', a hit for Petula Clark in 1961.)
72. Opening line of the Italian version of 'Let's Face the Music and Dance', written by Irving Berlin for the Astaire-Rogers film *Follow the Fleet* (1936), a poster for which (with the title *Danzare con te*) is seen earlier in the film outside the local cinema.
73. Traditional Mexican tune, made famous with words by Domenico Savino in the Hollywood film *Viva Villa!* (1934).
74. 1932, by (and performed by) Pippo Barzizza, Don Caslar and Michele Galdieri, an Italian number modelled on American big-band hits of the period (Borgna, 1992: 134).
75. That is, dance bands and the blind itinerant accordion player.
76. Cf. Fabe, 2004: 158–72.

77. Bruno Quaranta, 'Intervista l'amico occulto' (interview with Rol) in *La Stampa* 3 November 1993 (http://web.tiscalinet.it/pmusilli/gustavo_rol_articoli.htm, accessed 26 September 2009). An article in *La Repubblica* (19 October 2007) says that Fellini abandoned the film (already existing as graphic novel) when another magus, Arold of Turin, warned him that he would die on completing it (http://trovacinema.repubblica.it/news/dettaglio/i-viaggi-di-milo-manara-e-federico-fellini/334871, accessed 26 September 2009).

78. See Scardicchio, 2001; note also *Rabelaisiana*, 1977, using texts by the notably pagan monk Rabelais (De Santi, 1983: 167).

79. Cf. Brown, 1994: 221, for further discussion.

80. Albeit in relation to a different instrument, this recalls the reverend Hilyer's ecstatic vision on hearing the angel's trumpet in *La visita meravigliosa*.

81. He quotes Solmi, 1962: 153, in this connection.

82. 'Arrivava alla fine, quando lo stress per le riprese, il montaggio, il doppiaggio era al massimo ma come arrivava lo stress spariva e tutto si trasformava in una festa, il film entrava in una zona lieta, serena, fantastica, in un'atmosfera dalle quale riceveva come una nuova vita' (Fellini, 1986: 51).

Synopses

This is selective set of synopses of the less familiar films discussed dispersedly in the text, where filling in details of narrative development would clog up the development of the discussion.

ANNA
Sister Anna is a valued nurse in a Milanese hospital shortly to take her final vows as a nun. When her one-time fiancé Andrea is brought in as a result of an accident, she recalls the past. A night-club singer, she was engaged to Andrea but also involved in a masochistic relationship with the club's barman, Vittorio. On the eve of her wedding, staying at Andrea's country home, Vittorio came to confront her; in the ensuing struggle, Andrea killed Vittorio. This is why Anna decided to become a nun. When Andrea recovers he asks her to come back to him. She wavers but in the end decides to go through with her vows.

ANNI FACILI
Luigi De Francesco is a somewhat radical, incorrupt secondary school teacher from Rome in Palermo. He is transferred back to Rome, much to his alarm given the cost of living in the city, but to the delight of his wife and daughter. To make ends meet, he agrees to take on the task of securing from the commissar Lario a patent for the hormone-boosting drug Virilon. This involves endless, tedious and fruitless visits from official to official and in the end Lario accepts a bribe for the patent from a fellow Sicilian. Meanwhile, after much pressure, Luigi agrees to take a bribe to pass a dim-witted pupil in his exams. Both Luigi and Lario are found out, but while the first is sent to prison, the second is merely transferred to a similar job in Milan.

APPASSIONATAMENTE
The aristocratic Elena, in love with a poor doctor, Carlo, agrees to marry the rising engineer Andrea to save the family from further financial problems. On their wedding night he realises that she has not married for love. The marriage is cold but begins to thaw as Elena comes to appreciate his qualities. She arranges a ball to celebrate the opening of Andrea's mines and they dance a waltz that seems to bring them together at last. However, two of the servants, Paola and Antonio, jealous of what they see as Elena's usurpation of their previous power, find an amorous letter from Carlo to Elena and, later in the course of the ball, show it to Andrea, who rejects further advances from Elena. When he is wounded in a disaster in the mine, Elena nurses him, not knowing that the medicine she is giving him so devotedly has been poisoned by Paola. When an up-and-coming doctor is summoned to give advice, it turns out to be Carlo. Andrea's feelings for Elena have been rekindled by her loving care, but he now again thinks that she is still in love with Carlo. Distractedly she wanders from the house. Her maid Giannina tells Andrea what Elena's true feelings are for him and he pursues her in time to rescue her from being thrown over a cliff by Antonio. The couple are at last reconciled.

LA BELLA DI ROMA

Nannina, in love with the boxer Mario, wants to set up a trattoria. He gets into a brawl and is sent to prison. She gets a job in a café, where she is pursued by the owner, the ageing widower Oreste, and by one of the customers, the married Gracco. She strings them along, hoping they will invest in the trattoria and feigning not to be involved with Mario. With Nannina allowing him to have the impression she would marry him, Oreste agrees to set up the trattoria until he realises that Nannina is in love with Mario. The latter is released from prison and takes up his boxing again. Nannina still plays Gracco along; however, when his young son goes missing, he makes a vow to the Virgin that he will be faithful to his wife if the boy is found. Nannina tricks him into paying for the trattoria (to be called 'La bella di Roma') and starts to arrange her marriage to Mario. (The film is based on Carlo Goldoni's classic comedy *La locandiera*, 1751.)

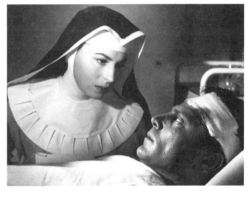

Anna: Nurse Sister Anna (Silvana Mangano) watches over her ex-fiancé Andrea (Raf Vallone); night-club singer Anna performs 'El Negro Zumbon'; Anna's sadistic lover Vittorio (Vittorio Gassman)

CAMPANE A MARTELLO

Agostina, with her friend Australia, returns from Livorno, where both had been working as prostitutes with US GIs, to Agostina's home, Ischia. Agostina had been sending her earnings for safe-keeping to the local priest, but when she gets there she discovers his successor, Don Andrea, used the money to set up an orphanage for the illegitimate daughters of GIs. Agostina wants the money so that she and Australia can go somewhere to set up in a dress-making business, although Agostina also has the possibility of going away with her old boyfriend Marco. However, because of her past, Agostina can only leave Ischia if the local marshal signs papers permitting her to do so. Australia and Don Andrea try to persuade the local council to divert money from a planned statue on honour of Napoleon to supporting the orphanage. Don Andrea eventually finds the money and, on his

death bed, gives it to Agostina. She, however, leaves the money in his room. When the local marshal discovers it, he too leaves it there, telling the local dignitaries that he is not prepared to take it and anyone who wants to can. The marshal signs the paper permitting Agostina to leave. At the jetty for the boat for the mainland, as Agostina, Australia and Marco embark, the townspeople, who have learnt of Agostina's generosity (in not taking back her money), gather and the marshal tells her that it has been decided to keep the orphanage going.

CITTÀ DI NOTTE

Fifteen-year-old Marina is a member of a fringe theatre group and enamoured of its leader, Alberto. Annoyed with her father for refusing to subsidise a tour for the group, upset to discover her best friend Lidia is carrying on with Alberto, and enraged when the latter rejects her advances, she spends the night wandering around Rome, while her father, Alberto and her brother look for her. In the end she returns home.

È PRIMAVERA

Beppe is a bread delivery boy in Florence, much given to flirting with his housewife clients. He is called up to do his military service, first in Catania in Sicily, where he marries local girl Maria Antonia, whom he meets through a fellow soldier, Cavalluccio, whose girlfriend she is when he first meets her. He is then transferred to Milan, where he marries another local girl, Lucia. After completing his military service, he gets a job (through his new mother-in-law) as a travelling salesman selling sweets, with particular responsibility for Sicily. He assumes this way he can keep his two marriages going. However, Maria Antonia travels to Milan and finds out the truth, leading to a court case for bigamy. The second marriage is annulled, Maria Antonia stays with him and Cavalluccio courts Lucia.

FILM D'AMORE E D'ANARCHIA

A peasant farmer, Tunin, sees his older, anarchist friend Michele killed by fascist militia. He travels to Rome intent on assassinating Mussolini in revenge. He stays with a fellow anarchist from his region, Salomè, who works in a casa di tolleranza (a state-regulated brothel) and falls in love with another of the girls, Tripolina. When the latter realises what he is going to do in two days' time, she arranges with the madam to spend the time left with him outside the casa (in return for his helping to carry out one of the clients who has had a heart attack, whom they abandon in the Forum). On the day of the assassination, Salomè and Tripolina decide not to wake him; when he realises he has lost his opportunity, he goes berserk, firing at random at the police who are doing a regular check of the casa. He is arrested, beaten up and killed; the authorities give out a notice saying that he committed suicide.

FILUMENA MARTURANO

Domenico Soriano and his housekeeper Filumena Marturano, an ex prostitute, have lived together for twenty years in perfect respectability, to all intents and purposes as man and wife. When Domenico decides to marry, Filumena fakes a fatal illness to inveigle him in to marrying her. When he discovers her trick, he wants to annul the marriage, but she then reveals that one of her (now grown-up) three sons from her former life is also his. She will not tell him which, and he tries to find out, but when this proves impossible he agrees to stay with her and to treat all the sons as his.

THE GLASS MOUNTAIN

Richard is an English composer, happily married to Anne. During the war, his plane is shot down over the Italian Alps and he is rescued by partisans, among whom is Alida, with whom he falls in love. She tells him of the legend of the nearby Glass Mountain, to which the ghost of a young woman lures with her song a young man to his death, after he has married another woman. After the war Richard cannot get Alida out of his mind, as Anne recognises; he returns to the village where he was rescued and composes an opera, commissioned by La Fenice opera house in Venice, based on the legend of the Glass Mountain. Despite their estrangement, Anne travels by private plane to the opening night, but the plane crashes in a storm before she can get there. On hearing the news, Richard rushes to be with her, realising she is his true love.

LA LEGGE È LEGGE
Ferdinand Pastorelli is a customs officer in the village of Assola on the French-Italian border and a proud Frenchman. He arrests the perennial smuggler Giuseppe la Paglia red-handed. However, Ferdinand then discovers that when he, Ferdinand, was born, in the village inn, the part of the inn that he was born in was at that time in Italy, so that he is technically an Italian and has no right to arrest Giuseppe. Various complications arise until Ferdinand eventually regains his French citizenship.

IL MAESTRO DI VIGEVANO
Antonio Mombelli is a secondary school teacher in Vigevano (a centre of the shoe trade), who takes pride in the status he believes his job gives him. His wife Ada, however, despises the low income it brings in. Against his wishes, she goes to work in a shoe factory. She persuades him to leave his job and to go into shoe manufacturing with her brother Carlo, although he proves himself incompetent. To set this up, she borrows money from local magnate Bugatti, with whom she develops an affair. Learning of the latter, Antonio sets out to kill them; they get away but Ada is killed in a car accident in the process. Antonio returns to his job at the school.

MOLTI SOGNI PER LE STRADE
Despite his best efforts, Paolo is unable to find employment, for which his wife Linda blames him. He is persuaded to steal a car and drive it to a dealer in the country. Linda is about to leave him but, thinking he has found a legitimate employment, decides instead to go with him and their little boy, Romoletto, on what she thinks is a country outing. The dealer, however, gets cold feet and Linda works out what the situation is. She persuades Paolo to give himself up to the police and he agrees, but then he abandons Linda and Romoletto at a fairground rather than actually go to the police. When he takes the car back to where he stole it, he finds that it has not been missed.

LA NAVE DELLE DONNE MALADETTE
On the occasion of her marriage to Manuel De Havilland, it is discovered that Isabella di Silveris previously abandoned an illegitimate child. Isabella's cousin Consuelo is persuaded to confess that the baby was hers, on the understanding that she will not have to serve any consequent sentence. However, Pedro Da Silva, the lawyer who defends her, is inexperienced and she ends up on a ship transporting women prisoners to the colonies. Also on the ship are the now married Isabella and Manuel, who owns colonial property, and, as a stowaway, Pedro. Conditions for the prisoners are bad and Consuelo becomes ill. In the infirmary she is visited by Isabella, who makes her promise not to tell the true story about the baby in return for freedom when they arrive at their destination. However, they are overheard by Pedro who denounces Isabella. Also eavesdropping is the Captain of the ship, who, though he believes in Consuelo's innocence, arrests Pedro to curry favour with Isabella, with whom he has fallen in love. He has Pedro and Consuelo whipped, but this is the trigger for a revolt of all the prisoners who overcome the guards, take over the ship and kill the Captain and crew. The ship is wrecked in a storm and only Pedro and Consuelo survive.

QUEL BANDITO SONO IO
Naples. Leo the American is the head of gang of forgers. His great rival is Faccia d'angelo (Angel Face), currently in prison, whose one-time girlfriend Rosana now lives with Leo, who has another girlfriend, Stellina.

Caradotti, a gangster from Genoa, plays Leo and Faccia d'angelo off against each other for the purchase of the control of the Northern business.

Leo discovers that he is the spitting image of Antonio Pellegrini, a meek bank clerk, married to an English woman, Dorothy, with a son, Ciocio. Stellina breaks up with Leo and goes to work as a maid in the Pellegrini household. Rosana and two of Leo's henchmen send Antonio a threatening note (intending to lure him out of the house and kidnap him, so that Leo can replace him in the home and at the bank); the Pellegrini's neighbour, the lawyer Catoni, helps them escape to his place in Sorrento, disguised as monks.

At a party in Sorrento, Faccia d'angelo, who has escaped from prison, mistakes Antonio for Leo and they fight. Catoni knocks them both out and all return to Naples, thinking that Faccia d'angelo is Leo the American and therefore they are now safe. Faccia d'angelo himself is put back in prison.

Back in Naples, Ciocio sees Leo out with Rosana and tells Dorothy that he has seen papa with another woman. The family upbraid the baffled Antonio when he comes home.

Leo now has Antonio kidnapped, luring him out of the house with a note telling him to report unexpectedly to the bank. At a night club, Dorothy (unaware of what has happened to Antonio), sees Leo and Rosana together, confirming, as she thinks, what Ciocio has told her. She confronts him and Leo, realising she has mistaken him for Antonio, pretends to be Antonio and goes home with her. Here he proceeds to throw his weight about and to kiss Dorothy in a most un-Antonio-like manner.

Stellina, realising what has happened, rescues Antonio from Leo's flat, while Leo, posing as Antonio, is robbing the bank. Antonio and Leo both return to the Pellegrini flat, but when the police arrive, alerted by Stellina, in the ensuing confusion Antonio is arrested and Leo gets away.

At the police station, all are convinced that Antonio the bank clerk *is* Leo the American. Only when Faccia d'angelo, who has again escaped from gaol, gets into a shoot-out with Leo on the streets does the mix-up become clear.

Leo is arrested. Antonio realises that Dorothy liked some aspects of Antonio's character (he has the 'Latin blood in his veins' that she says she hoped for) and begins to act more authoritatively and more passionately.

ROMA CITTÀ LIBERA

A thief enters a flat and finds a young man about to commit suicide; he dissuades him and they go out together, lifting a pearl necklace from a dead man. A young typist, desperate for money, decides to work the streets but when she is picked up cannot go through with it. A distinguished gentleman wanders the streets having lost his memory. All end up in a bar. The thief sneaks off, the distinguished gentleman recovers his memory and realises he is a member of parliament and the young man and woman strike up a relationship.

SPARA FORTE, PIÙ FORTE, NON CAPISCO

Alberto lives with his uncle Nicola, who, in despair at the world, communicates only by means of fireworks, which only Alberto can interpret. Alberto meets a scantily dressed woman, Tania, when she comes to have her fortune told at the neighbours'. Alberto's friend Aniello disappears without explanation and Alberto thinks he sees evidence that the neighbours, the Cimmaruta family, have killed him; when he goes out and hails a passing car to take him to the police station, it turns out to be Tania's, with a bloody glove in the glove compartment; but she seduces him nonetheless. Later he thinks that he merely dreamt all this. The neighbours, however, convince themselves that one of their number has killed Aniello and one by one they denounce each other to Alberto; however, they do not wish him to take their confessions to the police and so the father, Pasquale, attempts, unsuccessfully, to drown him. At last Aniello turns up. Nicola sets off a huge set of fireworks that kills him.

THIS ANGRY AGE

In Indo-China, Madame Dufresne and her two grown-up children, Suzanne and Joseph, eke out a living from land reclaimed from the sea. The children want to sell up but Madame Dufresne will not hear of it. During a damaging storm, they are helped out by Michel Forrestier, who falls in love with Suzanne. Meanwhile, Joseph goes to the city seeking work, without success, and strikes up a relationship with Claude, an older woman. The family find the money needed to build a stronger dam and Madame Dufresne dies at peace in her home.

TOTÒ AL GIRO D'ITALIA

Professor Totò falls in love with the winner of a beauty contest he is judging and proposes to her. To put him off, she says that she'll marry him if he wins the Giro d'Italia. Although he has never ridden a bike in his life, he starts to learn but is useless. When he says out loud that he'd sell his soul to the devil if he'd fix it for him to win, the devil appears and gets him to sign an agreement. Totò wins every stage of the race literally effortlessly, only to realise the implications of his deal with the devil; he does everything he can to loose, but in vain. The race nearly over, the devil goes to Totò's mother's house to await the winner and puts three dolls on the table, representing the leading contestants in the race; she slips him a sleeping pill and then knocks over the Totò doll, and the real Totò immediately falls off his bike. Happily the beauty queen has now fallen in love with him anyway.

TOTÒ E I RE DI ROMA

Ercole Pappalardo is a state archivist, married with five daughters. One day his boss, His Excellency Badalozzi, visits his home and there Ercole's parrot says the rude words about Badalozzi that it has picked up from Ercole. Badalozzi discovers that Ercole does not have an elementary school qualification, which makes him technically ineligible for his post. He is made to take an exam, which he fails. He decides to die, and from paradise whispers to his wife the winning numbers in the lottery.

ZAZÀ

A Parisian businessman, Alberto, visits the café chantant in St Etienne and falls into an affair with its star singer, Zazà. He tries to break it off but cannot. One of her fellow artistes, Cascard, aware that she is ruining her (and his) prospects, tells her that Alberto has another woman. Zazà goes to confront the latter in Paris, only to discover that it is his wife and that they have a little daughter, Totò. Back in St Etienne, Alberto tells Zazà he is going to leave his wife, but she says she wants to pursue her career and sends him back to his family.

Re-uses

This is a list of all the instances I know of in which Rota re-used his own material.

First use	Re-use	Second re-use
8½ (passerella)	clowns, I	
8½ (press conference)	fiera di Bari, La (concert overture)[8]	
americano in vacanza, Un (waltz)	Appassionatamente	gattopardo, Il
Appassionatamente (polka)	gattopardo, Il	
bidone, Il (fanfare)	Fortunella	
bidone, Il (tune at party)	notti di Cabiria, Le (prostitutes' motif)	
birichino di papà, Il	giornalino di Gian Burrasca, Il	cappello di paglia di Firenze, Il
Boccaccio '70 ('Le tentazione del Dottor Antonio')	Napoli milionaria (opera)[1]	
Casanova, di Federico Fellini, Il (male mantis theme)	Molière imaginaire, Le (Agnès' theme)	
clowns, I (mermaid, Anita Ekberg)	Amarcord (second part of Cantarel/accordionist's music)	
clowns, I (funeral march)	Godfather, The (Michael's theme)	Casanova, di Federico Fellini, Il (Wittenberg 'cantata')
Come scopersi l'America (Lisa's solo)	cappello di paglia di Firenze, Il	
Concerto soirée ('Can-can')	8½	strada, La (ballet)
Daniele Cortis	Piano Concerto in E (second movement)[2]	
delitto di Giovanni Episcopo, Il (soppy love tune)	cappello di paglia di Firenze, Il	
dolce vita, La (main title)	'Le tentazioni del Dottor Antonio'	Roma
dolce vita, La (Cadillac)	8½ (at open-air night club)	Napoli milionaria (opera) (the Americans)
dolce vita, La (Via Veneto 1)	Giulietta degli spiriti	Spara forte, più forte, non capisco[3]
dolce vita, La (Via Veneto 2)	'Toby Dammit'	Roma
dolce vita, La (canzonetta)	Napoli milionaria (opera) (the Americans)	
donna della montagna, La	Sinfonia sopra una canzone d'amore	Glass Mountain, The
È primavera (not title song)	Abdication, The	

First use	Re-use	Second re-use
Fantasmi a Roma (one of ghosts' themes)	*Film d'amore e d'anarchia* ('Canzone arrabbiata')[4]	
Fellini-Satyricon (refrain at Vernacchio's theatre and Trimalchio's feast)	*Godfather* films (main theme)	
Filumena Marturano	*Napoli milionaria* (opera)	
Fortunella (comic motif)	*Godfather, The* (love theme)	
giornalino di Gian Burrasco, Il	*Godfather II* (Kay's theme)	
Giulietta degli spiriti (circus flashback music)	*clowns, I*	
impresario delle Smirne, L'	*Godfather II*	
Ippolita gioca	*Symphony* 1[5]	
Look Homeward Angel[6]	*dolce vita, La* 'Cavallino' (Morelli Candore 422)	
Melodie immortali (theme at religious procession in Puglia)	*Rocco e i suoi fratelli* 'Paese mio'	
miserie del signor Travet, Le (jealousy motif)	*Il cappello di paglia di Firenze*	
Napoli milionaria (film)	*Napoli milionaria* (opera)[7]	
notti di Cabiria, Le	*Napoli milionaria* (opera)	
Plein soleil	*Much Ado About Nothing*[9]	*Napoli milionaria* (opera)
Rocco e i suoi fratelli	*strada, La* (ballet)	*Napoli milionaria* (opera)
Roma capomunni	*natale degli innocenti, Il*[10]	
Roma capomunni (finale)	*Amarcord* (Gradisca)	
Roma città libera (song)	*vitelloni, I* (boys' theme)	
Romeo and Juliet[11] (stage version)	*Romeo and Juliet* (film)	
Romeo and Juliet	*vita da Maria, La*[12]	
sceiccco bianco, Lo (main theme)	1. *La strada* (film)	2. *cappello di paglia di Firenze, Il* (finale)
	3. *Clowns, I*	4. *strada, La* (ballet)
sceicco bianco, Lo (Wanda's theme)	*Roma* (epic film)	
sceicco bianco, Lo	*Much Ado About Nothing*	
Sinfonia sopra una canzone d'amore	*gattopardo, Il*	
Sotto il sole di Roma	*Anni facili*	
strada, La (film)	*strada, La* (ballet)	
suo cavallo, Il[13]	*cappello di paglia di Firenze, Il*	
'Tis Pity She's a Whore[14]	*Abdication, The*	
Tre passi nel delirio 'Toby Dammit'	*Roma* (American tourist bus)	*Napoli milionaria*
Two Waltzes on the Name of Bach	*Casanova, di Federico Fellini, Il*	
vitelloni, I	*clowns, I*	
Vita da cani	*Accadde al penitenziario*	*cappello di paglia di Firenze, Il*
Waterloo	*Napoli milionaria* (opera)	
Zazà ('Zazà')	*Prova d'orchestra* (improvised by players during rehearsal)	

NOTES

1. The re-uses in *Napoli milionaria* are all noted in De Santi, 1983: 167.
2. Named 'Piccolo mondo antico', which could be used to evoke the world of *Daniele Cortis*.
3. 'G.Gr.' (Giovanni Grazzini) in the *Corriere della sera* (28 October 1966) considered the music in Alberto's dream (which is the 'Via Veneto' theme) a 'declaration' of the sequence's 'obvious derivation' from Fellini. (Quoted in Quarenghi, 1995: 159.)
4. Cf. De Santi, 1983: 98; Comuzio, 1986a: 42.
5. Cf. Gavezzani, 1987: 62.
6. Visconti's production of Kitty Frings' adaptation of Thomas Wolfe's novel, Rome, 1958.
7. Comuzio (1986a: 41) notes also the use of music from *Il bidone*, *La dolce vita*, *Fortunella*, *Le notti di Cabiria*, *8½*, *Rocco e i suoi fratelli*, *Lo sceicco bianco*, 'Le tentazioni del Dottor Antonio' and the *Concerto soirée*.
8. Composed in the same year.
9. Production by Franco Zeffirelli, London, 1965.
10. Cf. Scardicchio, 2001: 349ff.
11. Production by Franco Zeffirelli, London, 1960.
12. Scardicchio, 2001: 348–9.
13. Revue by Castellani, Longanesi and Steno, 1944.
14. Production of John Ford's play by Luchino Visconti, Paris, 1961.

Filmography

As it is now easy through the internet to check out the credits and details of films I have only given basic information here as an immediate aide mémoire. The most complete Rota filmography is Borin, 1999.

I list the title in the language of its principle country of production (and this is the title used in the text). In the second column, I give first a literal translation; then in the case of co-productions I give the title in the language of the secondary partner involved; finally, I give any title (if this differs) by which the film was distributed in the UK or USA.

8½		1963 Fellini
Abdication, The		1974 Harvey
Accadde al penitenziario	It Happened in the Prison	1955 Bianchi
Albergo Luna, Camera 34	Luna Hotel, Room 34	1947 Bragaglia
Alle origini della Mafia	How the Mafia Began	1976 (TV: 5 episodes)[1]
amante di Paride, L'	The Loves of Paris/Hélène de Troie	1953[2]
Amanti senza amore	Lovers without Love	1947 Franciolin
Amarcord		1973 Fellini
americano in vacanza, Un	An American on Holiday/US: A Yank in Rome	1945 Zampa
Amici per la pelle	Best Friends/Friends for Life	1955 Rossi
angeli del quartiere, Gli	The Neighbourhood Angels	1951 Borghesio
Anna		1951 Lattuada[3]
Anni facili	Easy Years	1953 Zampa
Appassionatamente	Passionately	1954 Gentilomo
Arrivederci Papa!	Goodbye Daddy	1948 Mastrocinque
bella di Roma, La	The Roman Beauty	1955 Comencini
Bella, non piangere!	Beautiful One, Don't Cry	1954 Carbonari
Best of Enemies, The	I due nemici	1961[4] Hamilton
bidone, Il	The Swindle	1955 Fellini
birichino di papà, Il	Daddy's Little Rascal	1942 Matarazzo
Bloc-notes di un regista	A Director's Notebook	1969 Fellini
Boccaccio '70		1962
'Il lavoro'	'The Job'	Visconti
'Le tentazioni del Dottor Antonio'	'The Temptations of Dr Antonio'	1962 Fellini

Boulanger de Valorgue, Le	The Valorgue Baker/Mi li mangio vivi	1953 Verneuil
brigante, Il	The Brigand	1961 Castellani
Campane a martello	Alarm Bells	1948 Zampa
Caro Michele	Dear Michele	1976 Monicelli
Casanova di Federico Fellini, Il		1976 Fellini[5]
Cento anni d'amore	A Hundred Years of Love	1953 De Felice
'Garibaldina'		
'Pendolin'		1953
Chi legge? Viaggio lungo le rive del Tirreno	Who Reads? Journey along the Banks of the Tirreno	1960 TV: Soldati
Città di notte	City at Night	1956 Trieste
clowns, I		1970 Fellini
Come persi la guerra	How I Lost the War	1947 Borghesio
Come scopersi l'America	How I Discovered America	1949 Borghesio
Daniele Cortis		1947 Soldati
Death on the Nile		1978 Guillermin
delitto di Giovanni Episcopo, Il	The Crime of Giovanni Episcopo	1947 Lattuada[6]
Divisione folgore	Lightning Squad	1954 Coletti
dolce vita, La		1960 Fellini
domenica della buona gente, La	The Decent Folks' Sunday	1953 Majano
donna della montagna, La	The Mountain Woman	1943 Castellani
Donne e briganti	Women and Bandits	1950 Soldati
Due mogli sono troppe	Two Wives Are Too Much	1950 Camerini
due orfanelle, Le	The Two Orphans	1954 Gentilomo
È arrivato il cavaliere	Here Come the Cavalier	1950 Steno and Monicelli
ennemi public no 1, L'	Public Enemy Number One/Il nemico pubblico N. 1	1953 Verneuil
È più facile che un cammello	It is Easier for a Camel	1950 Zampa
È primavera	Spring is Here	1949 Castellani
Era lui … sì! sì!	It Was Him … Yes! Yes!	1951 Metz and Marchesi
eroe dei nostri tempi, Un	A Hero of Our Time	1955 Monicelli
eroe della strada, L'	The Street Hero	1948 Borghesio
ettaro di cielo, Un	A Hectare of Sky	1957 Casadio
Europa di notte	Europe By Night	1959 Blasetti
'Il prestigiatore'	'The Conjuror'	
Fanciulle di lusso	Luxury Girls	1952 Vorhaus
Fantasmi a Roma	Ghosts in Rome	1961 Pietrangeli
Fellini-Satyricon		1969 Fellini
Femmine di lusso	Luxury Women	1960 Bianchi[7]
Film d'amore e d'anarchia ovvera: 'Stamattina alle 10 in Via dei Fiori nella nota casa di tolleranza …'	A Film of Love and Anarchy, or 'At 10 this morning in Via dei Fiori in the well-known casa di tolleranza …'[8]/Love and Anarchy	1973 Wertmüller
Filumena Marturano		1951 De Filippo

Fortunella		1957 De Filippo
freccia nel fianco, La	An Arrow in the Thigh	1944 Lattuada
Fuga in Francia	Flight to France	1948 Soldati
furto della Giocanda, Il	The Theft of the Mona Lisa	1978 Castellani (TV: 2 episodes)
gattopardo, Il	The Leopard[9]	1963 Visconti
giornalino di Gian Burrasca, Il	Gian Burrasca's Diary	1965 Wertmüller (TV: 8 episodes)
Giorno di nozze	Wedding Day	1942 Matarazzo
Giulietta degli spiriti	Juliet of the Spirits	1965 Fellini
Glass Mountain, The		1948 Cass
Gli italiani sono matti	The Italians They are Crazy	1958 Coletti
Godfather, The		1971 Coppola
Godfather II		1974 Coppola
grande guerra, La	The Great War	1959 Monicelli
grande speranza, La	The Great Hope / Submarine Attack	1953 Coletti
Handicap		1954 (UNICEF cartoon)
Hi wa shizumi hi wa noboro	Sunrise Sunset	1973 Kurahara
Hurricane		1979 Troell
Italia piccola	Little Italy	1956 Soldati
italiani sono matti, Gli	Italians are Mad	1957 Coletti
Jolanda la figlia del Corsaro Nero	Yolande, Daughter of the Black Corsair	1952 Soldati
ladro in paradiso, Un	A Thief in Paradise	1952 Paolella
legge è legge, La	The Law is the Law / La Loi c'est la loi	1957 Christian-Jaque
Londra chiama Polo Nord	London Calling North Pole	1955 Coletti
maestro di Vigevano, Il	The Teacher from Vigevano	1963 Petri
Mambo		1954 Rossen[10]
mano dello straniero, La	The Stranger's Hand	1953 Soldati
Marito e moglie	Husband and Wife	1952 De Filippo
medico e lo stregone, Il	The Doctor and the Warlock	1957 Monicelli
Melodie immortali	Immortal Melodies	1952 Gentilomo
meravigliose avventure di Guerin Meschino, Le	The Marvellous Adventures of Guerin Meschino	1951 Francisci
Mio figlio professore	My Son the Professor	1946 Castellani
miserie del signor Travet, Le	The Miseries of Mr Travet	1946 Soldati
Molti sogni per la strada	Many Dreams along the Way	1948 Camerini
momento più bello, Il	The Most Beautiful Moment	1956 Emmer
monello della strada, Il	The Street Rascal	1950 Borghesio
Musoduro		1953 Bennati
Napoleone		1951 Borghesio
Napoli milionaria		1949 De Filippo
nave delle donne maledette, La	The Ship of the Cursed Women	1953 Matarazzo
Noi due soli	Only We Two	1952 Metz and Marchesi
notti bianche, Le	White Nights	1957 Visconti
notti di Cabiria, Le	Nights of Cabiria	1957 Fellini

Obsession		1949 Dmytryk
Oggi, domani, dopodomani 'L'ora di punta'	Today, Tomorrow, the Day After 'Rush Hour'	1965 De Filippo
Peppino e Violetta	Never Take No for an Answer	1951 Cloche
pirati di Capri, I	The Pirates of Capri/Captain Sirocco	1948 Ulmer[11]
Plein soleil	Full Sun/Purple Noon	1959 Clément
Proibito	Forbidden	1954 Monicelli
Proibito rubare	Thieving Forbidden	1948 Comencini
Prova d'orchestra	Orchestra Rehearsal	1979 Fellini
Quei figuri di trent' anni fa	Those Characters from Thirty Years Ago	1956 De Filippo
Quel bandito sono io	I Am That Bandit/UK: Her Favourite Husband	1949 Soldati
Ragazze al mare aka *In vacanza al mare*	Girls by the Sea/Seaside Holiday	1956 Biagetti
Ragazze da marito	Marriageable Girls	1952 De Filippo
Ragazzo di borgata	Village Boy	1976[12] Paradisi
regina di Saba, La	The Queen of Sheba	1952 Francisci
Reluctant Saint, The	Cronache di un convento (A Monastery Story)	1962 Dmytryk
Riscatto	Ransom	1953 Girolami
Rocco e i suoi fratelli	Rocco and His Brothers	1960 Visconti
Roma		1972 Fellini
Roma città libera aka *La notte porta consiglio*	Rome Free City/Night Brings Advice	1946 Pagliero
Romeo and Juliet		1968 Zeffirelli
sbaglio di essere vivo, Lo	The Error of Being Alive	1945 Bragaglia
Scampolo '53		1953 Bianchi
sceicco bianco, Lo	The White Sheik	1952 Fellini
segreto di Don Giovanni, Il	The Secret of Don Juan	1947 Mastrocinque
Senso		1954 Visconti
Senza pietà	Pitiless	1947 Lattuada
sette dell'orsa maggiore, I	The Great Bear Seven	1952 Coletti
Something Money Can't Buy		1952 Jackson
Sotto dieci bandiere	Under Ten Flags	1960 Coletti
Sotto il sole di Roma	Beneath the Roman Sun	1947 Castellani
Spara forte, più forte, non capisco	Shoot Louder, Louder, I Don't Understand	1967 De Filippo
Star of India	La stella d'India	1953 Lubin
strada, La		1954 Fellini
Taming of the Shrew, The		1967 Zeffirelli
This Angry Age	Barrage contre le pacifique	1956 Clément
Totò al Giro d'Italia	Totò on the Tour of Italy	1948 Mattoli
Totò e i re di Roma	Totò and the Kings of Rome	1951 Steno and Monicelli
tre corsari, I	The Three Corsairs	1952 Soldati

Treno popolare	The People's Train	1933 Matarazzo
Tre passi nel delirio 'Toby Dammit'	Three Steps into Delirium/ Histoires extraordinaires/ Spirits of the Dead	1968 Fellini
Tutti i bambini	All the Children	1979 (UNICEF cartoon)
uomini, che mascalzoni, Gli	What Wretches Men Are!	1953 Pellegrini
uomini sono nemici, Gli	Men Are Enemies/Carrefour des passions	1947 Giannini
Valley of the Eagles, The	La valle delle aquile	1951 Young
Vanità	Vanity	1948 Pástina
Venetian Bird, The aka *The Assassin*		1952 Thomas
Vergine moderna	Modern Virgins	1954 Pagliero
via del successo con le donne, La	How to Succeed with Women	1955 Bianchi
Via Padova 46[13]		1953 Bianchi
Viaggio lungo la valle del Po alla ricerca …	Journey along the Po Valley in search of …	1957 Soldati
Vita da cane	A Dog's Life	1950 Steno and Monicelli
vitelloni, I		1953 Fellini
Vivere in pace	To Live in Peace	1947 Zampa
War and Peace		1955 Vidor
Waterloo		1970 Bondarchuk
White Corridors		1951 Jackson[14]
Zazà		1943 Castellani

NOTES

1. There is also music by Gion Marinuzzi Jr and some of the arrangements are by Ennio Morricone.
2. The only existing copy that I have been able to consult of this film, under the title *The Loves of Three Queens*, bears no resemblance to the film described in Borin (1999: 104–5) and does not have a music credit to Rota. Comuzio (1979: 71) says that Rota wrote the music for the '"mythlogical" inserts' in the film.
3. Songs by Armando Trovajoli.
4. I have viewed the Italian version.
5. Carlo Savina was involved as assistant composer and arranger for this film, not just, as in previous films, as conductor (itself, of course, a role contributing to the final character of the music); see Perugini, 2009: 11ff.
6. The credits list only Felice Lattuada as the composer, but Comuzio, 1986b: 118, for instance, notes that the music was a collaboration. One theme for soppy love is re-used in Rota's opera *Il cappello di paglia di Firenze*.
7. Music credit shared with Carlo Rustichelli and title song by Domenico Domugno. Film later rereleased, re-edited, as *Intrigo a Taormina*; this is the version I have seen.
8. 'Casa di tolleranza' means literally 'tolerate house' and referred to legally permitted brothels.
9. Not a strictly accurate translation; a gattopardo is a mythic beast.
10. According to De Santi (1983: 64), most of the score is by Angelo Lavagnino; the songs are by Bernardo Noriega and Dave Gilbert (with lyrics by Katherine Dunham). This implies that Rota's only contribution is the dance numbers.

11. I have watched the American version.
12. Themes by Rota developed by Carol Savina (Comuzio, 1986b: 162).
13. Later rerelease, re-edited to give more prominence to the Sordi character, as *Lo scocciatore* (The Pain in the Neck); this is the version I have seen.
14. The only music here is over the beginning and (very brief) end credits.

Bibliography

Alovisio, Silvio, Massimo Arvat and Claudia Gianetto (1991) '*La mano del straniero*: un "noir" a metà' in Squarotti et al. 1991: 217–23.

Alpert, Hollis (1986) *Fellini: A Life*, New York: Atheneum.

Aristarco, Guido and Gaetano Carancini (eds) (1960) *Luchino Visconti: Rocco e i suoi fratelli*, Bologna: Cappelli.

Bacon, Henry (1998) *Visconti: Explorations of Beauty and Decay*, Cambridge: Cambridge University Press.

Barzelon, Irwin (1975) *Knowing the Score: Notes on Film Music*, New York: Van Nostrand Reinhold.

Baxter, John (1993) *Fellini*, New York: St Martin's Press.

Bentley, Eric (1954) 'Son of Pulcinella' in *In Search of Theater*, London: Dennis Dobson: 281–95.

Bertetto, Paolo (2000) '*Il gattopardo*: Il simulacro e la figurazione. Strategie di messa in scena' in Pravadelli, 2000a: 175–86.

Blanchard, Gérard (1984) *Images de la musique au cinéma*, Paris: Edilig.

Bondanella, Peter (ed.) (1978) *Federico Fellini: Essays in Criticism*, Oxford: Oxford University Press.

Borgna, Gianni (1992) *Storia della canzone italiana*, Milan: Mondadori.

Borin, Fabrizio (1999) *La filmografia di Nino Rota*, Venice: Leo S. Olschki.

Boyer, Dreena (1978) *The Two Hundred Days of '8½'*, New York: Garland.

Brett, Philip, Elizabeth Wood and Gary C. Thomas (eds) (1994) *Queering the Pitch: The New Gay and Lesbian Musicology*, New York: Routledge.

Brown, Royal S. (1994) *Overtones and Undertones: Reading Film Music*, Berkeley: University of California Press.

Brownrigg, Mark (2003) 'Film Music and Film Genre', PhD thesis, University of Stirling.

Buhler, James, Caryl Flinn and David Neumeyer (eds) (2000) *Music and Cinema*, Hanover, NH: Wesleyan University Press.

Burke, Frank (1989) 'Fellini: Changing the Subject', *Film Quarterly* 43, 1: 36–48.

Burke, Frank (1996) *Fellini's Films: from Postwar to Postmodern*, New York: Dewayne.

Burke, Frank and Margaret Waller (eds) (2002) *Federico Fellini: Contemporary Perspectives*, Toronto: University of Toronto Press.

Calabretto, Roberto (2000) 'Gatti, Rota e la musica Lux. La nascita delle colonne sonore d'autore' in Alberto Farassino (ed.) *Lux Film*, Milan: Il Castoro: 89–101.

Calabretto, Roberto (2001) 'Luchino Visconti: *Senso*, musica di Nino Rota', in Rizzardi, 2001: 75–135.

Caldiron, Orio (1980) *Totò*, Rome: Gremese.

Caldiron, Orio (1999) 'Le fortune del cinema d'appendice' in Caldiron and Della Casa, 1999: 29–43.

Caldiron, Orio and Stefano Della Casa (eds) (1999) Appassionatamente: *Il mélo nel cinema italiano*, Turin: Lindau.

Cano, Cristina and Giorgio Cremonini (1990) *Cinema e musica: Il racconto per sovrapposizioni*, Florence: Vallecchi.

Canova, Gianni (2000) '*Rocco e i suoi fratelli*: Visconti e le aporie anestetiche della modernità' in Pravadelli, 2000a: 175–87.

Carcassonne, Philippe (1979) 'Nino Rota, carême-prenant', *Cinématographe* 47: 59–60.

Cardullo, Bert (ed.) (2006) *Federico Fellini: Interviews*, Jackson: University of Mississippi Press.

Carreri, Romeo (2000) 'I commenti di Nino Rota per la Lux Film' in Lombardi 2000: 38–40. (First published *Libera arte*, June–July 1947.)

Casadio, Gianfranco (1995) *Opera e cinema: La musica lirica nel cinema italiano dall'avvento del sonoro ad oggi*, Ravenna: Longo.

Catucci, Stefano (1996) *Novecento: La musica del secolo*, Rome: L'Unità Magazine.

Cecchi D'Amico, Suso (ed.) (1963) *Il film 'Il gattopardo' e la regia di Visconti*, Bologna: Cappelli.

Cecchi D'Amico, Suso (with Margherita d'Amico) (1996) *Storie di cinema (e d'altro)*, Milan: Garzanti.

Champenier, Serge (1979) 'L'héritage de Nino Rota (1911–1979)', *Image et son* 3421: 28–32.

Chiarelli, Cristina Gastel (1997) *Luchino Visconti: Music e memoria*, Milan: Archinto.

Chion, Michel (1985) *Le Son au cinéma*, Paris: Cahiers du cinéma/Editions de l'Etoile.

Chion, Michel (1994) *Audio-Vision: Sound on Screen* (edited and translated by Claudia Gorbman), New York: Columbia University Press. (First published as *L'Audio-vision*, Paris: Editions Nathan, 1990.)

Chion, Michel (2003) *Un Art sonore, le cinéma: Histoire, esthétique, poétique*, Paris: Cahiers du cinéma.

Cine Club Napoli (ed.) (1985) *Eduardo e il cinema*, Naples: Tempi Moderni.

Citron, Marcia J. (2005) 'Operatic Style and Structure in Coppola's *Godfather* Trilogy', *The Musical Quarterly* 87, 3: 423–67.

Colón, Carlos (1981) *Rota–Fellini (La música en la Películas de Federico Fellini)*, Seville: Publicaciones de la Universidad de Sevilla.

Comuzio, Ermanno (1979) 'Fellini/Rota: un matrimonio concertato', *Bianco e nero* XL, 4: 63–94.

Comuzio, Ermanno (1986a) 'Nino Rota antico e moderno, ossia là dove l'immagine modella il suono' in Comuzio and Vecchi, 1986: 19–45.

Comuzio, Ermanno (1986b) 'Centotrentotto film e mezzo' in Comuzio and Vecchi, 1986: 113–62.

Comuzio, Ermanno and Paolo Vecchi (eds) (1986) *138½: I film di Nino Rota*, Reggio Emilia: Comune di Reggio Emilia.

Cowie, Peter (1997) *The Godfather^{TM} Book*, London: Faber and Faber.

Cumbow, Robert C. (1975) 'Morricone Encomium', *Movietone News* 70: 22–6.

Curchod, Olivier (1984) 'Le sourire et la fresque: La représentation de l'antiquité dans *Fellini-Satyricon*', *Positif* 276: 30–7.

D'Andrea, Renzo (1986) 'Le musiche di Rota da Visconti a Fellini' in Comuzio and Vecchi, 1986: 88–92. (First published *Cinema nuovo*, 274 (1981).)

De Santi, Pier Marco (1978) 'La clownerie e la musica nei film di Fellini' in Pier Marco De Santi and Raffaelle Monti (eds) '*Il Casanova*' di Federico Fellini (*Quaderni dell'Istituto di storia dell'arte dell'Università de Pisa*, 1. Cinema), Pisa: University of Pisa: 98–117.

De Santi, Pier Marco (1983) *La musica di Nino Rota*, Bari: Laterza. All quotations from Rota cited as from this source are based on interviews conducted by De Santi and incorporated into the book; where he draws on other interview material I indicate this in the footnotes.

De Santi, Pier Marco (1992) *Nino Rota: Le immagini e la musica*, Florence: Giunti.

Degrada, Francesco (ed.) (2000) *Giuseppe Verdi: L'uomo, l'opera, il mito*, Milan, Skira.

Di Franco, Fiorenza (1975) *Il teatro di Eduardo*, Bari: Laterza.

Duloquin, René (1963) '*Rocco et ses frères* II. Une thématique musicale' in Estève, 1963: 84–94.

Dyer, Richard (2001) 'The Notion of Pastiche' in Jostein Gripsrud (ed.) *The Aesthetics of Popular Art*, Kristiansand: Høyskoleforlaget, 77–90.

Dyer, Richard (2002) '*L'Air de Paris*: No Place for Homosexuality' in Richard Dyer *The Culture of Queers*, London: Routledge: 137–51.

Dyer, Richard (2004) 'The Talented Mr Rota', *Sight and Sound* 14, 9 NS: 42–5.

Dyer, Richard (2005) 'Film, Musik und Gefühl – Ironische Anbindung' in Mattias Brütsch et al. (eds) *Kinogefühl: Emotionalität und Film*, Marburg: Schüren: 121–35.

Dyer, Richard (2006) 'Music, People and Reality: the Case of Italian Neo-realism' in Miguel Mera and David Burnand (eds) *European Film Music*, Aldershot: Aldgate: 28–40.

Dyer, Richard (2007a) *Pastiche*, London: Routledge.

Dyer, Richard (2007b) 'Side by Side: Nino Rota, Music, and Film' in Goldmark et al., 2007: 246–59.

Dyer, Richard (2009) 'Tales of Plagiarism and Pastiche: *The Godfather*, *Il gattopardo* and *The Glass Mountain*', *Anglistica*, http://www.anglistica.unior.it/content/tales-plagiarism-and-pastiche-music-godfather-il-gattopardo-and-glass-mountain

Dyer, Richard (2010) '*8½*' in Tom Brown and James Walters (eds) *Moments in Film*, London: BFI/Palgrave (forthcoming).

Estève, Michel (ed.) (1963) '*Luchino Visconti: l'histoire et l'esthétique*', *Etudes cinématographiques* 26–7.

Fabe, Marilyn (2004) *Closely Watched Films*, Berkley: University of California Press.

Fabris, Dinko (ed.) (1987) *Nino Rota compositore del nostro tempo*, Bari: Orchestra Sinfonica di Bari.

Farassino, Alberto (1989) 'Il cinema come premio' in Alberto Farassino (ed.) *Neorealismo: Cinema italiano 1945–1949*, Turin: EDT: 140–1.

Fava, Claudio G. (2003) *Alberto Sordi*, Rome: Gremese.

Fellini, Federico (1986) 'L'amico magico' in Comuzio and Vecchi, 1986: 47–51. (First published *Il Messagero*, 15 April 1979 (on the occasion of Rota's death five days before); English translation in Sciannameo, 2005: 15–17.)

Finotti, Fabio (2001) 'La vendetta dell'angelo: Le poetiche del candore e Nino Rota' in Morelli, 2001a: 1–20.

Flinn, Caryl (1992) *Strains of Utopia: Gender, Nostalgia, and Hollywood Film Music*, Berkeley: University of California Press.

Floyd, Samuel A. (1995) *The Power of Black Music: Interpreting Its History from Africa to the United States*, New York: Oxford University Press.

Frith, Simon (1988) 'Sound and Vision: Ennio Morricone' in *Music for Pleasure*, London: Polity: 141–5.

Fuller, Sophie and Lloyd Whitesell (eds) (2002) *Queer Episodes in Music and Modern Identity*, Urbana: University of Illinois Press.

Gabbard, Krin (2008) *Hotter Than That: The Trumpet, Jazz, and American Culture*, New York: Faber and Faber.

Gaudenzi, Cosetta (2002) 'Memory, Dialect, Politics: Linguistic Strategies in Fellini's *Amarcord*' in Burke and Waller, 2002: 155–68.

Gavezzani, Gianandrea (1987) 'Brevi capitoli su Nino Rota' in Fabris, 1987: 56–62. (First published in his *Musicisti d'Europa: Studi sui contemporanei*, Milan: Suvini Zerboni, 1955: 255–66.)

Giacovelli, Enrico (1990) *La commedia all'italiana*, Rome: Gremese.

Giannelli, Franco (1987) 'Petite Offrande Musicale' in Fabris, 1987: 71. (First published in programme notes to concert of Rota's chamber music, Bari, 1981.)

Giannetti, Louis D. (1976) '*Amarcord*: The Impure Art of Federico Fellini', *Western Humanities Review* 30: 153–62.

Goldmark, Daniel, Lawrence Kramer and Richard Leppert (eds) (2007) *Beyond the Soundtrack: Representing Music in Cinema*, Berkeley: University of California Press.

Gorbman, Claudia (1978) 'Music as Salvation: Notes on Fellini and Rota', in Bondanella, 1978: 80–94. (First published *Film Quarterly* 28, 2 (1974–5): 17–25.)

Gorbman, Claudia (1987) *Unheard Melodies: Narrative Film Music*, Bloomington: Indiana University Press.

Gorbman, Claudia (2007) 'Auteur Music' in Goldmark et al. 2007: 149–62.

Grasso, Aldo (1991) 'Viaggio lungo la televisione di Mario Soldati' in Squarotti et al., 1991: 205–11.

Harcourt, Peter (1974) 'The Secret Life of Federico Fellini' in *Six European Directors*, Harmondsworth: Penguin: 183–211.

Holbrook, Morris B. (2003) 'A Book-Review Essay on the Role of Ambi-Diegetic Film Music in the Product Design of Hollywood Movies: Macromarketing in La-La-Land', *Consumption Markets and Culture* 6, 3: 207–30.

Kalinak, Kathryn (1992) *Settling the Score: Music and the Classical Hollywood Film*, Madison: University of Wisconsin Press.

Kassabian, Anahid (2001) *Hearing Film: Tracking Identifications in Contemporary Hollywood Film Music*, New York: Routledge.

Kermol, Enzo and Mariselda Tessarolo (eds) (1996) *La musica del cinema*, Rome: Bulzoni.

Kezich, Tullio (2006) *Federico Fellini: His Life and Work*, New York: Faber and Faber.

Kranz, David (2008) 'Tracking the Sounds of Franco Zeffirelli's *Taming of the Shrew*', *Literature/Film Quarterly* 36, 2: 94–112.

Labroca, Mario (1959) 'Corsi e ricorsi negli incontri fra il cinematogrofo e la musica' in S. G. Biamonte (ed.) (1959) *Musica e film*, Rome: Edizioni dell'Ateneo: 11–20.

Larsen, Peter (2004) 'From Bayreuth to Los Angeles: Classical Hollywood Music and the Leitmotif Technique' in Dominique Nasta and Didier Hivelle (eds) *Le Son en perspective: nouvelles recherches/New Perspectives in Sound Studies*, Brussels: PIE – Peter Lang.

Latorre, José María (1989) *Nino Rota: la imagen de la música*, Barcelona: Editorial Montesinos.

Lefebvre, Cyril (1983) 'La Musique chez Luigi Zampa', *L'Avant-Scène du Cinéma* 17: 224–5 (booklet accompanying video).

Lombardi, Francesco (ed.) (2000) *Fra cinema e musica del novecento: il caso Nino Rota*, Venice: Leo S. Olschki.

Lombardi, Francesco (2001) 'Nino Rota e la riproduzione del suono' in Rizzardi, 2001: 161–78.

London, Justin (2000) 'Leitmotifs and Musical Reference in the Classical Film Score' in Buhler et al., 2000: 85–96.

Malorgio, Cosimo (2001) '*Evangélion* di Mario Castelnuovo-Tedesco, dedicato a Nino', in Morelli, 2001a: 91–100.

Mangini, Giorgio (2001) 'Nino Rota, il cinema, le canzoni, ovvero: "Quanta gente c'era da contentare!"' in Rizzardi, 2001: 137–60.

Mannino, Franco (1994) *Visconti e la musica*, Lucca: Libreria Musicale Italiana.

Miccichè, Lino (ed.) (1996) *Il gattopardo*, Naples: Electa (for Centro Sperimentale di Cinematografia).

Miceli, Sergio (1996) 'Le musiche del film. Una breve analisi' in Miccichè, 1996: 28–39.

Miceli, Sergio (1982) *La musica nel film: Arte e artigianato*, Florence: Discanto. (Republished as *Musica e cinema nella cultura del Novecento*, Florence: Sansoni, 2000.)

Morelli, Giovanni (ed.) (2001a) *Storia del candore: Studi in memoria di Nino Rota nel ventesimo della scomparsa*, Venice: Leo S. Olschki.

Morelli, Giovanni (2001b) 'Mackie? Messer? Nino Rota e la quarta persona singolare del soggetto lirico' in Morelli, 2001a: 355–429. (Also in Rizzardi, 2001: 3–74.)

Morricone, Ennio and Sergio Miceli (2001) *Comporre per il cinema: Teoria e prassi della musica nel film*, Venice: Bianco e Nero/Marsilio.

Nowell-Smith, Geoffrey (2003) *Luchino Visconti*, London: BFI (revised edition).

Parker, Roger (2000) 'Il "vate del Risorgimento": *Nabucco* e "Va pensiero"' in Degrada, 2000: 35–44.

Pellicciotti, Giacomo (1998) 'Suso Cecchi: così ha vinto l'Oscar', *La Repubblica* 1 December 1998: 45 (interview with Suso Cecchi D'Amico).

Perugini, Simone (2009) *Nino Rota e le musiche per 'Il Casanova di Federico Fellini'*, Cantalupo in Sabina: Edizioni Sabinae.

Pravadelli, Veronica (ed.) (2000a) *Il cinema di Luchino Visconti*, Venice: Marsilio (Biblioteca di *Bianco e nero* – Quaderni, 2.)

Pravadelli, Veronica (2000b) '*Le notti bianche*: Natalia, o la luce dell'utopia' in Pravadelli, 2000a: 157–74.

Prudenzi, Angela (1991) *Raffaello Matarazzo*, Florence: La nuova Italia.

Puppa, Paolo (1990) *Teatro e spettacolo nel secondo novecento*, Bari: Laterza.

Quarenghi, Paola (1995) *Lo spettatore col binocolo: Eduardo De Filippo dalla scena allo schermo*, Rome: Edizioni Kappa.

Rausa, Giuseppe (2009) '*Come persi la guerra, L'eroe della strada, Molti sogni per le strade, Proibito rubare* e *Il barone Carlo Mazza*: l'epoca dei furti (1947–48)', http://www.giusepperausa.it/come_persi_la_guerra__l_eroe_d.html (accessed 18 May 2009).

Rizzardi, Veniero (ed.) (2001) *L'undicesima musa: Nino Rota e i suoi media*, Rome: RAI – ERI.

Rohdie, Sam (1992) *Rocco and His Brothers*, London: BFI.

Rostagno, Antonio (2000) 'Verdi politico' in Degrada, 2000: 180–1.

Rothwell, Kenneth (1977) 'Zeffirelli's *Rome and Juliet*: Words into Picture and Music', *Literature/Film Quarterly* 5, 4: 326–31.

Saponaro, Giorgio (1987) 'Protagonisti della nuova Bari: Nino Rota' in Fabris, 1987: 31–2. (First published *Il Tempo*, 5 November 1967: 4.)

Savio, Francesco (1975) *Ma l'amore no: Realismo, formalismo, propaganda e telefoni bianche nel cinema italiano di regime (1930–1943)*, Milan: Sonzogno.

Scardicchio, Nicola (2001) 'Il mistero della natività ne "Il Natale degli Innocenti" di Nino Rota: Simbli e rivelazione' in Morelli, 2001a: 341–54.

Scheurer, Timothy E. (2007) *Music and Mythmaking in Film: Genre and the Role of the Composer*, Jefferson, NC: McFarland.

Sciannameo, Franco (2005) *Nino Rota, Federico Fellini, and the Making of an Italian Cinematic Folk Opera 'Amarcord'*, Lewiston: Edward Mellen Press.

Severi, Stefania (2001) 'L'arte figurativa e *Il gattopardo* di Visconti: presenza, citazione, ispirazione' in Francesco Petrucci (ed.) *Visconti e il Gattopardo: La scena del Principe*, Milan: De Agostini Rizzoli: 72–81.

Soldati, Mario (1986) 'I silenzi di un musicista' in Comuzio and Vecchi, 1986: 51–5.

Solmi, Angelo (1962) *Storia di Federico Fellini*, Milan: Rizzoli.

Solomon, Maynard (1993) 'Franz Schubert and the Peacocks of Benvenuto Cellini', *19th Century Music* 17: 193–206.

Spinazzola, Vittorio (1985) *Cinema e pubblico: Lo spettacolo filmico in Italia 1945–1965*, Rome: Bulzoni.

Squarotti, Giorgio Barberi, Paolo Bertetto and Marziano Guglielminetti (eds) (1991) *Mario Soldati: La scrittura e lo sguardo*, Turin: Lindau/Museo Nazionale del Cinema.

Steffan, Carlida (2001) 'Putti, angeli e anime. Un'occhiata all'antiserena barocca' in Morelli, 2001a: 55–65.

Stilwell, Robynn J. (2007) 'The Fantastical Gap between Diegetic and Nondiegetic' in Goldmark et al., 184–202.

Stoddart, Helen (2002) 'Subtle Wasted Traces: Fellini and the Circus' in Burke and Waller, 2002: 47–64.

Tassone, Aldo (1978) 'From Romagna to Rome: the Voyage of a Visionary Chronicler (*Roma* and *Amarcord*)' in Bondanella, 1978: 261–88. (First published in *La Revue du cinéma: Image et son* 290 (1974): 17–38.)

Tomasi, Gioacchino Lanza (1963) 'Verdi al balla del gattopardo', *Discoteca* 15 April–15 May: 18–19.

Trasatti, Sergio (1984) *Renato Castellani*, Florence: La nuova Italia.

Van Order, M. Thomas (2009) *Listening to Fellini: Music and Meaning in Black and White*, Madison/Teaneck: Fairleigh Dickinson University Press.

Verdone, Mario (1994) *Federico Fellini*, Milan: Il Castoro.

Vignal, Marc (ed.) (1995) *Dizionario della musica italiana*, Rome: Gremese.

Vinay, Gianfranco (2002) 'Fellini/Rota: innocence et ésotérisme' in Marie-Noëlle Masson and Gilles Mouëllic (eds) *Musiques et images au cinéma*, Rennes: Presses Universitaires de Renes.

Vincendeau, Ginette (ed.) (1995) *Encyclopaedia of European Cinema*, London: Cassell/BFI.

Wells, H. G. (1895) *The Wonderful Visit*, London: J. M. Dent.

Wiley, Mason and Damien Bona (1986) *Inside Oscar: The Unofficial History of the Academy Awards*, New York: Ballantine.

Index

LIST OF ILLUSTRATIONS

While considerable effort has been made to correctly identify the copyright holders, this has not been possible in all cases. We apologise for any apparent negligence and any omissions or corrections brought to our attention will be remedied in any future editions.

The Godfather, © Paramount Picture Corporation; *Il gattopardo*, © Twentieth Century-Fox; *The Glass Mountain*, Victoria Films (Productions); *Vivere in pace*, Lux Film; *Casanova*, © Kapustan Industries N.V.; *Satyricon*, Produzioni Europee Associate; *Amici per la pelle*, Cines; *La Merveilleuse visite*, Société Nouvelle Paris Films Production/Mandala Films/Office de Radiodiffusion Télévision Française/Zafes, Catania; *La strada*, © Ponti-De Laurentiis; *Death on the Nile*, © EMI Films Limited; *È primavera*, Universal-Cine; *Il bacio*, Francesco Hayez, 1859; *Zaʒà*, Lux Film; *Rocco e i suoi fratelli*, Titanus/Films Marceau; *The Godfather Part II*, © Paramount Pictures Corporation; *La Regina di Saba*, Oro; *Senʒa pieta*, Lux Film; *This Angry Age*, Dino De Laurentiis Cinematografica; *I pirati di Capri*, Industrie Cinematografiche Sociali; *War and Peace*, Ponti-De Laurentiis; *Fuga in Francia*, Lux Film; *Appassionatamente*, Rizzoli Editore; *Un americano in vacanʒa*, Lux Film/Ponti; *Giorno di noʒʒe*, Lux Film; *La grande speranʒa*, Excelsa Film; *Il lavoro*, Concordia Compagnia Cinematografica/Cineriz di Angelo Rizzoli/Francinex/Gray Films; *Obsession*, Independent Sovereign Films; *Vita da cani*, Carlo Ponti Cinematografica; *Campane a Martello*, Lux Film; *L'eroe della strada*, Lux Film; *La grande Guerra*, Dino De Laurentiis Cinematografica; *Quel bandito sono io!*, Lux Film/Renown Pictures Corporation; *Amarcord*, © F.C. Produzioni/P.E.C.F.; *Le notti di Cabiria*, Dino De Laurentiis Cinematografica; *8½*, Cineriz di Angelo Rizzoli; *Prova d'orchestra*, RAI/Daimo Cinematografica; *La dolce vita*, Riama Film/Pathé Consortium Cinéma/Gray Films; *Anna*, Lux Film.